CHINA UNBOUND

A NEW WORLD DISORDER

JOANNA CHIU

ANANSI

Published in Canada in 2021 and the USA in 2021 by House of Anansi Press Inc.
www.houseofanansi.com

House of Anansi Press is committed to protecting our natural environment. This book is made of material from well-managed FSC®-certified forests, recycled materials, and other controlled sources.

House of Anansi Press is a Global Certified Accessible™ (GCA by Benetech) publisher. The ebook version of this book meets stringent accessibility standards and is available to students and readers with print disabilities.

25 25 24 23 22   3 4 5 6 7

Library and Archives Canada Cataloguing in Publication

Title: China unbound : a new world disorder / Joanna Chiu.
Names: Chiu, Joanna, author.
Identifiers: Canadiana (print) 20210221755 | Canadiana (ebook) 20210221860 |
ISBN 9781487007676 (softcover) | ISBN 9781487007683 (EPUB)
Subjects: LCSH: China—Politics and government—2002- | LCSH: China—
Economic conditions—2000- | LCSH: China—Foreign relations—21st century. |
LCSH: China—Social policy.
Classification: LCC DS779.4 .C55 2021 | DDC 951.06—dc23

Book design: Alysia Shewchuk

House of Anansi Press respectfully acknowledges that the land on which we operate is the Traditional Territory of many Nations, including the Anishinabeg, the Wendat, and the Haudenosaunee. It is also the Treaty Lands of the Mississaugas of the Credit.

Canada Council   Conseil des Arts
for the Arts   du Canada

ONTARIO ARTS COUNCIL
CONSEIL DES ARTS DE L'ONTARIO
an Ontario government agency
un organisme du gouvernement de l'Ontario

With the participation of the Government of Canada
Avec la participation du gouvernement du Canada | Canadä

We acknowledge for their financial support of our publishing program the Canada Council for the Arts, the Ontario Arts Council, and the Government of Canada.

Printed and bound in Canada

PRAISE FOR *CHINA UNBOUND*

"Chiu's book is very well written and researched, with plenty of firsthand accounts from the author. I recommend the book for everyone interested in China." — Jorge Guajardo, *Los Angeles Review of Books*

"Drawing on a decade of professional experience, Joanna Chiu offers a passionate and powerful account of the challenges we face in dealing with China today—challenges rooted in the West as much as those born in Beijing. A critical voice we need to hear." —Timothy Cheek, Institute of Asian Research, the University of British Columbia, and author of *The Intellectual in Modern Chinese History*

"Joanna Chiu, a reporter for the *Toronto Star*, provides a powerful, heartfelt account of Chinese immigrants and their fraught encounters with Beijing's United Front Work Department, a lavishly funded government agency that works with the Ministry of State Security. Chiu tells gripping stories of influence operations in such disparate places as Australia, Canada, the U.S., Italy, Greece, Turkey, and Russia ... Chiu's stories demonstrate in human terms just how formidable a task it will be to put the U.S. and China on any kind of co-operative path." — *New York Review of Books*

"Brilliantly researched and beautifully written." — *Globe and Mail*

"By taking the China story global, Chiu shows how an increasingly powerful China is challenging not only our economies, but our institutions, our principles, and our communities. Reporting from the frontlines of China's influence operations from Australia, Canada, and the United States to Italy, Greece, Turkey, and Russia, Chiu reveals embattled diasporas and critics under pressure as hypocrisy runs rampant in business and government, and a new world order begins to form. *China Unbound* is a vital, illuminating read." — Madeleine O'Dea, author of *The Phoenix Years: Art, Resistance, and the Making of Modern China*

"Doggedly reported and fiercely argued, this cri de coeur offers essential insight into Beijing's "aims and activities." — *Publishers Weekly*

"A timely and fascinating book looking at China's rise and the impacts on the current global order. A very-needed account at a time of fast geopolitical changes with smart analysis and engaging writing." — Karoline Kan, author of *Under Red Skies: Three Generations of Life, Loss, and Hope in China*, and reporter, Bloomberg

"*China Unbound* reveals Chiu to be an intrepid reporter and cogent analyst of Chinese politics and society . . . She has produced a valuable contribution to public debate, illuminating the enigmatic Chinese state which is characterized by repression at home and an ambitious agenda abroad." — *Winnipeg Free Press*

For my family

CONTENTS

CONTENTS

就仿佛站起来的世界有赖于
你能用单腿独立在优美睡眠中。
风大一点，对我们来说，就不方便 ...

世界有极限，才会有你
尖锐地对立在人类的麻木中。

The world rising to its feet depends
on whether you can sleep on one leg gracefully
The wind would make it difficult for us...

The world has limits, so that we can see you stand
sharply against the numbness of humanity

— "The Books of Cranes" by poet
Zang Di (1964–), translated by
Ming Di and Neil Aitken

A NOTE ON TERMS

Mainland China is the geographical area of the People's Republic of China (PRC). It doesn't include the semi-independent Chinese cities of Hong Kong and Macau.

Mandarin is the standard language of mainland China. The romanization system is Pinyin, which is used over the older Wade-Giles system, where Beijing was "Peking." Some non-conventional spellings for historical figures are common, however, such as Chiang Kai-shek and Sun Yat-sen.

Cantonese is spoken primarily in Hong Kong, Macau, and south eastern China's Guangdong province.

For both Mandarin and Cantonese names, surnames come first, before personal names.

Uyghur: The minority ethnic group is pronounced WEE-guhr.

Tibetan names: Family surnames are rare. For example, a common Tibetan name is Tenzin, which means "holder of the teaching" and is the personal name of the fourteenth Dalai Lama.

Chinese women generally do not take the surname of their husband. Some surnames are very common, so it's best to not assume that people sharing the same name are related.

This book uses the terms "Belt and Road" and "The New Silk Road" interchangeably.

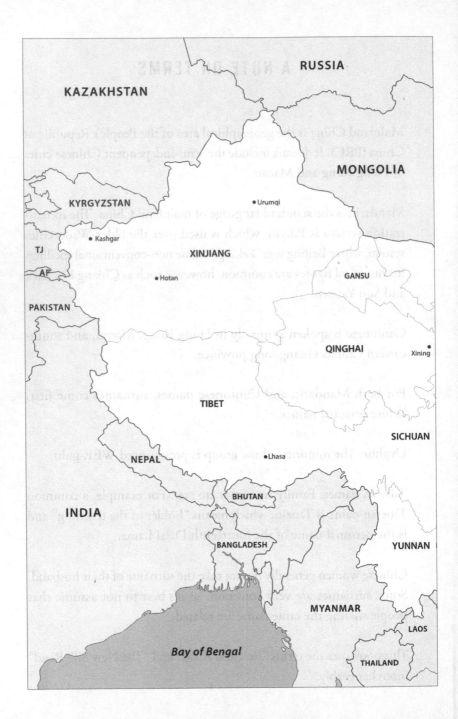

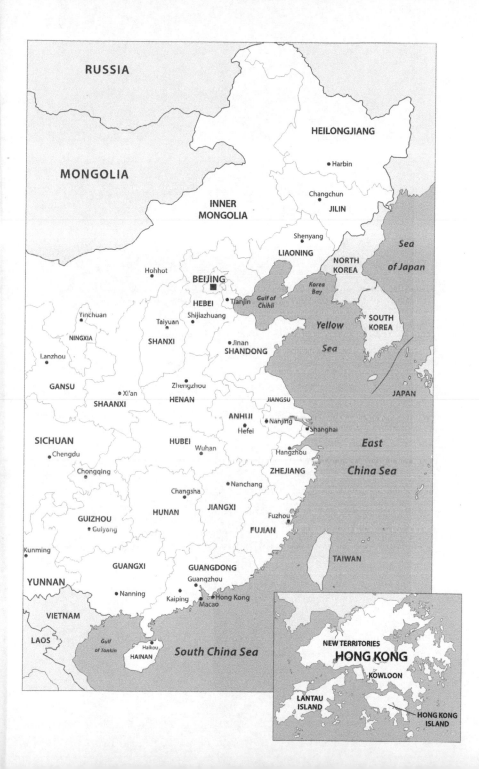

INTRODUCTION

Like rolling thunder, 2,008 drummers in shimmering robes drummed to the same beat, marking the start of the four-hour spectacle that was the Summer Olympics opening ceremony in Beijing.

As they danced around the traditional bronze drums, the musicians sang out a quote from the Analects of Confucius: "Isn't it delightful to have friends coming from afar?"

Following close behind, fifteen thousand performers in elaborate costumes swept across the Bird's Nest stadium in a carefully choreographed celebration of Chinese history. They showcased the nation's "four great inventions" — the compass, gunpowder, paper, and the printing press — and then artifacts gave way to a kaleidoscopic light show representing China's hopes of harmony between the peoples of the world.

By all measures, the 2008 ceremony was a fantastic success, its scale easily outstripping that of any Olympic opening of the past. The Summer Games were an opportunity for Beijing to present its best and most benign face to the world, from its long history and multi-ethnic cultures to its many technological innovations. It brought a surge of hope in the country, as well as around the world, that as China rose in global status its ascent would be beneficial to global communities.

Despite all the messages of friendship, however, Chinese Olympic athletes were under great pressure from the government to trounce the competition. Thousands of dedicated sports schools in the country had trained children intensively from six years old, leaving little time for an academic education. Many athletes developed chronic health problems, while others faced limited prospects if they failed to become stars. China wanted to present a friendly face to the international community, but it also wanted respect.

More than a dozen years after that triumphant ceremony, Beijing is no longer broadcasting songs of friendship to the world. Now Chinese officials engage in "wolf warrior" diplomacy, uttering threats at any perceived slight to their country's pride.

Was that grand show of affection always just fiction?

I sought the opinion of Jan Wong, the first Canadian journalist of Chinese descent to serve as bureau chief of the *Globe and Mail* newspaper's Beijing outpost, from 1988 to 1994. Before that, in 1972, Wong had travelled from her hometown of Montreal to Beijing as an international university student. China was closed off to most Western visitors until the 1970s, as it suffered tumultuous years of internal conflict during the Cultural Revolution.

Wong recalled coming to China at a time of tentative social recovery when Chinese leaders and citizens expressed a genuine desire for global friendship. "I remember in those days, if you just showed up in China, they were so grateful you were there. Because everyone was tilting to [formal diplomatic relations with] Taiwan. And the Chinese were always talking about the friendship between their country and your country.

"The Canadian hockey team went to China, and they were playing at the recently built Capital Indoor Stadium. I got a ticket, and they were playing a team from Harbin. And everyone was chanting, *You yi di yi. bi sai di er.* The whole stadium. 'Friendship first, competition second.'

"So it's completely different now, and now they are bullies. China went from being the underdogs to the bullies. They're still not confident; they still have this residual complex, like they want respect and everything is about respect. They're really thin-skinned and jump to conclusions, thinking other countries don't respect them. But they have so much clout now."

Wong and I were speaking in mid-2019, in the aftermath of Beijing's arrest of two Canadians in China: my friend Michael Kovrig, who is a diplomat-on-leave, and Michael Spavor, an entrepreneur. The move was in retaliation for Canada's detention of Huawei CFO Meng Wanzhou at the request of American authorities. The Americans wanted Meng extradited to the United States to face fraud charges, but authorities seemed to underestimate the tech executive's level of influence and how her arrest would enrage China's leaders.

The hostage-taking of the Canadian men took the Western world by surprise; until then, it had been widely ignorant of the many times China had taken foreigners of Asian descent as political prisoners. The cruel treatment of the "two Michaels" also dismantled a longstanding myth that China was heading in a liberal direction.

Many Westerners had accepted the idea that as China opened up to the world, things would get better. By the early 1980s, the People's Republic of China was introducing market reforms and establishing diplomatic ties with more countries. The Communist world was gradually liberalizing its authoritarian systems and would soon become "just like us."

The 1989 Tiananmen massacre of mostly young pro-reform protesters in Beijing shattered these hopes. People around the world watched in shock; they couldn't believe Chinese troops had opened fire on their own people, killing hundreds, perhaps thousands, of peaceful demonstrators.

Decades later, however, the myth of a liberalizing China still persisted, and it wasn't just Americans who believed it. China became a member of the World Trade Organization (WTO) on December 11, 2001, after a lengthy process of debate and negotiation. Beijing's successful entry into the WTO was, at the time, deeply symbolic of the country's integration into a global order based on the rule of law.

Western leaders were optimistic. Bill Clinton said in a memorable 2000 speech, "The WTO agreement will...advance the goals America has worked for in China for the past three decades." Membership in the WTO would not create a free society in China "overnight" or guarantee that China would always play by global rules, but over time, Clinton said, China would move in the right direction.

But the opposite happened. As China became richer, it became more authoritarian. The state retained significant control over its economy and mammoth state-owned enterprises under a philosophy called "socialism with Chinese characteristics." Officials have returned to large-scale persecution of scholars, lawyers, artists, activists, and minorities. Targets include an estimated million Uyghurs in internment camps.

For far too long, Western societies have mishandled or simply ignored Beijing's actions out of narrow self-interest.

Decades of wilful misinterpretation have, over time, become complicity in the toxic diplomacy, human rights abuses, and foreign interference China engages in today.

I USE THE TERM "the West" in this book intentionally, because it is crucial to recognize the colonial histories in which modern frictions arose. The Western world view was one where the "East," encompassing Asia, North Africa, and the Middle East, represented newly discovered territories that early European colonizers depicted as static and undeveloped, and therefore deserving of domination.

Beijing has reason to feel that the Chinese people have been grievously insulted. The emotional baggage of China's so-called "century of humiliation," from 1839 to 1949, at the hands of allied European powers and Japan helps explain contemporary Chinese leaders' great sensitivity and their compulsion to best the West.

Some 140 years ago, Canadian officials tricked my great-great-grandfather into leaving his home in southern China for the promise of mining gold in Canada. When he arrived, after an expensive journey, he found he had little choice but to toil alongside thousands of other Chinese men to build the Canadian Pacific Railway. It was brutal work in harsh conditions for little pay, and at least six hundred workers lost their lives. Few of those who survived the ordeal were able to settle in Canada with their families, since the "head tax" placed exorbitant fees on subsequent entry of Chinese migrants. My great-great-grandfather returned to China with little to show for his years of hard labour. Then, in the early mid-twentieth century, before the Chinese Civil War broke out, my grandparents fled from southern Guangdong province to British-controlled Hong Kong in search of stability.

I was born in Hong Kong several years before the Tiananmen massacre in Beijing. Like everyone in Hong Kong, my parents were horrified by what the Chinese government had done to the youthful protesters. Already, Hong Kongers' sense of identity was very different from that of Chinese mainlanders. To protect ourselves from the region's uncertain future, my family decided to leave Hong Kong before the British handed the city back to Chinese rule in 1997.

This time, we were accepted as immigrants to Canada, and I was lucky to grow up taking basic freedoms for granted. But as I started to read about the one-child policy and other draconian rules in China that profoundly affected its citizens' lives, I felt guilty. There I was, playing sports and gunning for top grades at my middle school in Canada, while in mainland China, infant girls were being abandoned at birth, most in orphanages but some in wells or ditches on the side of the street, their parents choosing to abandon and even kill them because they couldn't afford the fines they would incur if they tried for a coveted male child.

By the late 1990s, I started to notice signs of Beijing's influence at home in Vancouver. My father worked for a Canadian media company offering programming in Mandarin and Cantonese, and I heard whispers about popular commentators being fired or pressured to censor their commentary on Chinese politics. Later I would learn these efforts were part of Beijing's attempts to win influence abroad through economic and political enticements, or otherwise through intimidation and harassment.

An irresistible sense of an important unfolding story led

me to learn Mandarin in preparation to move to China. As a teenager, I pored over books about China in public libraries, devising a self-study program where I'd assign myself essays to write. Then I took all the Chinese history, politics, and sociology courses I could fit into my university schedule, and I wrote my undergraduate thesis on the role of Chinese women revolutionaries in the twentieth century.

Meanwhile, given all the questions I fielded about where I was "from" and why my English was so good, I was aware that people in the West viewed me as an outsider. But I thought this outsider status would benefit me as a journalist, that a lack of belonging could help me see things more objectively.

I wanted to be in China to chronicle its rapid economic development and help people around the world understand the country's complex social issues. Instead, I got a front-row seat as China veered toward totalitarianism. My time in Hong Kong and Beijing coincided with the rise of Xi Jinping as general secretary of the Chinese Communist Party (CCP). Before he took power in 2012, some thought Xi would be a liberal reformer, but those expectations were dashed as human rights and press freedom plunged to new lows. Under Xi's leadership, China has imprisoned thousands of people for even mild social criticism as the country's censorship and surveillance apparatus becomes ever more sophisticated.

Torture and forced confessions are common in China's legal system, though the number of executions each year is a state secret. In the last decade of front-line reporting, I have seen grieving mothers of Tiananmen Square massacre victims dragged away by police and have interviewed dozens of persecuted artists, underground church leaders, writers, lawyers, and activists. Chinese police have far-reaching rights to detain suspects without charge in secret makeshift prisons for up to six months. The Orwellian system is called "residential surveillance in a designated place." It is excruciating for family members, who have no idea where their loved ones have gone.

Some of the most haunting moments I had as a journalist in China came during interviews conducted via online messaging. On occasion, the messages would abruptly stop coming, leaving me to stare at the time stamp showing when my interview subject had last been online.

On plane rides home to Canada for the holidays, I would feel numb, as if a video recording of what I had witnessed were replaying on fast-forward in my head. For my friends working in different fields in China, it was a dynamic place with a lot to offer, but reporting on human rights and politics in Beijing was a truly dystopian experience.

A sliver of hope for many in China, and for observers of Chinese politics, was that once Xi stepped down after the customary ten-year term, his successor would discontinue the sweeping crackdowns on civil society. But then, on March 10, 2018, Xi won a lifetime mandate to rule. I was in the upper stands of the Great Hall of the People when it happened, squinting down at the stage where the country's collected leadership sat stiffly in matching black suits. After the ballots were counted in the parliamentary vote to amend China's constitution so that Xi could serve indefinitely, thousands of Chinese legislators erupted into fervent applause. In one stroke, the son of a revolutionary veteran had become the most powerful leader in modern China since Chairman Mao Zedong, consolidating the growing might of the military, economy, and state in the hands of one man.

The amended constitution said the abolishment of term limits "will be conducive to safeguarding the authority and the unified leadership of the CCP Central Committee with Comrade Xi Jinping as the core." Xi is still only in his sixties, meaning that China's authoritarian trajectory could continue for decades.

SEVERAL MONTHS AFTER XI'S coronation, when I couldn't take any more of Beijing's air pollution — which required me to take constant drags from my inhaler and occasional trips to the hospital — I packed my bags to return to Canada.

I regretted having to leave the China story behind with many fascinating topics left unexplored. But within months of my departure, Meng Wanzhou was arrested in Vancouver, and days later came the stunning news that Kovrig and Spavor were among the Canadians ensnared in the diplomatic fallout. Dystopian China had followed me home.

At the same time, tensions have ratcheted up between China and other countries over abuses in Xinjiang, a security law in Hong Kong affecting the freedoms of foreign citizens, international trade disputes and clashing territorial claims in the South China Sea, and the India-China border.

Canadian officials promised to announce a new comprehensive strategy to deal with an increasingly authoritarian Beijing. But several years later, no shift in policy has been announced.

Meanwhile, in the U.S., government leaders and pundits alike seemed to be gearing up for a second Cold War along ideological battle lines, where America represented Western democracies and China was the encroaching superpower of the East. Washington's message to its allies was clear: You're with China, or you're with us.

Technology giant Huawei has become a proxy for U.S. struggles with Beijing, thanks to the Chinese government's aggressive backing of its private companies. The U.S., U.K., Australia, New Zealand, and Canada cooperate on intelligence matters in an alliance referred to as the "Five Eyes." All members except for Canada have either banned or restricted Huawei from supplying equipment for their 5G networks.

Then, after the COVID-19 pandemic originated in Wuhan, China, some politicians across the Western world were careless in their language about the outbreak. Pandemic scapegoating led to a devastating rise in hate crimes against people of Asian descent, and advocates took officials to task for their role in branding the coronavirus the "China Flu," or in U.S. president Donald Trump's words, the "kung flu."

There has, of course, long been racism in many countries against people of Chinese descent, who, compared to other ethnic groups, seem most often conflated with a government's actions. It doesn't matter if an individual's family has been settled outside of China for generations. This has been highly detrimental to the quality of international research and dialogue on China, since people of Chinese descent have been subject to blanket suspicion and their valuable contributions overlooked.

In the wake of the March 2021 murders of Asian massage parlour workers in Atlanta, Georgia, American cybersecurity intelligence expert Amy Chang shared her experiences of trying to build a career in Washington, DC. She said the most egregious question she and many other Asians in Washington receive on a regular basis is "Are you a Chinese spy?"

Informing my travels for this book, from late 2018 to 2020, and my choice of people to interview, was a need to cut through the simplistic rhetoric that all too often obscures reality. I sought out individuals with unique lived experiences related to China, who aren't often provided platforms from which they can inform the decisions of countries or multinational companies.

Members of the Chinese diaspora had, after all, tried to warn Western policymakers that Beijing was working clandestinely to spread its will around the world, but those warnings mostly went unheeded. Only recently have egregious cases prompted high-level responses.

Mayors and city councillors have expressed complete surprise when I've informed them that photos of them shaking hands at Lunar New Year events have shown up in propaganda boasting of China's influence abroad. Some seemed unaware of the implications even when granting interviews to Chinese state-owned media. I could only shake my head when a Canadian politician complained to me that the state-run Xinhua news agency had twisted his words.

It is even more galling to watch governments accept investments and even sell off parcels of key infrastructure without due consideration. Even if Beijing is genuine in its reassurances that its massive New Silk Road global infrastructure investment plan isn't part of a bid for political power, national oversight of such deals only makes sense. In Greece, for example, citizens are concerned about their government's apparent willingness to take China's side on issues at the United Nations so as to increase the likelihood of more Chinese investment.

Experts have also expressed fears that China and other authoritarian countries like Russia, Turkey, and Iran might forge formal alliances to challenge democracies. The on-the-ground reporting in this book in Turkey and Russia examines these claims.

All the while, Beijing uses racism from the West to deflect criticism, as noted by Yangyang Cheng, a China-born, U.S.-based particle physicist, in an essay for the *Guardian*. The Chinese Communist Party, Cheng wrote, "makes self-orientalising gestures, mirroring the worst of the China watchers, by defending its policies as suited to China's 'unique national condition': disputed borderlands are described as 'part of China since prehistoric times,' and authoritarianism is welcomed by a people with 'Confucian values.'"

Many in the West are primed to accept these lies. But when we pay attention to people like Cheng who have their feet in different worlds, it helps to cut through propaganda and, to put it bluntly, reveal the hypocrisy on all sides.

It is difficult to step back and find the best paths forward for these complex geopolitical problems when the human crises are so urgent. My goal with this book is to provide necessary nuance and context, cross-country comparisons as well as important individual stories that can help ground public debate and inform governments' and organizations' policies on China.

To that end, I am deeply grateful to all those who spoke with me who are vulnerable to repercussions.

This book starts with a chapter set mostly in Beijing that lays out the background of China's crackdowns on civil society and its forging of an ambitious foreign strategy and vision for an alternative world order. Chapter 2 draws on my years of reporting on Hong Kong's pro-democracy movement and its struggles to counteract both the shadowy forms of influence by the CCP's "United Front" agents and the blunt-force use of laws and policing to quash dissent. Chapters 3 to 6 provide comprehensive case studies as well as individual stories in "middle power" countries—Canada, Australia, Italy, and Greece—that have faced economic and political pressure and coercion from Beijing. Chapters 5 and 6 also discuss China-EU relations more broadly. The last part of the book, featuring reporting in the U.S., Turkey, and Russia, gathers evidence on potential arenas of future global conflict, with clues to what can be done to avoid disastrous confrontations.

PART I
ONE CHINA, ONE SYSTEM

1.
BEIJING

Rule by Law

I learned about the underground church from a member of a basketball group I joined after moving to Beijing in late 2014. The gym we rented was in a large public school complex tucked in the *hutongs*, a maze of ancient alleyways in the old walled city that now only exists in a few central neighbourhoods.

Every Tuesday, if the air quality was decent, I pedalled my bicycle to the gym after work. With my phone poking precariously out of my purse so I could hear directions from Baidu Maps, I careened around parked scooters and food vendors. Out of tiny metal pushcarts, the vendors sold delicious *jianbing* egg crepes or bright red skewers of candied hawthorn fruit, or strawberries if they were in season. The voice of the Baidu lady called out quick twists and turns and the unfamiliar alley names in Mandarin.

I had to use a Chinese app because, nearly five years earlier, in 2010, Google products had been blocked. The American technology giant had refused to self-censor its search results and elected instead to shut down its China search engine. Thousands of international websites are now only accessible in the country through a VPN, software that allows people to surf the internet as if they were in another country, but that doesn't always work well. I had lived in Hong Kong previously, and though freedom of expression was under constant threat, at least the semi-autonomous city had fast and unfettered internet.

Our basketball group was made up of young male professionals, a few female university students, a youth basketball coach from Serbia, and me. There were plenty of bars and entertainment options in the city, but these tended to be raucous, and it was much easier to meet my first local friends while playing the most popular sport in China. The NBA was probably the most beloved American institution in the country.

After our game one night, one of my new friends — a particularly tall and athletic man in his late twenties — asked me what I was working on.

I bit my tongue. I had just received a freelance assignment from the *Economist* to investigate state suppression of religion in China — not really a subject for polite conversation in an authoritarian country. And I didn't know this man well enough to guess how he would react.

So I told him I was researching Christianity. You know, in general.

His face brightened, and he immediately invited me to visit his Protestant church.

"Oh, is it an official one?" I asked, trying to be subtle.

"No," he said, nonchalantly admitting to a subversive act against the state.

My mind was swimming with questions, but I didn't get the chance to probe further; our time slot at the gym was up.

So he sent me the church's address over the ubiquitous social media app WeChat and said he would introduce me to his congregation's leaders at the very next Sunday service.

CHRISTIANITY FIRST APPEARED in China in the seventh century, but it didn't gain a significant presence until Jesuit missionaries arrived some nine hundred years later, late in the Ming dynasty, in the sixteenth century. The Jesuits played a key role not only in spreading the religion but in acting as intermediaries between Western and Chinese elites. Later, as relations with the West deteriorated, Christianity became associated with the aggression of Western imperial powers, and hostility in China grew against missionaries. In 1812, the Qing dynasty banned Europeans from spreading Christianity and later made violations of the new prohibition punishable by death. Chinese subjects who refused to reverse their conversions were given as slaves to Muslim leaders in the country, who at the time enjoyed better social standing in China than Christians did.

The role of missionaries in China grew when first Britain and then Britain and France defeated the Qing during the First and Second Opium Wars (1839–1842 and 1856–1860, respectively) and forced the dynasty to sign treaties that made Hong Kong a British colony and gave Westerners special privileges at various other ports. It was also during this time that Hong Xiuquan, an ambitious schoolteacher who failed the notoriously difficult national imperial examination several times and was therefore unable to become a civil servant, was exposed to missionary tracts.

Hong turned his frustration into an anti-imperial movement, initially preaching to friends and relatives who had also failed the civil service examinations. He soon mobilized millions of similarly disgruntled people in southern China and led the massive Taiping Rebellion against the Qing dynasty from 1850 to 1864. The religious insurgents called for a complete shift in the political and social system and rejected traditional Confucian values, so they wanted to do more than simply topple the dynasty and replace the Qing emperor with Hong. They also wanted to convert the masses to a new kind of Christianity that included elements of Chinese folk religion. The uprising was the bloodiest civil war of the nineteenth century, in any part of the world, with an estimated twenty to seventy million casualties. The conflict also drove millions of civilians to flee to other parts of China or to emigrate abroad. Twentieth-century revolutionaries would later consider "God's Chinese Son" a hero for trying to rid China of its rigid and feudal structures, though historians have noted that, in practice, Hong and other Taiping leaders took on many of the trappings of traditional power holders and often behaved similarly in the areas they controlled.

To this day, because of its associations with Western imperialism and civil uprising, Christianity continues to be one of the most restricted religions in the country. The government vets the appointment of all pastors in official churches, and no church is allowed to declare allegiance to any particular branch of Christianity. The Chinese Communist Party is officially atheist, and it prohibits its ninety million party members from holding any religious beliefs. And while the nation's constitution purports to protect citizens' religious freedoms, religious activity is in reality tightly monitored. China has one of the world's largest populations of prisoners persecuted in relation to their religion. Some groups, such as the quasi-Christian Church of Almighty God and the Falun Gong spiritual movement, are outright banned, and their followers are subject to arrest. A relentless crackdown on Falun Gong began in 1999 after the group organized a peaceful demonstration outside CCP headquarters to push for greater freedom to practise.

In short, Beijing seems highly suspicious of anything that involves large numbers of people pledging loyalty to a higher power than the Chinese Communist Party.

For years, police have been harassing and intimidating members of Christian "house churches," unofficial congregations that refuse to register with authorities to operate under government oversight. Since mid-2014, authorities in the coastal province of Zhejiang have been tearing down the crosses that adorned the roofs of many such independent churches, including makeshift converted apartments and office buildings; protesting pastors were arrested and sentenced to as much as fourteen years in prison. In the winter of 2015, Christians around the country were wondering if this might portend a broader crackdown.

I TOOK A CAB to my friend's church, which was out on the "fourth ring" expressway, a route that runs in a loop around the megacity. It was hard to find, because all I could see were identical rows of towering Soviet-style concrete apartment buildings. Eventually, I found a narrow unmarked entranceway next to a convenience store, which led into the courtyard of one of the apartment blocks.

Underground it may have been, but once you knew where to look, the church was far from clandestine. A large red cross plastered to a ground-level window advertised its presence. Posters of Bible verses with cartoon illustrations inside the building were also visible from the courtyard. Down a flight of stairs, I saw that its rooms included a high-ceilinged hall with neat rows of folding chairs and a much smaller space that doubled as a nursery and cloakroom.

In his sermon, the young pastor focused on analyzing passages of the Bible and avoided commentary on Chinese society. Afterwards, he asked me to stand and introduce myself. No one blinked an eye when I said I wasn't religious but wanted to learn about their church. I didn't want to announce to the group the fact that I was a journalist, in case undercover police were present, but I might not have needed to be so circumspect.

"We are not exactly lying low," a church leader assured me in an interview following the service. "We sing hymns so loudly, people in the community get curious and come down to see what's going on. Anyone is welcome."

He also explained that with only a couple hundred members, their unregistered church was relatively small. At least in Beijing, congregations of their size didn't normally attract official scrutiny. Still, he asked me not to name the church if I wrote about it.

As my unfailingly polite friend drove me back to my apartment in a central neighbourhood, I asked why he had converted to Christianity even though organized religion held such a precarious place in society.

"It gives me some meaning in life," he said simply. "China has changed so quickly, and young people are under a lot of pressure. I want to figure out how to live well."

TO UNDERSTAND BEIJING'S QUEST for global power, I first had to understand the lengths to which the CCP tries to maintain control over its 1.4 billion citizens. The modern Chinese state was founded on revolution, so its leaders know all too well the power of the masses. In order to maintain control of such a huge population, instead of rule of law in China, there is *rule by law*, and it's aided by high-tech surveillance.

Laws and regulations govern virtually every aspect of a person's life, controlling who you can marry, whether you can give birth, whether you can relocate within the country, whether you can post a satirical meme on the internet, and even your beliefs about the afterlife.

An extensive framework of legislation supports Beijing's ability to censor, punish, or restrict all forms of expression, including on the internet, in print publishing, and many types of speech. In 2000, China's State Council (the chief administrative authority of the People's Republic) made internet companies legally liable if they failed to ensure adequate compliance with censorship rules on their platforms.

In 2013, the government launched a campaign against the spreading of "false rumours." Hundreds of bloggers and journalists, as well as many prominent social media users who spoke on political matters, were arrested that year. Even if they used online aliases, they were tracked down by police through their IP addresses or the information they used to register for social media accounts. Research from Canada's Citizen Lab, a cybersecurity and human rights watchdog, has shown that popular Chinese-owned platforms like WeChat are able to read and instantaneously censor messages even in private conversations between two people.

At the Deutsche Presse-Agentur newsroom in Beijing,

working for Germany's largest multilingual news agency, I reported on the jailing of teenage bloggers, forced abortions, and illegal land grabs. Terms such as *daibu* (arrest), *Guo'an* (secret police), and *bigong* (forced confession) formed part of my daily lexicon. My Mandarin was still a work in progress, but I focused on improving my vocabulary on the most politically sensitive subjects, since I feared asking my Chinese colleagues for translation help could put them in danger.

In China's surreal legal system, lawyers receive rigorous training and judges cite legal precedent in their judgements, but the Chinese Communist Party is above the law. There is no watchdog to monitor the country's leaders. While the constitution enshrines liberal values like freedom of speech and freedom of demonstration and property rights, the document does not limit the Party's power—a vital detail that renders it meaningless.

Amnesty International estimates that more people in China receive death sentences than in the rest of the world combined. The exact number of executions is unknown, because the government considers them "state secrets." And Chinese courts have an astounding 99.9 percent conviction rate.

Since virtually everyone charged with a crime ends up being found guilty, the only variable is the magnitude of the prison sentence or fine. This has been the norm for decades. In 2003, the *People's Daily*, the Party's mouthpiece newspaper, reported that a court in Anhui province sentenced two men to prison terms of nine and seven years for "unlawful operation of a business." Their crime? Publishing love poems without government authorization.

I have tried and failed several times to make it inside a Chinese courtroom. Once, in the northern city of Tianjin,

I spotted a row of unmarked cars with surveillance cameras on their roofs parked outside the Tianjin First Intermediate People's Court, where a government official was being tried for corruption. The sidewalk was clear, and I thought I could make it close enough to the courthouse to at least observe the atmosphere outside.

Seemingly out of nowhere, a motley group of men appeared, wearing tracksuits or ill-fitting shirts tucked into khakis, and surrounded me. There was nothing to indicate I was a journalist; my phone and notebook were stashed in a pocket of my bag. "I'm just trying to walk down the street," I said innocently, but a thug with a buzz cut roughly pushed me back. They didn't stop yelling and jostling me until I managed to break away to call my editor. The men stepped back when they heard me speaking English.

Something about my demeanour could have aroused their suspicion, despite my appearance as an ordinary Chinese woman. Or they could have been tracking my movements. My colleagues have been stopped trying to do things like boarding a train out of Beijing to report on polluting factories, or even jogging near Tiananmen Square around the yearly anniversary of the 1989 massacre.

Security cameras with facial scanning technology — installed in busy public areas by government authorities as well as by private companies in premises such as banks — are ubiquitous in the country. Some police officers even sport high-tech sunglasses that can scan crowds to identify suspects through facial recognition. There are no national laws governing the collection of biometric data, including fingerprints, facial characteristics, and voice characteristics, creating an environment where people don't expect much privacy.

It wasn't healthy to be worried all the time, but in fields such as media, law, and NGO work, it was generally accepted good practice among foreigners and Chinese citizens alike to assume we were being surveilled at all times—through hacking of personal laptops and phones, or by people following us while we were travelling for work.

The Tianjin police let me go after a uniformed officer inspected my foreign press credentials, but a few plainclothesmen tailed me as I hurried toward a subway station. I jumped into a taxi instead and hollered at the driver to go quickly in any direction. It felt like a getaway scene in a movie, and I shudder to think what might have happened if they hadn't believed I was a foreign citizen.

I was glad the police hadn't asked to see my passport. Though it bore Canada's coat of arms on the cover, it listed my birthplace as Hong Kong. They might have suspected that I was actually a Chinese citizen, since the Chinese government doesn't recognize dual citizenship. In reality, I had renounced my Hong Kong citizenship-by-birthright years earlier as a precaution.

HISTORIANS SAY THE PARTY'S obsession with control has roots in the traditions of Confucianism and Legalism. According to the philosopher Confucius, who lived more than 2,500 years ago, proper behaviour is dictated by one's position within hierarchies of superior and subordinate relationships. Therefore, children must obey their parents, younger adults must heed their elders, and every citizen must be loyal to the emperor.

Legalism, which emerged in China around 400 BCE, was compatible with the Confucian world view because it empowered the emperor to rule effectively over a vast empire containing people of different ethnicities and cultures through sets of codified laws and edicts. It was a kind of absolute power through bureaucracy. This philosophy has been compared to Machiavellianism in the Western world, since it champions the rightful consolidation of autocratic power to achieve stability and security.

Within both traditions, there is little support for a pluralism of ideas or an individual's inalienable rights.

Since assuming power of the CCP in 2012, Chinese president Xi Jinping has declared his admiration for the Chinese classics and is particularly fond of quoting ancient Legalist scholars to justify why it is in his citizens' best interests to submit to a strong leader.

"When those who uphold the law are strong, the state is strong," Xi told a leadership forum in 2014, quoting Legalist scholar Han Fei (280–233 BCE) on monarchs taming social disorder. "When they are weak, the state is weak." In doing so, Xi compared himself to an emperor.

Born in 1953 as the son of Communist revolutionary-in-arms Xi Zhongxun, Xi Jinping is part of an elite cohort of "princelings": descendants of prominent senior Chinese Communist Party leaders. In recent years, this pedigree has afforded princelings advantages similar to those enjoyed by members of prominent American political families like the Kennedys, and the cohort tends to feel it has a special duty to safeguard CCP rule.

During the tumult of the tail end of the Cultural Revolution, in the mid-twentieth century, however, Xi's father fell out of political favour and spent years in prison. Xi was among the thousands of urban youth forced to spend years in the countryside to learn from the peasants. He would likely have ended up among the legions of "sent-down youth" regardless of his father's status anyway, since it was such a blanket policy. While several of Xi's family members suffered greatly, Xi's kinship with Chinese commoners in his time as a sent-down youth has since become part of his lore.

In his youth and middle age, Xi worked his way up the Party ranks, serving first as governor of the prosperous Fujian province, from 1999 to 2002, before becoming Party secretary of neighbouring Zhejiang province. In 2012, at the age of fifty-nine, he was elected general secretary of the Chinese Communist Party. The term "president" isn't commonly used in China, but in the English-speaking world, the leader of the People's Republic of China is widely referred to as "president," even though some experts think that using the title makes the role sound democratically elected.

Though he rarely expressed emotion, by all accounts Xi was a force to be reckoned with. Soon after he took the top job, he delivered a speech to party members on the "deeply profound" lessons the CCP should take from the breakup of the Soviet Union.

"Why did the Soviet Union disintegrate? Why did the Soviet Communist Party collapse? An important reason was that their ideals and convictions wavered," Xi said, according to a summary of his comments that circulated among Chinese officials and was published by the *New York Times*. He also cited political rot, ideological heresy, and military disloyalty as factors that the CCP strongly guarded against.

Within a few years, he oversaw the rapid modernization of the country's armed forces and placed himself at their very top as both chairman of the Central Military Commission and commander in chief of its joint battle command center, which was a new title. He reshuffled the military as well as other nodes of the CCP leadership structure to minimize the decision-making power of bureaucrats, making himself the central figure in virtually all governance matters.

BEIJING'S PREOCCUPATION WITH SOCIAL ORDER is deeply informed by "Chinese imperial histories of turbulence, collapse, and implosion, going back two millennia," according to Kerry Brown, director of the Lau China Institute at King's College, London. "No wonder Chinese leaders today place such a premium on order at any cost. But those outside engaging with this concept need to be clear—fear sits right beside it. It is an order predicated more on avoiding negative things happening, rather than outlining some bold, positive vision of how things can be different, and better."

China's leaders certainly act as if they greatly fear another mass social upheaval, but many ordinary citizens remember the chaos of recent decades as well. Among average Chinese citizens, a widespread wariness of history repeating itself plays a role in maintaining the Party's authoritarian rule.

Many people who were born before the 1970s have known civil war, famine, and waves of CCP attempts to "reform" and "re-educate" the masses in the name of socialist revolution. If the Mao era or the Cultural Revolution comes up in conversation, older people often sum up those decades with one word before changing the subject: *luan*, a state of confusion and turmoil bordering on chaos. The decades following the Second World War were tumultuous, to say the least.

After Sun Yat-sen's Nationalist revolutionary forces managed to topple the Qing dynasty in 1912, marking the end of monarchical rule in China, the new Republic of China soon faced a new challenger. The proletarian Russian Revolution and the principles of Marxism and Leninism had gained ardent admirers among some Chinese left-wing intellectuals, some of whom had spent formative youthful years in Moscow. The Chinese Communist Party was soon established by fifty intellectuals in Shanghai in 1921, led mostly by Chen Duxiu and Li Dazhao. The group was passionate about finding ways to adapt the tenets of Marxism-Leninism to forge a strong and modern new China. At first, the privileged scholars had no intention to seize control of the country by force.

What began as a subtle rivalry developed into an armed conflict after the Nationalist general Chiang Kai-shek unexpectedly ordered the massacre of five thousand Communists in Shanghai in 1927. The fact that the Communists were able to recover from the killing spree had a lot to do with the actions of a relatively junior party member at the time. Mao Zedong was the son of a rich farmer in Shaoshan, central Hunan province. Throughout his life, and especially over two decades of civil war between the Nationalists and the CCP, he relied on the support of the peasant class to survive and rise to power.

As a teenager, Mao had read widely on politics, taking a keen interest in the military campaigns of George Washington and Napoleon Bonaparte. In 1917, while studying to become a teacher at the First Normal School of Changsha, he commanded the students' volunteer army. Later that year, Mao moved to Beijing and got a job as an assistant to the university librarian Li Dazhao. Mao's time in Beijing and tutelage under intellectuals like Li and Chen had turned him into a staunch Marxist and believer in the Communist cause.

After the massacre of Communist Party members, which forced survivors to flee to other parts of the country, Mao rallied support among the commoners and co-founded the Chinese Workers' and Peasants' Red Army. His insistence on the adoption of guerrilla military tactics proved to be a boon for the ragtag force, and he was chosen as the leader of the CCP during the Long March of 1934 to 1935, when various Communist armies narrowly escaped Nationalist strongholds to establish a new base in Yan'an, Shaanxi province.

During the Second Sino-Japanese War, from 1937 to 1945, coinciding with the Second World War, the Red Army agreed to a truce and allied with the Nationalists to resist the Japanese. But the Communists largely left the hard fighting work to the Nationalists, led by Chiang Kai-shek. The Chinese Civil War resumed immediately after Japan's surrender, and the Red Army was able to defeat the weakened Nationalists, driving them to Taiwan, a southern island previously controlled by Japan.

The People's Republic of China (PRC) was established on October 1, 1949, and Mao served as the paramount leader of the country until his death in 1976.

The Chinese Communist Party, later referred to simply as "the Party," had the task of turning a war-torn country into the kind of utopian Communist society it had promised its followers. Chairman Mao may have been a shrewd guerrilla military leader, but he proved a far less competent statesman. He thought that grouping previously separate farms together into massive agricultural communes would help drive China's transformation from an agrarian economy into a modern industrialized nation. Overnight, traditional farming practices were upended, and local officials came under pressure to quickly increase crop yields. The disastrous "Great Leap Forward" agricultural collectivization project (from 1958 to 1962) led fearful officials to compete to ship unrealistic quotas of grain to the cities, leaving farmers to starve. Many higher officials did not dare to report the failures of Mao's scheme, and by the time it became obvious that the countryside was starving, it was too late.

An estimated thirty million people died in the countryside, making it the worst famine in history.

In cities, however, the Party's policy guaranteed that urbanites in the military, civil service, or state-owned enterprises could enjoy job security and social benefits for life. The system became known as the "iron rice bowl." The term came from a story about a beautiful housemaid who kept breaking her squire's rice bowls. Because of her beauty, she wasn't punished, and the squire eventually replaced his ceramic bowls with iron ones. Even though the maid wasn't doing her job well, she was still rewarded.

But people paid for "iron rice bowl" security by having little control over their career paths and personal lives. The Party enabled work unit managers to decide who could marry and when, and whether they were allowed to have children. They also shuttled people from job to job with no accounting for personal preferences.

In 1966, facing internal criticism and seeing his status as leader diminishing, Mao mobilized his youthful supporters to stamp out "bourgeois" elements that had infiltrated government and society. He called them the "Red Guards," and across the country, paramilitary gangs embarked on unspeakable acts of violence against people they deemed "class enemies," such as intellectuals and landowners. This was the beginning of the Cultural Revolution, which would last a decade.

At this point of the country's development, China resembled a "hermit kingdom," in some respects like North Korea is today, closed off to the world, with few formal diplomatic ties to non-Communist countries. Between 1949 and 1974, the borders of the People's Republic were closed to most Western countries, even for short-term tourism. China only started to develop its tourism industry in the late 1970s, as part of Deng Xiaoping's economic reforms. In its state of virtual global isolation beforehand, the Cultural Revolution tore at the basic foundation of Chinese society, pitting even family members against one another to commit horrors.

ZHANG HONGBING WAS SIXTEEN years old when he and his father sent his mother to the executioner.

On the evening of February 13, 1970, in a small town in Anhui province, Zhang's mother, Fang Zhongmou, railed against Mao in an argument in her home with her zealous family members. More than a million people had already been killed in the Cultural Revolution, one of the bloodiest eras in Chinese history, and many millions more had been beaten, humiliated, and harassed.

"Why is Mao Zedong making himself a personality cult? His pictures are everywhere!" she said.

"I told her, 'Shut up! I will smash your dog head if you go against our beloved great leader, Chairman Mao,'" Zhang told me. Calling a person a dog, or a relation of a dog, is a common Chinese insult.

His uncle begged Zhang's mother to take her words back, warning that she would be killed, but she said, "I am not scared," then tore down Mao's portrait and burned it.

"After that, Father asked us to watch Mother, and he left to report her," Zhang said. "I also wrote a letter and reported her as well."

Zhang attended his mother's trial, but he did not go to witness her execution. "I chose to run away. I didn't want to see the bloody, cruel moment of my mother's death."

Zhang agreed to speak with me for a story I wrote in 2016 marking the fiftieth anniversary of the start of the Cultural Revolution. The CCP now officially views the revolution as "ten years of catastrophe" that caused "the heaviest losses suffered by the Party, the country, and the people since the founding of the People's Republic." But it does not tolerate discussion of the events that attempts to hold instigators accountable.

Zhang Hongbing is an anomaly—a man so haunted by guilt that he is willing to speak out. Now a Beijing-based lawyer, he warns that as people's memories fade and the younger generation isn't taught about the tragic side of modern China's rise, the Cultural Revolution could "happen again—only in a different form."

More often than not, when I asked older people about their experiences, they would scold me for being annoying. They didn't want to dwell on the past. They wanted to believe in a better future.

COLLECTIVE AMNESIA ABOUT TRAUMATIC EVENTS, and the public's desire to focus on the future, is a good thing for Chinese government. It makes it easier for Beijing to manage its citizenry through a carrot-and-stick approach. The carrot is mostly economic incentives, and the stick is legal or economic punishment.

While this approach has been central to CCP statecraft for decades, under Xi, the Party has energetically propagandized about its strength and ability to provide economic prosperity. Xi has stated passionately in his public speeches that the collapse of the Soviet Union should be a cautionary tale and that defence against economic vulnerability and ideological resistance is central to maintaining domestic stability.

Today, China is not an egalitarian society by any means. The underclass is a literal reality, living in slums and cavernous underground apartments. Poor migrant workers are shunted aside whenever a new highway or shopping mall has to be built. Paper eviction notices in red ink can be slapped on their shanty doors and that is that, even though their jobs as construction workers and street sweepers, for example, are essential to the running of cities. Officials cut the electricity to their homes and set up barbed-wire fences to keep people out, and the demolition crews go to work.

Yet even those in low-income jobs are relatively hopeful about the future. The Pew Research Center found that in 2016 roughly eight in ten people in China believed their children would be financially better off than they were. As the reputable global surveys have shown year after year, the Chinese public tends to be one of the world's most optimistic about its future economic prospects. Seven in ten Chinese expect that their personal economic situation will improve in the next twelve months. This contrasts with the gloomy outlook for North American millennials compared to their parents' generation.

You can see the entrepreneurial spirit everywhere: in the *jianbing* cart owners in Beijing and elsewhere who move around the city to serve their savoury stuffed crepes wherever the hungriest people congregate, and in the endless advertisements for new businesses, gadgets, nightclubs, and restaurants. When I travelled to smaller cities and used apps to hire drivers, they would often stop multiple times to pick up more passengers to maximize their income. This kind of hustle is quite normal among the working class in China. One driver even took a video call from his toddler daughter in the car; it was clear he was working hard for her sake.

Government anti-poverty campaigns do provide assistance to the ultra-poor in remote areas. But officials have used methods that wouldn't be feasible in democratic countries, such as demolishing villages and forcing residents to move to different parts of a province, reportedly so that residents can access better resources and economic opportunities. The rural poor also take care of each other; a network of grassroots and state-supported "barefoot social workers" has sprung up since 2010 to help children affected by disease and destitution.

Studies on the Chinese middle class show moderate to high levels of support for the central government. About 40 percent of entrepreneurs are members of the Communist Party, often sitting on representative bodies and local government associations. "This is seen by businesspeople themselves as good business practice," according to David Goodman, a professor at the University of Sydney.

According to the experts I have interviewed, people's faith in the Party on economic matters can be credited in large part to the enduring influence of Deng Xiaoping, who gradually took power as China's leader after Mao died in 1976. In addition to steering the country in a dramatic shift from collectivized economic models to a pseudo-capitalist system with limited state ownership of key industries, Deng also established trade ties with many democratic countries.

"Let some people get rich first" and "socialism with Chinese characteristics" were popular slogans of the Deng Xiaoping era. Known as the "architect of modern China," Deng occupied different senior roles within the CCP but was effectively its paramount leader from 1978 until his retirement in 1989, although he remained highly influential until his death in 1997.

Through memorable speeches, the charismatic leader touted his plan to gradually allow free-market capitalism into the country while delaying socialist goals such as distributing wealth equally among the people.

His economic policy was similar to the "trickle-down" theory popularized by American president Ronald Reagan in the 1980s, which postulated that giving large businesses and wealthy people tax breaks would stimulate economic growth and benefit wider society in the longer term. Like the "American Dream," the Chinese equivalent appealed to individual interests. You shouldn't be alarmed if others got very rich first, said Deng and the Chinese leaders who followed him, because you could be next.

But while he was a remarkably liberal reformer when it came to the economy, Deng chose to maintain staunch controls on civil society. When the 1989 Tiananmen Square protests in Beijing spread to around four hundred other Chinese cities, Deng and other hardliners within the Party argued that society would devolve into anarchy if they didn't use force.

International condemnation of the Tiananmen Square massacre weakened Deng's reputation within the Party. He "retired" in November 1989, and his economic reforms faltered in his absence. Deng was still highly influential in the Party, however, and enjoyed popular support as well. In a bid to rebuild momentum for his vision of letting capitalism propel the country's economy forward, he embarked on his famous 1992 southern tour of the cities he thought had the economic potential to open up China's business to the world, drumming up widespread local support and international approval. The speeches he made during that tour contain axioms that Deng is still respected for and that remain influential today. He said the set-up of free-market economic zones in China was "socialist in nature" and urged citizens not to be afraid of doing business with foreign enterprises.

In 2001, China joined the World Trade Organization after a lengthy process of international debate and negotiation. But while some Chinese citizens grew fabulously wealthy from the ongoing reforms and opening of the economy to global markets, the average citizen remained very poor. In 2010, China surpassed Japan to become the world's second-largest economy. Yet by 2018, the average annual income per capita was just US$12,473 — far below the global average. Income inequality in China is still among the highest in the world.

As Beijing offered billions of dollars in subsidies and other forms of state support to entrepreneurs and industry leaders, the distance widened between rich and poor in China, and it is now bigger than it has ever been in the U.S.

According to the World Bank, after nearly four decades of double-digit growth per year on average, China's economy is finally slowing down. In the summer of 2015, China's stock markets were nearly in free fall, diving to levels not seen since the dawn of the global financial crisis in 2007. In response, central authorities rolled out a dizzying array of stimulus and loosening measures, including multiple interest rate cuts and devaluing the Chinese currency. These efforts helped prevent a crash, but experts say a sense of unease about the faltering economy has persisted. The slowdown has continued, and in 2019 China's economy grew only 6.1 percent from the previous year, which was a big step down from the pace of earlier years.

"I sold off most of my China shares, and I'm planning to invest in overseas companies instead," Mason Zhao, a major Beijing-based investor, told me in 2015. As the rich scrambled to park their money outside the country, the poor were bearing the brunt of the slowdown. Prices of staple goods rose, while companies shed jobs and automation made many factory workers obsolete.

With the economy no longer expanding at a breakneck speed, the notion that the Party would provide prosperity to citizens in exchange for totalitarian control was becoming untenable. But President Xi has stuck with his message that the Soviet Union is a cautionary tale. The CCP wasn't going to allow space for public criticism to flourish and undermine the Party's political principles.

WITHOUT A FREE CIVIL SOCIETY in which Chinese people can lobby the government to address their concerns, immigration to a freer country is a popular option for citizens with the means. Those who have no ability or intention to leave typically try to focus on their personal circumstances. Caring about politics is *ma fan*—too troublesome—yet at the same time, many bristle at state control over the most intimate aspects of their lives.

Giving birth to boys has traditionally been highly preferred over girls, because only male children can continue a family line. The one-child policy from 1979 to 2015 was intended to control the size of the population to avoid overwhelming the country's resources, but it also led to millions of sex-selective abortions and an estimated one hundred million infant girls being killed or abandoned by parents who wanted to try again for a boy.

In October 2015, after more than three decades of brutal government interference in citizens' reproductive choices, there seemed to be a breakthrough. Beijing suddenly announced it would allow all married couples to have two children.

China's population is rapidly aging, and with low birth rates, there won't be enough young people to take care of the elderly and supply the labour force. The economy could collapse under the strain. But the change in policy doesn't meant that anyone can have two children for the sake of the country's future. For same-sex couples, unmarried couples, and single parents, the bureaucratic nightmares continue.

For Xiao Min, a very pragmatic thirty-six-year-old single woman in Shanghai, the solution was to find a fake husband — a marriage of convenience that would look good on paper.

Over cocktails with me at a restaurant on an elegant leafy boulevard of Shanghai's former French concession, she explained that as a single mother she would have to pay a hefty fine to bear a child out of wedlock. Even then, there was no guarantee that her child would get an identity card, which was needed to access public services, secure a bank account, and travel long-distance. Social stigma would be the least of her child's worries.

A successful businesswoman, Xiao approached life in an authoritarian country as a puzzle to be solved. She persuaded a friend to donate his sperm and enter into a sham marriage with her. Armed with a marriage certificate and the approval of family planning officials, she gave birth to a happy and healthy daughter. Her "husband" lives separately from them and visits from time to time, and no one has given them any trouble.

"I have a career that allows me to hire a full-time nanny. I do not want to rush to find someone to marry just so I can have children," she said, raking her fingers through her coiffed hair. I admired her pluck and creativity, but her story made me realize that China's harsh legal system isn't applied to everyone equally. Wealth and connections matter.

Poor parents from less prosperous inland regions often feel they have no choice but to leave their children in the care of relatives so they can seek work in a big city. According to UNICEF, there are about seventy million of these "left-behind children" in China.

People who want to move for work get stuck in limbo because of the household registration, or *hukou*, system, which makes them temporary residents anywhere outside their home province. As temporary residents, they lack access to welfare services and educational opportunities even decades after they relocate.

With so many families living vast distances apart, and unable to afford air travel, the two-week Lunar New Year festival is such a special time in China because it's the only time of the year when migrant workers have enough time off work to take long-haul train trips home to reunite with their families.

I often think about Zhang Jing, a thirty-five-year-old who left her rural town in southeastern Anhui province at the age of nineteen to search for work in the capital. She beat the odds to rise through the ranks to become a manager at a shipping company, but still, none of her family members have Beijing *hukou*. This means her daughter is ineligible to take local university entrance exams. Once Zhang's daughter reaches high school age, the family will have to move back to Anhui.

"If not for her education, why would we go back? Most of our relatives have moved to Beijing already. We know barely anyone in Anhui," she told me.

But Zhang still counts herself lucky. Though her daughter's future is uncertain, other parents from Zhang's hometown are toiling in factories or working long hours in big-city restaurants or as cleaners on subsistence-level wages, thousands of miles away from their children.

Government land seizures are another common source of discontent. According to Chinese property law, individuals cannot privately own land and can only lease land-use rights for a number of years, giving them little leverage to challenge government decisions. Small-scale protests are frequent when citizens are offered very little compensation for their homes.

After I changed jobs in 2017 to work for the Agence France-Presse in Beijing, I often paired up with photographer Nicolas Asfouri. Together, we trekked to far-flung communities to witness lightning-speed social change before entire ways of life were gone. We visited a travelling circus, spent weeks in a close-knit migrant workers' village due for demolition, and rode a speedboat down a river to glimpse daily life in North Korea during the height of missile test tensions.

In the southern Chinese city of Kaiping, in a historic neighbourhood, we met several dozen people who were holding out against government pressure to sell their properties to make way for a "heritage theme park." In 2007, UNESCO had listed the town of Chikan, with its unique European-inspired architectural flourishes, as a World Heritage Site. Locals considered the international honour a curse, since city leaders later brokered a US$900 million deal with an investment firm to turn Old Chikan into a tourist attraction emptied of the families who had lived there for many generations. Developers wanted to build a wall around the village, set up trinket shops, and charge entrance fees.

Years ago, customers would line up around the block for Grandma Wu's red bean and coconut puddings. But when

Asfouri and I visited on a sweltering summer evening, the agile sixty-year-old Grandma Wu had to show us how to vault a barricade to get to her dessert shop.

After insisting that we try her puddings, which she was still making and delivering to loyal customers, she pointed out the eviction notices tacked to her door. Chikan residents were offered compensation of between ¥3,200 and ¥3,900 (US$472 and US$575) per square metre, which was nowhere near enough to purchase a small apartment in the area. When Wu and some neighbours staged a protest the previous autumn, they were arrested and jailed for several days.

Listening to Wu speak about how she felt she had no future, I imagined the popular outrage if a mayor in France or Germany tried to do the same to a historic town. While Wu and her neighbours were defiant, they accepted their lot. They stayed out of principle, and because they had nowhere else to go, but were essentially waiting for police to force them out.

For those who didn't own property and were therefore ineligible for cash buyouts, the city government provided subsidized rental housing. But these were essentially rows of metal containers stacked atop one another and unbearably hot in the summer.

We visited a relative of Grandma Wu's who was living by herself in one such metal box on the barren outskirts of the city. Two rotating fans circulated the air around the small apartment but did little to cut the stifling heat. Outside, there were no sitting areas for the displaced villagers to gather. Children who had once played in the shade of beautiful trees in their ancient village occupied themselves in the spaces between the rows of metal homes with nothing to shield them from the sun.

PROTESTS OF ANY SORT are very rare considering the size of China's population, but they do occur regularly. I kept track of labour protests by factory workers calling for higher wages and better conditions. They are too small in size to attract much media attention, but they happen continually all across the country. The Hong Kong–based watchdog group China Labour Bulletin recorded 2,509 strikes and protests by workers and employees in China in 2015 alone. The main reasons for these strikes are factory closures and layoffs as Beijing steers the country away from a manufacturing-based economy to higher-tech innovation- and consumer-oriented industries. The global market is also a factor, with factories in Southeast Asia undercutting many Chinese factories by offering even lower manufacturing and labour costs.

To some extent, these labour protests are permitted, as long as their targets are considered low-level, such as local factory owners. But when wider criticism implicates the Party, governments respond to the potential risk of organized opposition by stifling even the mildest expressions of dissatisfaction.

Under Xi's leadership, there have been fewer carrots and more sticks.

On the eve of International Women's Day in 2015, police in Beijing, Guangzhou, and Hangzhou arrested five young women simply because they were planning to distribute stickers with messages against sexual harassment on subway trains and buses. The women gained international support as the "Feminist Five" and spent months in jail under constant interrogation. Hillary Clinton, an American presidential candidate at the time, tweeted that the treatment of the five women was "inexcusable."

In the past, the feminist movement in China had more leeway than many other causes because the Communist revolution was predicated in part on liberating women from a feudal system that entrenched their lower status. But the arrests of these women pointed to the likelihood that all types of activism were risky under Xi's more authoritarian brand of leadership.

Later that summer, police swept across the country in a ruthless campaign to detain or question more than two hundred Chinese human rights lawyers and activists in the largest clampdown on the legal profession in recent history. The group included prominent lawyer Wang Quanzhang, who has defended many political activists and victims of land seizures. After Wang disappeared into the bowels of the detention system, I met his wife, Li Wenzu, at a restaurant on the outskirts of Beijing. Tears streamed down her face when she told me she didn't know if her husband was dead or alive; she hadn't received any word from him for a thousand days since his arrest.

In July 2017, I travelled to a hospital in the industrial city of Shenyang, in northeast Liaoning province, to try to find the Chinese dissident who is perhaps the best known in the West: Nobel Peace Prize laureate Liu Xiaobo. The writer and philosopher had been sentenced in 2009 to eleven years in prison for "subversion" after co-authoring Charter 08, a petition calling for democratic reforms. Before that, he was a Tiananmen Square student leader and had written many books and essays on political reform. His wife, poet Liu Xia, had been under de facto house arrest since he won the Nobel in 2010, even though she was never charged with any crime. Liu Xiaobo was fighting advanced liver cancer, which he had developed in prison, and it was likely to kill him any day.

Armed police guarded the entrances of the sprawling medical complex where Liu was being kept. Unlike foreign reporters with heavy camera equipment, who had been roughed up and shoved away in recent days, I was able to slip past because I look like an ordinary Chinese woman clutching a sparkly pink phone. (To blend in even better, I wore a bright-purple dress; in many cities, Chinese women tend to have bold tastes in fashion.) I took the stairs instead of an elevator to avoid surveillance cameras.

Once in the oncology department on the eleventh floor, I stopped to catch my breath before walking down the hallway. I spotted patients wearing the same blue-and-white striped pyjamas that Liu had been wearing in photos his family members had sneaked to the press. I watched as nurses paced and bored-looking men who might have been police sat on benches just outside a wing that looked like it had been recently closed off from the public. Makeshift paper signs taped to the walls read: "Closed for renovations."

I headed to the reception desk to ask a nurse if I could see a man by the name of Liu Xiaobo. She searched on a computer but said she couldn't find anyone of that name in the hospital records. (Just that morning, the hospital had posted an online statement about the famous democracy advocate's condition and the top quality of care he was receiving.)

Two weeks later, on July 13, 2017, Liu succumbed to liver cancer in that hospital. He was the first Nobel Peace Prize winner to die in police custody since the days of Nazi Germany.

Following his cancer diagnosis, Liu had asked to receive treatment abroad—a request that friends believe was, in reality, an attempt to secure his wife's safety after he died. Hospitals in the U.S. and Germany offered to accept him, but Chinese authorities refused to let the couple go.

Although online censorship in China was becoming increasingly sophisticated—private messages can disappear without the user knowing their words were never sent—people found ways to express their sadness over Liu Xiaobo's death. All over WeChat, people posted candle emojis and "RIP," though administrators quickly caught on and removed the posts for "violating relevant laws and regulations."

OFTEN, BEIJING'S RELENTLESS PERSECUTION of so-called "dissidents" results in baffling cruelty toward their hapless spouses and children.

In late 2015, state harassment against Professor Chen Guiqiu and her two daughters, aged four and fifteen, reached such an unbearable level that they fled their home in the freezing winter with only the bare essentials in backpacks. Chen was giving up her job in the Environmental Science department at Hunan University in central China, but that was the least of her worries. A few months earlier, in the summer of 2015, during the country-wide crackdown on hundreds of human rights lawyers and activists, authorities had taken away Chen's husband, Xie Yang.

Xie was a lawyer, and like so many of China's public interest defenders, he was brought to a secret detention facility for questioning. He was missing for months, and Chen feared the worst. A court later charged him with "inciting subversion of state power," a very serious crime defined as an attempt to undermine the state and socialist system by spreading rumours or slander. Before Xie's arrest, his clients had included underground Christians, a victim of police violence, and supporters of democracy in Hong Kong.

While Xie was in detention, police tortured him to extract a confession. "Your only right is to obey," the officers allegedly told him, right before the violence began. "They'd split up the work: one or two would grab my arms while someone used their fists to punch me in the stomach, kneed me in the stomach, or kicked me," Xie said, according to transcripts of interviews with his lawyers.

Chen became a vocal advocate for her husband. She agreed to speak with international journalists like me and formed a sisterhood with wives of other detained human rights lawyers, marching outside police stations with the names of their husbands sewn in red cloth on their white clothes, demanding their freedom. Most of them also had young children who were struggling to understand what had happened to their fathers.

While many others were also in Xie's position, his case garnered special attention on the international stage. The United Nations repeatedly condemned the treatment of the lawyer, including in a letter from the UN Human Rights Council saying that China should immediately release Xie and two others from "arbitrary detention" and pay them compensation.

This made Chen more of a target. Officials interrogated her repeatedly and threatened to evict her from her home and have her fired from her university job if she continued to speak out about her husband.

First, Chen and her children tried to leave the country by train. Security officials blocked them, separating Chen from her elder daughter before letting them go with a warning. Chen knew then that she needed to attempt a daring escape to protect what was left of her family.

Supporters escorted Chen and her daughters across towns, villages, long roads, and forest thickets on their way to Thailand, travelling by foot and by car on different legs of the journey. The ordeal took over a week. They walked long distances through

rough terrain in the dead of night to evade border guards. Finally, the family arrived at a safe house in Bangkok, in an affluent neighbourhood with leafy tropical trees. It seemed like an oasis.

The respite was brief. Thai police soon arrived at the house, and an immigration court judge ordered the family to leave the country immediately. But Chen's confidence didn't waver, she told me. She knew that American friends had arranged permits for them to travel on to the U.S. She knew also that because her younger daughter is an American citizen by birth, their family would have the right to consular assistance.

While Chen and her daughters were waiting inside a Bangkok immigration detention centre, Chinese agents showed up outside and swarmed the facility. That was when the family began to panic. Several U.S. diplomats intervened and convinced Thai officials to let the group leave through a back door. But the Chinese agents did not give up pursuit so easily. They chased them to the international airport, where the three countries' representatives engaged in a noisy argument. Eventually, a diplomatic deal was struck and the family was able to board a plane to America.

This international drama unfolded on March 3, 2017 — several weeks before President Xi Jinping and President Donald Trump met for the first time at the Mar-a-Lago resort in Florida. When, in my role as a foreign correspondent in Beijing, I asked a Chinese foreign ministry spokesperson about the case of Chen Guiqiu and Xie Yang, he only repeated the ministry's talking points.

Two years later, Xie was relatively fortunate to be released from prison. But to Chen he sounded "strange" in phone calls to his family. Chen confessed to me that she fears her husband's health has been permanently damaged, and she feels powerless to help him from afar. It is unclear whether the family will ever be reunited, because police have confiscated Xie's passport.

I reached out to Chen again in 2019 after she settled in Texas. We used an encrypted app to communicate. "Inside the immigration prison, I was not expecting any rescue," she told me in Mandarin, her voice calm and strong. She was relieved to see her daughters unwind after what they had endured every day in China, she said. The girls immediately took a liking to Texas because the police there did not follow them everywhere.

EVEN EXPERIENCED CHINA WATCHERS have found it hard to explain why Xi Jinping and his cohort have ramped up attacks on civil society to such unprecedented levels. Surely Chinese society is strong enough to stay intact in the face of defence lawyers doing their jobs and a handful of feminists distributing stickers on some buses?

Analysts can't decide whether the increasingly heavy-handed repression means the CCP regime is on the brink of collapse— or preparing to create an alternative world order.

In the early 1990s, Deng Xiaoping, wary of Beijing claiming global leadership too soon, promoted a dictum that his country should "hide our capabilities and bide our time." Evidently, Xi thinks it is now time for China to shed its low-profile foreign strategy. More than any other Chinese leader, he has been upfront about Beijing's ever-expanding global ambitions.

Ever since Beijing hosted the 2008 Summer Olympics, the state has emphasized pomp and ceremony at major events to bolster its world image. This was certainly true in September 2016, when China became the second Asian country to host a summit of the Group of 20 (G20) major economies. Xi presided over the carefully orchestrated two days of meetings in Hangzhou, a lush eastern city famed for its ancient waterways and picturesque West Lake.

I had already seen how Beijing locks down its city centre and puts a halt on polluting factories to set the stage for important political meetings, but I was stunned at the lengths officials went to ensure the Hangzhou G20 summit would be a success.

They closed off entire blocks so dignitaries staying in five-star hotels could be shuttled to the glittering summit venue without spotting a single local resident on streets lined with freshly manicured lawns, trees, and flowering bushes. In the weeks leading up to the summit, Chinese authorities quietly blocked international civil society groups from monitoring the event, which has been the tradition, and also rounded up local activists to make sure no one spoke about political rights while the world's attention was on the city.

A key objective of the meeting was to discuss climate change. Earlier, environmentalists had expressed doubts that the summit would make much of a difference to the sluggish global effort to cut emissions. But as host, Xi immediately took a bombastic stance, as if scolding other leaders for being slow and ineffective. He opened the summit on a Sunday afternoon with a speech calling for the body to become "an action team instead of a talk shop."

Xi reiterated the point at a welcome dinner for the G20 leaders, including Turkish president Recep Tayyip Erdoğan, Canadian prime minister Justin Trudeau, and British prime minister Theresa May. "It is imperative that the G20 take the lead and blaze a trail," he said, looking statesmanlike with both his hands on the table in front of him.

That weekend, U.S. president Barack Obama and Xi entered their two countries into the Paris Agreement on climate change, and by the conclusion of the summit, all of the G20 members had joined the accord. The pact set out a global framework to reduce emissions enough to limit global warming to below two degrees Celsius and to provide financial assistance to developing countries affected by a changing climate.

To cap off the fruitful gathering, participants visited the lush shores of West Lake to watch a breathtaking performance, where it seemed as if dancers were skating and leaping on the surface of the water.

Xi's decision to focus initially on assuming the role of global leader to fight climate change was savvy; it was a relatively apolitical cause that didn't invite criticism on China's dismal human rights record.

A year later, in 2017, at the largest-ever international meeting Beijing had hosted to date, nearly three hundred foreign political leaders signed a document praising President Xi's contribution to world peace. The "global interparty dialogue" involved hundreds of politicians from mostly developing nations, including Burmese state counsellor Aung San Suu Kyi and Cambodian prime minister Hun Sen. New Zealand's Labour Party, Italy's Democratic Party, South Korea's Democratic Party, and Japan's Komeito party also sent representatives.

It was a dull event, and most people took no notice, but those paying attention were astounded that so many leaders would endorse Xi as a *peacemaker*, of all things, given the violent manner in which the Chinese state has cracked down on its detractors at home and abroad.

"Many political parties in the world are confused and struggling and searching for a new path," stated Wang Yiwei, director of the Institute of International Affairs at Renmin University of China, who spoke at the event. "As Brexit and Trump have shown, there's no teacher of liberal democracy and teachers have made mistakes. There is no universal model of development."

In other words, there was a power vacuum in global leadership from Western nations, and China was stepping in.

THROUGH IT ALL, Beijing has been remarkably clear about its goals. Under Xi, many official government documents have explained that China isn't content to be just an economic heavyweight, or to have its manufacturers serve as the world's factory. It wants to alter existing international norms and global governance to suit its broader vision.

In September 2019, the State Council, Beijing's chief administrative authority, issued a white paper outlining China's goals to rise as a leader among democratic nations, "fundamentally altering the international structures of power" for a "new era." The paper emphasized China's contributions to the world economy and claimed that the country has no intention to challenge or "replace" the United States as the world's dominant power.

It warned, however, that continual attempts from Western countries to "interfere" with China's domestic issues would be a "strategic miscalculation" that "risks turning conflict and confrontation into a self-fulfilling prophecy." The paper called instead for a harmonious "new model of international relations" and a "community of common destiny" that would be built on the principles of mutually beneficial cooperation and respect for other countries' political systems. "All should oppose power politics, hegemony, and interference in other countries' domestic affairs," the paper argued. It employed the flowery and obtuse language that is also commonly found in Beijing diplomats' fiery rebuffs of any international criticism.

It all sounds very nice, these slogans of "win-win" cooperation and global dialogue. But many analysts have commented that such language is really a self-interested manifesto for the right of authoritarian countries to do as they wish, without the interference of global institutions like the United Nations or international courts, although China has never called for the dismantling of such organizations.

"Can you construct a new world order using the structure of the existing world order? That increasingly seems to be Xi Jinping's goal, couched amidst calls to 'safeguard the UN-centered international system, preserve the international order underpinned by international law,'" China expert Bill Bishop wrote in an analysis for the *Sinocism* newsletter, quoting from Xi's latest speech on international governance in April 2021.

It is a deliberate twist on the concept of "democracy" that suits Beijing's interests, where there is equality and equal legitimacy of all nations regardless of regime type, including authoritarian governments that subject their citizens to draconian laws and cruel treatment.

2.

HONG KONG

Century of Humiliation

In the spring of 2014, Hong Kong was on the precipice.

For months, a trio of veteran political reform advocates had been planning a civil disobedience campaign, to fight for fully democratic elections. While there are some opportunities for Hong Kong residents to vote for government representatives at lower levels, only a small number can vote for the city's leader, and only for Beijing-vetted candidates. The campaign, named "Occupy Central with Love and Peace," called on Hong Kong's 7.4 million people to block the streets of the central business district if the government refused to meet their demands for universal suffrage. Clogging the financial heart of this capitalist hub would force Hong Kong's leaders *and* Beijing's central leaders to pay attention.

So the thinking went.

As a city affairs reporter for the *South China Morning Post* since 2012, it was my job to understand the planned occupation. One day, I left my apartment in a traditional *tonglou* row house at the foot of the western side of Hong Kong Island and hiked uphill toward the University of Hong Kong campus. There I met law professor Benny Tai, one of the three instigators of Occupy Central. The other two were a middle-aged sociologist and an elderly Baptist minister. Every inch of spare space in Tai's office was stacked high with books and papers.

"I'm sure my office is bugged, but it'll be impossible to find the device in this mess," Tai joked, adjusting his glasses.

The soft-spoken scholar explained that protesters would simply ask the government to fulfill its obligations under the territory's constitution. The Basic Law stipulated that the city's chief executive should be selected in accordance with the principles of universal suffrage (in practice, candidates for the office were nominated by a largely pro-Beijing nominating committee). Civil disobedience, Tai said, would be the people's last resort.

I left Tai's office with a notebook full of facts and legal arguments but little clue as to what would happen in the fall if the threatened occupation began.

It was clear from my own experience at a local English-language newspaper that the city's institutions were under pressure. Time and again, articles on politically sensitive subjects got pulled just minutes before the paper hit the presses. Once, *South China Morning Post* editors scrubbed an entire story from the website because a senior official found my interview of him unflattering. One night, even the paper's CEO got involved to complain about a straightforward news story about Hong Kong's declining press freedom, and editors were forced to cut it down to a stub. The self-censorship and lack of clarity about what was off limits were demoralizing, and the paper's staff was quitting in droves.

People in the city were also still reeling after Kevin Lau, a prominent Chinese-language newspaper editor, was brutally attacked a few months after he collaborated with international journalists to produce an investigative story exposing the offshore holdings of family members of Chinese Communist Party leaders. In broad daylight, the attacker used a cleaver to hack his target from behind, leaving him in critical condition. Lau survived, and nine men were later arrested in connection with the assault—but they were only hired hands. The instigators remain unidentified and at large.

The unsolved crime only made journalists more anxious. Our stories were being censored, and now violence? In 2002, Reporters Without Borders ranked Hong Kong's media the eighteenth most free in the world. That ranking had plummeted to eightieth by 2020.

CHINA'S BOUNDARIES HAVE EXPANDED and contracted for millennia, as shown by the earliest written records from the Shang dynasty, which, in the second millennium BCE, ruled a region around the Yellow River, an area that is only a small portion of China's extent today. Over thousands of years, successive emperors and warlords expanded their kingdom's borders through successful military campaigns and defended them from invaders, quite often being forced to retreat and give up swaths of land.

This was par for the course for major empires throughout history. But the loss of Hong Kong in 1842 to the British during a period of Western imperialism against the Qing dynasty, the last to rule in China, was a humiliation that cut deeply. Its repercussions continue to this day, with the uprisings in Hong

Kong stoking modern Chinese leaders' anger over a time when their ancestors were too weak to defend themselves against technologically advanced allied Western forces.

Beijing's concern over the restoration of its perceived traditional territories didn't start with President Xi. In 1950, one of the first acts of the Red Army after its civil war victory was to invade and annex Tibet, which for centuries had alternated between independence and rule by the Mongolians and Chinese dynasties. Today, Chinese leaders generally take a broad and sweeping view of the country's traditional territories to include areas that were at any time part of imperial Chinese territory, even if those lands were claimed for centuries by other nations and peoples. And a recent shift in China's global relations strategy that observers dubbed "wolf warrior diplomacy," after a *Rambo*-style Chinese nationalistic action film, has meant that Beijing is now asserting its claims without worrying about what the international community might think.

In the aftermath of the Tiananmen massacre and the run-up to the 2008 Summer Olympics, Chinese diplomats had been cautious in their interactions with other countries, especially the United States. "The idea was to win trust and persuade the world that China's rise wasn't a threat," says Peter Martin, a former Beijing-based foreign correspondent and author of *China's Civilian Army: The Making of Wolf Warrior Diplomacy.*

That former approach to diplomacy initially proved highly effective, Martin told me, but it frustrated a lot of Chinese citizens who felt that their diplomats were too deferential to their foreign counterparts. As China grew more powerful, many thought their country should assert its interests more forcefully, Martin found in his research, which drew on the memoirs of more than one hundred retired diplomats.

"Starting in 2008 [the year China hosted the Summer Olympics], and with increasing intensity after Xi Jinping came to power in 2012, the behaviour of Chinese diplomats became outright aggressive. The long-standing touchiness and insecurity of Chinese leaders was paired with a new sense of strength and entitlement," Martin said. "The outcome was wolf warrior diplomacy."

Liu Xiaoming, who served as China's ambassador to the U.K. for eleven years, is among a group of diplomats who have taken aggressive stances on social media platforms to champion Beijing's interests. "As I see it, there are so-called 'wolf warriors' because there are 'wolfs' in the world and you need warriors to fight them," Liu tweeted in February 2021. His hundreds of posts, including one that claims "people in Xinjiang live a happy life in a stable environment," are amplified by an army of fake Twitter accounts that have retweeted Chinese diplomats and state media tens of thousands of times, according to a 2021 investigation by the Associated Press and the Oxford Internet Institute. Many of these accounts impersonate U.K. citizens.

"Wolf warriors" frequently promote policies related to Taiwan and the South China Sea.

The CCP has always claimed Taiwan as part of its territory, even though the island has been self-governed since the Nationalists took it over after losing the Chinese Civil War in 1949. Beijing considers Taiwan a renegade Chinese province that must one day become "reunified" with the mainland — by force if necessary.

Most major countries of the world have followed along with Beijing's "One-China" policy, which claims there is only one legitimate government of China and that Taiwan is part of China. For decades, they have maintained only informal ties with Taiwan. As a result, Taiwan has been diplomatically isolated, despite the fact that the island has developed into a vibrant democracy. Even the United States officially recognizes — and has formal ties with — only Beijing, though in the final days of President Donald Trump's administration, U.S. Secretary of State Mike Pompeo announced that the U.S. would lift restrictions on official contact with Taiwan.

Still, Chinese officials now frequently react with explosive fury whenever a media outlet, academic, or company makes the "mistake" of even implying that Taiwan is a sovereign nation. Donatella Versace, chief creative officer of the luxury Italian brand Versace, personally issued a public apology for a T-shirt that listed many fashionable cities and implied Hong Kong and Taiwan were independent territories. Versace wrote on Instagram, "I am deeply sorry for the unfortunate recent error. . . . Never have I wanted to disrespect China's National Sovereignty and this is why I wanted to personally apologize."

In April 2018, China's Civil Aviation Administration (CAA) ordered a number of international airlines, including several from the U.S., to change how Taiwan is described on their websites and promotional material. The U.S. State Department swiftly pushed back in response to Beijing "dictating" policy, but some airlines still complied, likely fearing backlash from China that could impact flight routes and ticket sales.

Meanwhile, Beijing's aggressive claims over the South China Sea have stoked tensions across the Asia-Pacific. China claims about 90 percent of the South China Sea, spanning more than two million square kilometres, which holds key shipping lanes and may contain oil and gas deposits. Taiwan, Vietnam, and China have competing claims over the Paracels island chain. The Spratlys, another major archipelago in the South China Sea, are even more hotly contested, with about forty-five islands, reefs, and other maritime features occupied by militaries from China, Taiwan, Vietnam, the Philippines, and Malaysia.

Under the slogan of "big country diplomacy," Xi has asserted claims in the South China Sea much more boldly than his predecessors, resulting in a spike in confrontations. Beijing has reclaimed land from the sea to build airstrips at a frenetic pace, setting up military bases and deploying surface-to-air missiles.

In October 2015, the United States responded by sending a U.S. Navy destroyer through the Spratlys to conduct a freedom of navigation operation (FONOP). Admiral Harry Harris, head of the U.S. Navy's Pacific Command, said China was "changing the operational landscape" in the South China Sea and that the United States would increase FONOP patrols. Beijing has long protested America's involvement, accusing the U.S. of raising regional tensions with its patrols and surveillance.

The following year, an international arbitral tribunal sitting in the Hague delivered a sweeping rebuke of Beijing's historical claims in the South China Sea. The tribunal said the country violated international law by causing "irreparable harm" to the marine environment through its construction of artificial islands. Beijing refused to take part in the arbitration and said the verdict was null and void.

International law and tribunal rulings are having a diminishing impact on Beijing. China is doubling down on repression in places on the geopolitical periphery of its modern dominion, including Tibet, Xinjiang, Hong Kong, and Macau. Beijing rejects the assertion that it is empire-building, because, it says, territories including Taiwan and most of the South China Sea are indisputably China's. Many disagree.

TO UNDERSTAND THE GREAT TOUCHINESS of Chinese leaders, it's helpful to acknowledge that it wasn't very long ago when Western and Japanese forces invaded China and subjected Chinese emperors and then the first leaders of the Republic of China (1912–1949) to extensive economic and territorial concessions. The so-called "century of humiliation," from 1839 to 1949, is evidently still a sore point and is central to understanding Beijing's attitudes toward the West.

For many centuries, China was secure in its exalted place among the world's kingdoms. From its roots in the Han dynasty (206 BCE to 220 CE) until the nineteenth century, the "tributary system" (a term coined by Europeans) facilitated international relations under a framework where all those who sought to make contact with China would need to pay respects to the emperor through rituals such as kowtowing and giving gifts. Historians disagree on how asymmetrical the tributary system was and the degree to which Chinese emperors saw themselves as superior to the non-Chinese world. But records generally show the system was generally well accepted and facilitated smooth trade and diplomatic relations between China and its neighbours.

Early contact with the British, who did not agree that showing a great deal of respect to the Chinese emperor was necessary, proved disastrous. In 1793, Britain's first ambassador to China, George Macartney, arrived with a large entourage and six hundred crates of gifts to present to Emperor Qianlong in the hope of impressing the Qing dynasty leader and convincing him to lift trade restrictions on the British.

After an arduous journey that took nearly a year, the

Macartney mission formed a parade procession and marched into the Summer Palace grounds in Beijing, but to their utter embarrassment no one was there to meet them.

Eventually, an official helped them settle in and prepare to greet the emperor. Macartney did not consider Qianlong superior to the King of England, however, so he refused to perform the traditional kowtow ceremony of going down on both knees and bowing nine times. On entering the ornate tent used for the reception, he knelt on just one knee before the emperor and presented Qianlong with gifts, including an Oxford scholar's gown and some watches. Translators then read out a letter from King George in which the king requested to establish a British embassy in Beijing, the opening of additional ports, and the use of a small island off the Chinese coast.

Qianlong initially received the Macartney party with polite restraint, according to reports from both sides, but he became angry when Macartney refused to leave before negotiating better terms for trade. The emperor furiously sent them packing with a stinging response to King George's letter: "Strange and costly objects do not interest me.... We possess all things. I set no value on objects strange or ingenious, and have no use for your country's manufactures."

Then, in a second edict after Macartney still did not get the hint: "There is nothing we do not have. So we have never needed trade with foreign countries to give us anything we lacked." He argued that China's tea, porcelain, and silk were "essential needs" for countries that did not have them, and so the dynasty permitted foreign merchants "to satisfy your needs and to allow you to benefit from our surplus." Trade, in other words, was entirely a show of China's benevolence toward less fortunate nations.

After Macartney's failed mission, China continued its restrictions on overseas commerce, known as the Canton System, which confined all foreign trading to a southern port city now known as Guangzhou. Into the nineteenth century, silver from Europe was flowing into China as payment for the tea, silks, and porcelains that Westerners coveted, but the Qing dynasty's dismissive attitude toward foreign wares remained unchanged, and there were few items Chinese merchants requested as barter. Europe risked running out of silver as a result and needed to create demand for some kind of foreign product in China.

To address the unsustainable deficit, the frustrated British East India Company, which traded with and colonized large parts of the Indian subcontinent and Southeast Asia and also acted as an overseas military and administrative arm of the British government, turned to exporting Indian opium, made from poppy seeds, to China. After millions of Chinese became addicted and the emperor banned opium from entering the country, the company paid smugglers to continue the trade. The Chinese eventually used a show of force, essentially placing foreign traders under siege, to confiscate the illegal opium supply, and in response the British Royal Navy used its vastly superior fleet and firepower to brashly attack China's southern coast in a bombardment later described as "gunboat diplomacy."

This was the First Opium War. It resulted in the first of a series of "unequal treaties" that caused five new ports to be opened along China's coast to Britain and its allies France and Russia, and Hong Kong to be ceded to the British in perpetuity. Other Western countries then used pressure or sometimes force to gain similar prerogatives in China.

When the British seized the island of Hong Kong, on January 26, 1841, and raised the Union Jack over Possession

Point, the population of the island was less than eight thousand people, mainly Tanka and Hakka clans who subsisted largely on fishing in a smattering of coastal villages. At the time, the loss of Hong Kong had little economic impact on China, but it was still deeply gutting for the Qing dynasty. It was the result of an unprecedented war with the West that saw an estimated ninety million of its citizens becoming drug addicts from forced imports of opium.

The Opium War diminished the Chinese emperor's ability to govern over a still-vast empire, and the population of Hong Kong would soon swell with people from southern China fleeing famine, unrest, and civil wars. The British later demanded further territory, acquiring outright the Kowloon Peninsula, adjacent to Hong Kong, in 1860 after the Second Opium War, and then, in 1898, procuring another ninety-nine-year lease on what is known as the New Territories, which includes many small outlying islands, to grow the city of Hong Kong.

MOST HONG KONGERS LIVING today came of age under British rule. Despite being colonial subjects, they enjoyed free speech, human rights protections, rule of law, and relative stability and prosperity compared to those on the mainland.

The British implemented a system of nearly unbridled capitalism in Hong Kong. Taxes were low, but social safety net measures were also minimal, creating a cutthroat sink-or-swim environment. The city's proximity to China, along with a pro-business legal environment, helped transform it into a cosmopolitan economic powerhouse.

From the 1960s on, Hong Kong's economy boomed. The city became an important international banking and trading entrepôt and acted as a conduit to mainland China's steadily growing wealth, as well as a link to other Asian economies. Businesses could indirectly tap into the growing mainland Chinese economy without having to deal with the obstacles of operating in Communist China or other Asian countries with unfamiliar banking systems.

Hong Kong's gross domestic product (GDP) grew 180 times between 1961 and 1997, overtaking those of entire countries, such as Ireland and Israel. By the late twentieth century, Hong Kong was for several years the world's busiest container port. The city also developed a reputation for strong rule of law and adherence to global trade rules. It became a full member of the World Trade Organization in 1995 and continues to participate in the WTO as a full and separate member apart from mainland China.

MY PARENTS GREW UP in Hong Kong, and their experiences were very typical in the recovery years after the Second World War. Their childhoods were lived in poverty, with their entire families crowded into tiny apartments. They shared beds with siblings and needed to work as teenagers to contribute to the household. But by the time my parents were in their twenties, they were able to increase their salaries by taking evening courses to expand their skills, relentlessly job-hopping until they achieved a middle-class lifestyle. The city was ripe with opportunity for people who were willing to hustle, and since almost everybody started off poor, class privileges were not entrenched. Business magnate Li Ka-shing, the richest person in Hong Kong for twenty-one years, famously started off as a factory worker.

But while Hong Kong prospered and its airport became an international travel hub, most people in mainland China still did not have passports. In 1990, 280 million people in China's rural areas lived under the international poverty line of less than a dollar a day. Many Hong Kong residents, including some of my own friends and relatives, developed a sense of superiority as the income gap widened between themselves and the mainland Chinese.

There were cultural rifts too. It was rare for a Hong Kong family to choose to vacation in mainland China or to watch a movie or listen to songs in Mandarin; the mainland seemed to have little to offer them. Their city, meanwhile, produced hundreds of films a year in the 1990s. Heaps of pirated versions of these movies and records would find their way onto market stalls on the mainland, but almost never the other way around.

AS THE END of the ninety-nine-year lease for the New Territories drew closer, the British government was concerned about possible conflict if an arrangement wasn't in place for transfer of power in 1997. Hong Kong's financial institutions and function as a popular Asia headquarters for international firms were also important for the world economy, and the sudden dismantling of the capitalist system there by the Chinese government would be hugely disruptive.

Meanwhile, Beijing wanted to strike a deal to get all of Hong Kong back, including Hong Kong Island and Kowloon, which the United Kingdom had claimed for all time. After rounds of negotiations, the Sino-British Joint Declaration was signed in Beijing on December 9, 1984, between Chinese premier Zhao Ziyang and U.K. prime minister Margaret Thatcher.

The treaty stated that in 1997, the Chinese government would resume sovereign rule over Hong Kong, including Hong Kong Island and Kowloon. However, China had to agree to the "one country, two systems" principle, where it wouldn't immediately impose a socialist system on the city. Hong Kong's existing capitalist system, independent courts, and way of life would be unchanged for fifty years, until 2047.

Chinese newspapers rejoiced, heralding Hong Kong's coming "return to the dragon." But many people in Hong Kong dreaded the return to the "motherland." Over the course of more than a century, the residents of Hong Kong had naturally developed a distinct culture and identity and no longer considered themselves "Chinese."

Many Hong Kongers did not trust Beijing to honour the terms of the handover treaty and feared for the demise of their independent courts, freedom of expression, and freewheeling media. Protests became a way of life in anticipation of the coming repression. Those protests include demonstrations each year marking three anniversaries: the June 4 Tiananmen massacre; the July 1 handover from British colonial rule; and, on October 1, the creation of the People's Republic of China.

A consensus emerged among Hong Kong politicians, scholars, and activists that only democracy, which the British never offered to the city's residents, would ensure that their cherished way of life would remain unchanged for the fifty promised years.

Mass demonstrations, often bringing hundreds of thousands of people to the streets and in rare cases upwards of a million, have angered Chinese authorities but so far failed to change a political system in which Hong Kong's leader is nominated by a small committee of Beijing loyalists, then appointed by China's government.

ON THE NIGHT OF SEPTEMBER 26, 2014, the Hong Kong Federation of Students led a group of about a hundred over tall metal gates to occupy a courtyard right outside city government headquarters.

The students pumped their fists and chanted, "Hope stems from people, change begins with struggle!" But police were ready. Several student leaders, including rising political star Joshua Wong, aged seventeen, were arrested almost immediately as the rest of the occupiers fled into the night. Photos of Wong wincing in pain as he struggled with police were rapidly shared across the city, where people spend an average of three hours a day glued to their smartphones.

In the morning, it seemed like every person in Hong Kong had heard about the arrests, and activists rapidly organized a rally for the next day. On September 28, crowds streamed toward the government buildings, and it wasn't only students this time. Some middle-aged people skipped a day at the office to join the demonstration, with some wearing slacks and collared shirts, as if they had spontaneously made the decision to stop what they were doing and support the students.

As I spoke with tense protesters outside the locked gates of the city legislature, I heard shouting ahead: "*Hoi lou!*" "*Hoi lou!*" "*Hoi lou!*" — "Open the road!"

I weaved through the crowd, peering beyond placards and raised fists, and spotted rows of police with riot shields and masks. It was disorienting; I had never seen Hong Kong officers in riot gear before.

The protesters on my side of the street kept gesturing at something. I pushed closer. A huge crowd, easily hundreds of people, had gathered on the other side of the eight-lane highway. Officers were trying to prevent them from marching through traffic.

All at once, the mass of people began to cross toward us, and a double-decker bus had to screech to a halt. It felt like a moment of no return.

Police unfurled a large banner that read "DISPERSE OR WE FIRE." This only further riled the crowd, and officers kept shoving protesters back with their shields. They waited only minutes before unleashing a huge cloud of tear gas, a weapon that hadn't been used in the city for almost a decade. My eyes began to burn, but I stood transfixed as young people surged past me right into the stinging black haze.

Some protesters on the front lines instinctively used umbrellas to protect themselves and others from the unrelenting spray of tear gas. A photographer for Getty captured an image of a young man wearing only a flimsy surgical face mask for protection. He holds two black umbrellas up in the air—one broken—as thick smoke swirls around him.

The Umbrella Movement was born.

THE ICONIC IMAGES of mass protests sent a strong message about just how many citizens of Hong Kong were willing to risk their lives to secure democracy. According to a 2014 University of Hong Kong survey, the number of people in the city who identified as "Hong Kongers" that year had surged; the number of those proud of being Chinese citizens was at a record low. About 67 percent of respondents identified as Hong Kongers, whereas 31 percent identified as Chinese.

"We have to stand up and fight now, otherwise Hong Kong

will disappear to become just another Chinese city," a teenage
protester told me. He was wearing makeshift body armour
consisting of a bicycle helmet, wrist and knee pads, and swim
goggles, with a sturdy umbrella in his back pocket. He wanted
democracy for Hong Kong but didn't dispute that the city was
part of Chinese territory. Meanwhile, a full-out independence
movement was forming among a fringe but vocal minority of
protesters. For Beijing, this was hugely concerning, since losing
Hong Kong was not an option. It could set a precedent by
which people in other disputed or semi-autonomous territories,
like Taiwan, Tibet, or Xinjiang, would be inspired to agitate to
break away from China.

During the months-long Umbrella Movement protests—
which spread to other busy parts of the city, including the
shopping and entertainment districts of Mong Kok, on the
Kowloon Peninsula, and Causeway Bay—physical fights broke
out. Emotional older adults, including parents and teachers, often
stood among students, and some stepped between the youngsters
and baton-wielding police or in front of unidentifiable masked
thugs who came in the night to destroy camps where protesters
slept. I tried to avoid staying too late at the protest sites, but one
evening I found myself near a group of preteen girls, still in their
school uniforms, surrounded by jeering older men who were
jostling and verbally abusing them for taking part in the protests.
The girls stood stoically, avoiding eye contact with the men, while
nearby adults moved to stand protectively around them.

Nearly a thousand people were arrested in connection with
the "illegal Occupy movement," the Hong Kong government
later announced. Most protesters were released without charge,
as were some triad members (the masked thugs) accused of
attacking protest camps.

Hong Kong triad gangs had become "patriotic" after the 1997 handover, a former senior triad member alleged. "All the existing triad groups in Hong Kong are patriotic and follow the country's orders," said Michael Chan Wai-man, a Hong Kong actor and retired triad boss. No Hong Kong triad group dared to defy China's public security ministry, because "whoever tries to do so will not be able to operate anymore," Chan said in a December 2014 interview with the Chinese website NetEase.

Authorities also prosecuted student leaders Joshua Wong, Agnes Chow, and Nathan Law, and the original trio of Occupy Central leaders. Law professor Benny Tai and sociologist Chan Kin-man were both sentenced to sixteen months in prison for "conspiring to commit public nuisance"; seventy-five-year-old Reverend Chu Yiu-ming was spared jail time. None of it brought the city any closer to democracy.

Hong Kong citizens' fears about the lengths to which the Chinese government would go to attack their free speech were realized when, over a few weeks in late 2015, five Hong Kong–based booksellers vanished and then mysteriously appeared inside Chinese jails. These naked kidnappings represented a change in tactics that many had worried was coming.

Two of the men, Lee Bo and Gui Minhai, were foreign citizens: British and Swedish, respectively. All five had all worked at Causeway Bay Books, which sold titles containing unflattering gossip about Beijing's political elite, including scintillating tales about Chinese president Xi Jinping's wife.

Gui disappeared while on holiday in Thailand, and Lee was last seen in Hong Kong. When they turned up in Chinese police custody, they both publicly professed to have voluntarily decided to go to mainland China to assist in a court case. Experts on Chinese law derided the statements as forced confessions—all the more worrying because the booksellers' foreign passports seemed to provide little protection. In his "confession" on Chinese state television, Gui said, with head bowed and voice quavering, "I truly feel that I am Chinese." As of June 2021, he is still in custody.

When international reporters pressed Wang Yi, China's foreign minister, on Lee's case, Wang told them Lee was "first and foremost a Chinese citizen."

The cases showed that to Chinese leaders, people of Chinese descent were Chinese and would be treated accordingly, no matter where they lived or what citizenship they held.

IN XI JINPING'S PUBLIC SPEECHES, he has repeatedly asserted the need for unity.

"Unity is iron, steel, and strength, and it is the important guarantee for the Chinese people and Chinese nation that they will overcome all challenges and gain one victory after another," the state-run *China Daily* newspaper quoted him as saying, at a celebration of the seventieth anniversary of the founding of the People's Republic of China, on September 30, 2019.

Xi's expectation of unity extends beyond the question of national boundaries to lay claim to any person of Chinese descent living anywhere. In the same speech, Xi said, "We must cement the great unity of all our ethnic groups, and strengthen the great unity of all Chinese sons and daughters at home and abroad.... We must maintain the close bond between the [Party] and the people and promote patriotism. Thus we will create an unparalleled force that will power the ship of our national renewal."

The roots of such entitlement to the loyalties of anyone of Chinese descent has roots in imperial China. As more Chinese emigrated abroad, emperors gradually started to see the overseas diaspora as a potential asset. Through the centuries, different Chinese leaders have drawn on an old fable to legitimize its claims. The story went that all Chinese descended from the Yellow Emperor himself, so anywhere Chinese people went on earth, they were still Chinese, and their loyalties were always to lie with the motherland. The CCP later expand this to specifically include even ethnic minorities in China.

Currently, millions of ethnic "Chinese" families have deep multi-generational roots in countries all over the world. Some do not speak any of the languages of China and have never even visited China. But the "Yellow Emperor" myth paves the way for Chinese authorities to ignore foreign citizens' rights and to claim them as their own.

BEIJING'S BID FOR CONTROL over Hong Kong is part of a wider picture. The same set of party and state agencies responsible for influencing groups and political entities in Hong Kong has a similar mission all around the world.

It sounds like the stuff of spy novels, but the United Front Work Department is an official agency that is lavishly well resourced. The agency's primary goal is to target non-Communist people and entities internationally to ensure influential individuals and groups support Chinese Communist Party interests. Beijing says that United Front's work is collaborative and democratic, seeking consultation from people around the world, but its own documents show that the United Front works closely with the Ministry of State Security, China's secret police, which has been responsible for detaining or threatening scores of dissidents.

In her paper "Magic Weapons: China's Political Influence Activities under Xi Jinping," New Zealander academic Anne-Marie Brady drew from primary documents to show that the CCP's United Front concepts are being used by China in both its domestic and foreign policy. Brady explains that her pioneering research shows United Front activities involve "working with groups and prominent individuals in society; information management and propaganda; and it has also frequently been a means of facilitating espionage."

Chairman Mao Zedong introduced his adaptation of Leninist "united front work" strategies in a journal in 1939, during the twenty-two-year civil war between the Nationalists and the Chinese Communist Party. "The Party is the heroic warrior wielding the two magic weapons, the united front and the armed struggle, to storm and shatter the enemy's positions," Mao wrote. He meant that the CCP should rally as many allies as possible in conjunction with waging military campaigns.

When the Communists won the civil war and established the People's Republic of China in 1949, much of the population remained unconvinced of socialism's benefits, with many even fleeing the country in fear. And so the united front work continued. The CCP sent emissaries around the country to meet with local warlords, religious leaders, and major ethnic minority groups to bolster the party's legitimacy.

The United Front Work Department has been a main agency of the CCP since 1979, when Deng Xiaoping tasked it to collect information from sources around the world and advance global support for the party.

Until recently, Chinese leaders did not broadcast their international influence ambitions. A 2004 internal government publication of the State Council instructed agents to foster plausible deniability in their overseas activities. United Front officials were to avoid being seen as "leading" the overseas Chinese community and instead be perceived as a "guide" for them, the manual instructed.

This has changed under President Xi, who has been laying out his vision in various speeches printed in Chinese state media. These reports relate how Xi has taken steps to make sure the agency is lavishly well resourced and unhindered by bureaucracy so that it rises in importance for all Party members. In a 2014 speech printed in the *People's Daily*, Xi even evoked the "magic weapons" language of Chairman Mao. "The United Front is the victory of the Chinese Communist Party in creating revolution, construction and reform," he said. "The important magic weapon is integral for realizing the great rejuvenation of the Chinese nation."

China's United Front activities are more subtle than the heavy-handed approach of American intelligence agencies, which have been widely accused of meddling in the political systems of weaker countries, such as through military interventions that brought about regime changes. The United Front is primarily focused on influencing civilians and civil society organizations around the world to try to shape these individuals' and groups' attitudes toward Beijing.

The United Front recruits non-CCP members to work in China's interests, such as by offering payments and political donations to win influence over foreign politicians. For example, leaked screenshots published in the *Washington Post* in 2019 showed Chinese embassy officials in Ottawa instructing students of Chinese descent to find out information about a talk at McMaster University in Hamilton, Ontario, on rights of Uyghur minorities in China, and to collect data on whether Chinese nationals were involved in organizing the Canadian event. The Chinese embassy in Canada denied it had anything to do with the actions but stated, "We strongly support the just and patriotic actions of Chinese students."

In June 2020, the Australian Strategic Policy Institute think tank released a comprehensive report that mapped out the structures, methods, and effects of what it calls China's global foreign interference system. The report called the United Front's overseas expansion "an exportation of the CCP's political system. Overseas United Front work taken to its conclusion would give the CCP undue influence over political representation and expression in foreign political systems."

The report's author, Alex Joske, told me in an interview that experts and governments around the world seem to underestimate the United Front's impact. Officials might view the work as a form of aggressive diplomacy or propaganda, but they fail to appreciate the extent of how public and legal activities can sometimes facilitate the criminal espionage that countries do take seriously.

Governments should "carry out detailed studies of United Front work across their [countries] as well as in specific sectors" and communicate findings to the public to promote general understanding, Joske said.

IT'S IMPORTANT TO RECALL that until 1997 Hong Kong was a British territory in which Beijing had no legal jurisdiction. So before the return to Chinese rule, the CCP's main option was to use the United Front system to try to secure loyalty among influential Hong Kong residents.

Geoff Raby, former Australian ambassador to the People's Republic of China, wrote in a 2019 opinion column that "probably nowhere else on earth is the [United Front Work Department] so active and so well resourced as in Hong Kong." And yet, he wrote, Beijing seems to have lost the battle for the hearts and minds of the next generation in Hong Kong.

Some months after the Umbrella Movement protests waned in Hong Kong, pro-democracy lawmaker Claudia Mo told me that to get a sense of what might be in store for other countries where China seeks to police expression of dissent, international observers should pay close attention to what has happened in Hong Kong after the softer United Front tactics didn't work and subtle coercion and economic inducements gave way to outright harassment and steamrolling of civil rights.

A former journalist for international media at the time of the Umbrella Movement, Mo was a prominent member of Hong Kong's Legislative Council, an independent representing the Kowloon West constituency.

We met at a coffee shop across from the city's legislature, which had been furnished with enhanced surveillance apparatus and padlocked gates. The café was nearly empty.

Mo recalled that in the early nineties, with the 1989 Tiananmen Square massacre fresh on people's minds, few in Hong Kong were optimistic that their political rights and freedoms would expand under China's rule. Back then, Hong Kong journalists had felt free to report on whatever topics they wished, including human rights and political intrigue on the mainland, but that would soon change.

Slowly, Beijing co-opted tycoons who owned media outlets in the city. The Hong Kong Journalists Association's yearly surveys of its members linked an increasing occurrence of self-censorship orders to media owners' corporate business interests in the mainland. In its 2014 report, the association called the pressure to self-censor an "invisible hand" strangling freedom of speech, citing cases where newspapers lost advertising revenue from China-focused local businesses, and where managers working for media owners with business interests in China ordered editors to stop printing or broadcasting critical stories. The report noted that more than half of Hong Kong media owners had accepted patronage appointments to one of the main political assemblies of China.

Since 1997, the Beijing government and mainland Chinese tycoons have injected billions in capital into Hong Kong's economy. Hong Kong businesses also expanded into the huge mainland Chinese market, in pretty much every sector imaginable. Academics such as Sonny Lo have documented how Beijing secures the loyalty of influential Hong Kong public figures by appointing them to the Communist Party's top advisory group, the Chinese People's Political Consultative Conference (CPPCC).

The CPPCC is the main political organ of the United Front, meaning it is the highest-level political organization that deals with non–Communist Party groups and individuals to advance the Party's goals both domestically and internationally.

Hong Kong's elite CPPCC delegates now include movie star Jackie Chan, former city leader Tung Chee-hwa, and newspaper and tobacco tycoon Charles Ho Tsu-kwok. As a group, they have called on the city to use the full extent of law enforcement to bring rule-breaking protesters to justice, and supported "a need to strengthen the ranks of patriots among Hong Kong society," according to the *China Daily*.

Suddenly, the troubles at my previous newspaper made more sense. The *South China Morning Post*'s owner at the time,

Chinese Malaysian tycoon Robert Kuok, bought the paper in 1993. Kuok has a controlling interest in the Shangri-La chain of luxury hotels and other large real estate holdings in mainland China. One of Asia's richest men, he was among Beijing's selected advisers on Hong Kong's future in the run-up to the 1997 handover. Critics, including a former *Post* manager, told me Kuok had forced the departures of a string of editors and reporters critical of Beijing, accusations he denied. "Money is power," the former senior *Post* manager said.

Around the world, the United Front attempts to co-opt international politicians (which later chapters of this book will examine), using techniques such as donating to political campaigns, offering paid trips to China, and showering individuals with flattery.

China's efforts to endear itself to elites and tycoons may have met with some success, but in Hong Kong they've had the opposite effect with the masses. Many now hate the actor Jackie Chan, for example, because they believe he has "sold out" to Beijing. The public responds with revulsion whenever Chan is quoted saying things like "Chinese people need to be controlled" or appears on Chinese state television singing patriotic songs praising the motherland, such as the ballad "Amazing China." In 2013, I was reporting on the red carpet at a music awards event in Hong Kong when I saw Chan walking toward a gaggle of journalists. He waited for them to ask him questions, but everyone ignored him. He awkwardly lingered for several moments before moving on.

DURING THE UMBRELLA MOVEMENT in Hong Kong, officials in Beijing and Hong Kong, as well as a number of publications that support the Communist Party, accused teachers of corrupting the new generation. They directed much of the blame at a secondary-school course called Liberal Studies.

The problem, argued the *Ta Kung Pao* newspaper, was that teachers and university professors "lack a sense of nationhood and have blindly inculcated the young with Western ideas like universal values and democracy. . . . Textbooks have failed to shoulder the duty of propaganda."

In the fall of 2019, in Toronto, I met a former Hong Kong Catholic high school principal who had come under pressure as a scapegoat for the mostly youth-driven protests.

He arrived ahead of me at the Starbucks patio where we had arranged to meet, and I found him sitting in the shade of an umbrella in a black windbreaker and black pants, looking like he was trying to be as incognito as possible. He relaxed after I explained that my family is from Hong Kong too, and we switched from speaking in English to Cantonese. He told me the story of how he became a refugee in Canada. I will refer to him here as "F."

In March 2015, F. had run in a weekend marathon in Hong Kong. Pro-democracy activists were handing out joke race bibs after the race with the label "D-689"—a play on words in Cantonese that basically cussed out Hong Kong's chief executive, Leung Chun-ying—and F. had taken one without really thinking about it. An amused student shared a photo of the principal on Facebook.

That's when the phone calls started coming to F.'s office.

"I know about the shameful things you did. If you don't resign, I will tell your school, I will tell your wife," a man said in a calm and courteous voice. He called again and again, each time refusing to identify himself but repeating the same threats in an almost bored tone.

F. reported the incidents to his supervisors and sought advice from the school security liaison and a lawyer. They said there was nothing they could do, though some had heard of other principals and teachers receiving strange calls.

When the calls didn't provoke the intended resignation, the city's Education Bureau began to receive letters claiming to be from a group of parents concerned about the principal's "lewd" and "inappropriate" behaviour toward students. No parent signed their name. Education Bureau officials were already aware of the harassment F. and other teachers had received and ignored the dubious letters.

Soon, newly joined members of social media groups for school alumni and parents began to spread gossip. This time, there were examples of his alleged behaviour: "This school principal has slept with female students! He has had affairs with teachers!"

F. had managed to control his anxiety until then, but this was the last straw. "Of course, some alumni and parents didn't know the context," he told me.

I asked what went through his mind when he saw those posts.

Deep shame, he said. "They probably thought, 'Wow, what's going on? Why is there a principal like this?' It was very embarrassing when I was at school and saw parents looking at me with this look of distrust, likely wondering if the allegations were true."

The harassment brought on such severe depression and anxiety that F. turned to the only thing that helped him feel better: meditation. It worked so well that he applied for a master's in psychotherapy in Canada so he could help people in Hong Kong handle the pressure better too.

Still, he admitted, altruism was only part of the reason he left Hong Kong.

"It's kind of like a white terror," he said, referring to the anonymous acts of aggression, often from loyalist organized crime groups, against critics of Taiwan's government during four decades of martial law there from the 1950s to the 1980s. "For some famous activists, they might get arrested, but for people like us, who are not famous but still have positions of some influence, they use strategies like this to silence us."

Even when he was in Canada, before he received refugee status, his wife told him that security officers called her at their home in Hong Kong to check that he was in Toronto and not planning to return.

He showed me copies of letters and screenshots documenting the extended campaign of harassment against him. All to try to convince one man to leave his job in Hong Kong.

It shows that a key component of Beijing's strategy for political control is to target non-elite individuals and groups, a fact that can be overlooked when trending media stories focus mostly on high-level conflicts such as the trade war and war of words between the White House and Beijing.

As rhetorician Sharon Yam and historian Jeffrey Wasserstrom wrote in August 2020 in *Foreign Policy*, the Party's "local-centred approach focuses not on the rhythms of U.S.-China jabs but on that of successive state efforts to strike fear into different social sectors, striking at young activists one week, academics another, [then] journalists, publishers and political party founders."

BEIJING'S EFFORTS TO SILENCE the "city of protests" didn't work.

Starting in the spring of 2019, Hong Kongers turned out en masse again — nearly *two million* strong on one day in June — to oppose an extradition bill that would make it easier to transfer criminal suspects from Hong Kong to the mainland. The turnouts were likely the biggest in the city's history. Many feared the new law, though framed by the city government as a way to deal with murderers, was really intended to allow China to extradite political dissidents. There, they would face a justice system controlled by the Communist Party, with its 99.9 percent conviction rate.

This time, right from the beginning, protesters appealed directly to the world for support. They warned that the bill would not apply only to residents; any visitor or person transiting through Hong Kong International Airport could be subject to the law's unknown ramifications. Protesters raised HK$5 million to buy front-page newspaper ads in the U.S., U.K., Canada, France, Germany, Switzerland, and Japan, among other nations.

"Today, nobody is safe," read one full-page ad in Canada's *Globe and Mail.* "We are running out of time — but you can make a difference. Request your government to protect the 300,000 Canadians living in Hong Kong. . . . Fight for Freedom."

The Hong Kong government did not back down. Police fired thousands of canisters of tear gas at protesters and hauled out water cannons laced with blue dye and other irritants. That escalated to the firing of rubber bullets and beanbag rounds, then finally live ammunition — including a bullet fired into a teenager's chest in an alleged act of self-defence.

Perhaps police hoped the quick show of force would prevent another protracted occupation, but it only made people angrier. Police actions triggered outcry from many countries, including the U.S., Canada, and the U.K., as well as an unprecedented intervention by the United Nations Human Rights Office condemning the use of potentially lethal force. For the first time, the UN body called on Hong Kong authorities to investigate whether police actions complied with international standards.

Rather than set up camps and wait to be arrested, a contingent of young people adopted a novel approach: to "flow like water" and show up in flash protests in different parts of the city. This led to dramatic chases in shopping malls, subway stations, and alleyways. Onlookers captured images of police slipping on floors the officers had just doused with tear gas and a protester bringing down an officer with a flying kick. All around the world, people were glued to their screens.

The protesters who physically confronted police faced disapproval from the Hong Kong public as well as from fellow activists who stuck to their peaceful approach of applying for permits to protest. It's a testament to the strong culture of bureaucratic efficiency in the city that police still processed and approved some of these march permits even in the midst of chaotic street battles. The youngsters who opted for the flash mob approach—many barely in their teens—said the old ways hadn't worked and they were prepared to sacrifice themselves for Hong Kong's future. They knew a rioting charge could cost them ten years behind bars.

The first fatality came on June 15, when a thirty-five-year-old man fell after climbing bamboo scaffolding along the side of a shopping mall to unfurl a banner saying "No extradition to China."

On July 1, 2019, on the twenty-second anniversary of the city's return to Chinese sovereignty, dozens of protesters broke into the legislature building and destroyed furniture, defaced portraits, and sprayed protest graffiti all over the walls. The graffiti read "Hong Kong is not China, not yet" and "The government forced us to revolt."

I arrived in Hong Kong the next day to report for the *Toronto Star*. For weeks back home in Canada, I had stayed up late to watch from afar, along with many others around the world who shared a personal connection to the city or simply understood that what was unfolding could tell the world whether there was any hope of free speech and democracy on Chinese soil.

I met again with Claudia Mo, who described how she tried to stop a young man from storming the legislature. "He reminded me of my son, a rugby player," she said. "He was vowing to storm in, and I approached him, saying, 'Hey, look, think twice. The rioting charge could cost you ten years behind bars. It's just not worth it.' He put his arm around my shoulders and seemed to appreciate the concern, but told me to get out of the way . . . they would die for this fight."

On July 3, I walked to the government complex, which is near the central business district, and saw a yellow raincoat tied to a post, flapping in the wind — a tribute to the protester whose fatal fall from scaffolding had happened in that spot. Around the corner, a young woman was giving a tearful speech outside a metro station. The people of Hong Kong should not give up their peaceful resistance despite the deep sadness afflicting the city, she urged. The rest of her group, including an elderly man, were staging a hunger strike.

Shattered glass covered the ground outside the legislature, and police and security guards milled around, surveying the damage and collecting evidence. Graffiti was still up on the walls. The protesters' beloved "Grandma" Alexandra Wong was outside, pasting pro-democracy slogans on the fences around the government courtyard, even though she knew they would be quickly taken down. Young men with umbrellas shielded her from the sun, eyeing me and my camera warily. Wong would later be abducted by mainland state security, subjected to forcible re-education, and coerced into making a videotaped confession, she said.

The protests continued after Hong Kong's chief executive, Carrie Lam, said the extradition bill was "dead" but then failed to formally withdraw it. All summer long, organizers followed a similar pattern: a few events and demonstrations during the week followed by a big protest on the weekend. Many times, a fringe contingent would linger and engage with police, leading to bloody battles, arrests, and injuries for passersby.

I watched protesters pour into the streets of Kowloon, an entertainment district popular with tourists from mainland China, to do exactly what the Chinese Communist Party feared. They took their message directly to their mainland compatriots. Chanting in Mandarin "Democracy for Hong Kong" and "Love your country, come protest," they moved through the streets. They stopped outside malls to wave at mainland Chinese shoppers inside, encouraging them to come out and join them. Protesters also used the iPhone AirDrop function to send messages to people in the area explaining why they were marching.

I climbed a set of stairs to get a better look at the massive crowd. Some carried children on their shoulders and sang slogans, while others just walked in silence. Next to me, a woman from China's Guangdong province watched the procession with a look of wonder. When she asked what the protests were about, I told her the Hong Kongers were opposing an extradition bill because they don't trust China's legal system. She only nodded.

THIS WAS EXACTLY WHAT Beijing didn't want to happen.

That summer, Chinese government censors and state media worked in overdrive to prevent the movement from spilling into the mainland. State media focused on the idea of foreign interference to explain the magnitude of the protests. A *China Daily* editorial from June 9, 2019, declared that "some Hong Kong residents have been hoodwinked by the opposition camp and their foreign allies into supporting the anti-extradition campaign."

Overseas support for the protesters also rankled Regina Ip, a pro-Beijing lawmaker in Hong Kong and backer of the extradition bill. When I talked to her at her office, she told me she was interested in how the so-called leaderless protesters were so well organized and solidarity marches around the world came together so quickly.

She said she had no hard evidence that foreign governments had "interfered" but felt it was odd: "There are behind-the-scenes organizers no doubt, but it's not for me to point fingers. The [Hong Kong] government should be proactive in investigating."

I bit my tongue, because I had met some of those foreign supporters she found so suspicious. Many were Canadian, and while they were a mix of ethnicities, most were ethnically Chinese with family members and friends in Hong Kong. They were losing sleep to build a broad international network that kept in touch through mobile apps with people on the ground in Hong Kong to lend assistance and moral support. Some contributed to crowdfunding campaigns for things like first aid kits and protesters' legal fees.

More than ever before, the city's protest movement had become global, engaging communities around the world to put pressure on their respective foreign governments to speak up. There were solidarity marches in dozens of cities. Governments in countries such as Canada, the U.S., and Germany not only issued statements of concern but later accepted refugees fleeing the city. So Beijing went further.

"I expected to be older when 2047 came" was the darkly humorous meme that circulated among youth in Hong Kong over the news that China's parliament had approved a law that would effectively eradicate the "one country, two systems" agreement to respect freedoms in the city for fifty years.

On June 30, 2020, an hour before the twenty-third anniversary of the city's handover to China from British rule, the national security law came into effect. The law, which bans all activities Beijing deems a danger to its national security, was greeted with astonishment and drew widespread condemnation, not least because it purported to apply not just to the actions of everyone in Hong Kong but to the actions of anyone outside the region as well. Actions against China taken by individuals of any nationality outside the mainland may be considered violations of this law. The maximum sentence for the law's long list of vaguely defined offences is life imprisonment.

Hong Kong's first day under the new law saw more than 370 people arrested for various protest-related offences and several charged with violating the new restrictions. Countries around the world quickly moved to cancel their extradition treaties with Hong Kong for fear that Beijing would use such treaties to whisk people into the mainland.

The global reach is clear, and many international legal experts quickly sounded the alarm to advise people of any nationality who ever said anything critical of Chinese or Hong Kong authorities to avoid travelling to greater China.

On August 26, 2020, Hong Kong police issued a warrant for Samuel Chu, an American citizen living in Los Angeles, who had supported Hong Kong's pro-democracy movement from afar on social media.

Alvin Cheung, who previously practised as a Hong Kong barrister and is now a non-resident affiliated scholar of the U.S.-Asia Law Institute at New York University, pointed out that people should avoid boarding flights operated by Cathay Pacific and other vessels registered in Hong Kong, since the security law also states that it applies "aboard ships or aircraft registered in the Hong Kong Special Administrative Region."

In the end, it shouldn't have been surprising that such a brazen act of "lawfare," an attack on civil rights through legislation, would be connected to Hong Kong. Hong Kong was once taken away from the Chinese empire, and when it was returned, the people called for the meaningful autonomy that was promised to the territory in the Sino-British Declaration. In response, Beijing not only cracked down on the city but laid claim to foreign citizens' free speech. Having been rebuffed in its attempts to win the hearts and minds of Hong Kongers, Beijing chose to impose its criminal law on Hong Kong—and the rest of the world.

Cheung says the national security legislation hasn't gone as far as dismantling the "one country, two systems" framework, likely because Beijing doesn't want to weaken the city's legal system to the point where it can no longer act as an international financial hub. "As long as institutional facades remain in place, I think there will be plenty of investors who will turn a blind eye to the instances in which Beijing visibly puts a hand on the scales," Cheung told me. "The key is to retain just enough of the 'normative state' that ordinary commerce can continue."

To the legions of believers in democracy, the idea of a city of hollow institutions that would protect businesses while failing to protect the vulnerable is far from comforting.

BECAUSE OF THE PANDEMIC, I couldn't travel to Hong Kong in 2020, the first year I'd failed to spend any time in the city in over a decade. I missed the incomparable atmosphere of its bustling streets, the rugged hiking paths perched atop valleys filled with high-rises, and the endless culinary delights.

I spoke almost daily with friends and relatives in the city, partly out of homesickness for my birthplace, and partly just to keep up with an eventful year of political developments. It was as if Beijing was taking advantage of the world's preoccupation with the pandemic to chip away further at Hong Kongers' freedoms.

It seemed that the city was becoming divided into camps: elites and others who had supported Beijing all along, and ordinary Hong Kongers who feared losing legal and political rights but disagreed vehemently among each other on methods of protest.

In January 2021, while many people around the world started the new year with tentative hopes that the worst of the coronavirus crisis was behind them, Hong Kong braced for more political crackdowns. Among the dozens of former lawmakers and political advocates arrested that month for the crime of "subverting state power," more than fifty were netted for organizing or participating in a July 2020 primary election, in which hundreds of thousands of Hong Kongers voted to thin the field of potential pro-democracy candidates vying for seats in the city's legislature. This was meant to avoid a splitting of votes to increase the chance of having pro-democratic legislators in office.

Hong Kong secretary of security John Lee said the police operation was needed because election organizers were seeking to "paralyze the Hong Kong government" by winning a majority in the legislature as well as "mobilizing vast-scale riots in the streets." It didn't make much sense.

Even though the primary election would have been perfectly legal before the national security law was in place, authorities used the sweeping provisions of the law to punish the politicians. John Clancey, an American lawyer who had assisted in the primary polls, was also arrested, sparking outraged responses from U.S. officials.

Hong Kong–based journalists, meanwhile, told me they fear press freedom in the city will further erode as more journalists self-censor to avoid topics that might land them in jail. In April 2021, the Hong Kong High Court denied former lawmaker Claudia Mo bail because she had given numerous interviews on the "loss of human rights and freedom" in Hong Kong to international media. She faces life in prison on charges of "subversion." Some bookstores and literary event organizers stopped displaying or featuring new books about the city's protest movement. In June 2021, the unabashedly pro-democracy Hong Kong newspaper *Apple Daily* was forced to close after local police arrested their top executives under the national security law, and also froze the newspaper's assets.

Antony Dapiran, a Hong Kong-based lawyer and author, told me that the city is currently still a unique place in China where people can have wide-ranging public debates on politically sensitive topics related to the mainland, but there is a great deal of censorship related to Hong Kong's own political situation. "Hong Kong has fallen into this strange dynamic where Hong Kong itself has become the most sensitive topic of all, and many are consumed by self-censorship and second-guessing what the powers-that-be want. In the meantime, the Hong Kong government is using 'rule of law' and a ruthlessly efficient bureaucracy to prosecute every minor matter to the fullest extent possible, and pro-Beijing loyalists are trying to out-compete each other to see who can demonstrate the most 'patriotism.'

"It's all a pretty sad state of affairs."

PART II
MIDDLE POWERS
★

PART II

MIDDLE POWERS

3.
CANADA

Death Threat Diplomacy

Dear Joanna Chiu,

I am [Dan]. I am from China. I just graduated from [a Quebec university]. I hesitated for a whole night before deciding to write this email....

Now I am living in Canada, but I am living with fear from the Chinese government.

Dan, whose name I've changed to protect his identity, hails from one of China's picturesque and relatively laidback southwestern provinces. He studied English diligently and was elated when a top Canadian university accepted his application to study law.

About a month before the start of the September 2017 session, when Dan was still in China, the university issued his student credentials, and with them he received access to a

virtual private network (VPN). The tool allowed him—for the
first time in his life—to scale the "Great Firewall of China"
and access an uncensored internet.

Curious, the twenty-one-year-old thought he might check
out some overseas social media sites, connect with future classmates, and read world news; that way, he wouldn't seem so
out of touch once he arrived. He would be joining a cohort
of Chinese international students in Canada totalling around
140,000 that year.

He decided to take a few basic precautions, since he hadn't
left China yet. He signed up for Twitter using a fake name and
fake location, and even set his gender to female.

To his amazement, the platform was already full of
Chinese-language users. A whole network of bloggers, artists,
independent journalists, and scholars were engaging in a level
of dialogue on Chinese politics he had never seen.

Once Dan arrived in Canada and began adjusting to a new
city and a new university, he continued to browse Twitter in
his dorm room. He was too nervous to actually join in any
conversations. He retweeted only three posts: the news that
Nobel laureate and Chinese democracy advocate Liu Xiaobo
had died, a short satirical video about President Xi Jinping, and
a chart on levels of Chinese government corruption.

With only two followers, he wasn't making a splash—but
sharing those posts still gave him a thrill. His undergraduate
studies did offer some opportunities to discuss international
political systems, and the problem of lower-level government
corruption wasn't a completely taboo topic, but virtually all
Chinese people know that publicly supporting high-profile
dissidents or satirizing top leaders is strictly forbidden.

Months passed. Life got busy, and Dan didn't have time to

keep up his exploration of social media. He never got involved in any political activities on campus either. Rather, he focused on learning about the Canadian legal system in hopes of staying and working in the country.

Then his father called him out of the blue, clearly disturbed.

"Son, did you say something about the Chinese government on the internet? The public security bureau called us twice."

China's public security bureaus are police stations that also oversee some migration matters. They sometimes work with the United Front Work Department to monitor Chinese nationals living abroad, though the Ministry of State Security secret police typically handle higher-profile cases.

The year before, in 2016, the CCP had added a new bureau to the United Front Work Department to ensure that certain professionals and returning overseas Chinese students acted in accordance with CCP objectives.

Announcing the new unit—called the New Social Classes Work Bureau—the United Front's chairwoman, Sun Chunlan, said the initiative would target professionals in private and foreign-owned enterprises; people working in NGOs, including lawyers and accountants; "new media" professionals (those working for online news sources); and returning Chinese overseas students. "The new social classes are highly mobile, scattered, active in thinking and diverse in ideas. . . . [They] are the new focus as well as an innovative aspect of United Front work. They can be a highlight if the work is done well," she wrote.

The United Front seeks to turn potential threats into allies. As both an overseas student and a future lawyer studying at a Canadian university, Dan was an ideal target to coerce into someone who would support the motherland rather than become a detractor. "Diversity" and "active" thinking are positive attributes in the eyes of Chinese officials only as long as people don't develop critical views of the Party.

Soon after Dan got the warning from his father, a police officer contacted him on the WeChat social media app. Dan hadn't accepted a new friend request, but the officer was able to send him messages and call him anyway.

"I told him maybe they found the wrong person," Dan told me over a video call in mid-2019.

His email to me earlier that week contained a timeline of what happened, along with screenshots and audio recordings of his conversations with the public security agent. I was impressed by his detailed documentation.

On our video call, I could see a large library atrium behind him with floor-to-ceiling windows. Dan was dressed neatly in a white polo shirt and spoke precise and nearly fluent English.

"The police told me the Ministry of Public Security [China's internal policing department] tracked me by my IP address and knows where I live in Canada. They have evidence the Twitter account belongs to me," Dan said, his voice dropping to a whisper. Police never spelled out what Dan had done wrong, exactly, such as whether he violated any Chinese internet regulations or committed any crime.

Making use of his law school training, Dan had subtly tried to glean information from the police officer while not admitting to anything. But the officer only offered cryptic replies about a "classified" investigation and ordered Dan to immediately delete the offensive posts.

The officer never raised his voice, but his tone became sterner as the conversation went on. When Dan asked what would happen if he refused to accept responsibility for the

Twitter account, the agent told him in Mandarin, "You will face trouble."

"Trouble" is a well-known euphemism in China for state persecution. It can range from repeated visits and phone calls all the way to travel bans, rejection for jobs, and house arrest. Chinese authorities also routinely threaten relatives in China to silence dissidents abroad. In a report on the topic by the international NGO Human Rights Watch, a Vancouver technology consultant explained, "If I criticize the [CCP] publicly, my parents' retirement benefits, their health insurance benefits could all be taken away."

"To be honest, I'm terrified," Dan whispered to me, so students in the library wouldn't hear him.

Dan had confided in one of his professors, who expressed alarm about the threatening call and urged him to report it to local police. But when the student showed up with all his files, police officers said they couldn't do anything about activities that happened in China.

"You can delete the posts, but you don't have to," an officer said, shrugging.

That was never the question; Dan knew he had freedom of speech on Canadian soil. But while he hadn't been sure what police could do to help his parents in China, he'd thought they would at least accept his report so that, if something ever happened to him or his family, they would have something on file.

Crestfallen, Dan removed the retweets.

Back in his dorm room, he was left to wonder how Chinese authorities were able to track him overseas, why they would care about his influence on an audience of two — and how a democratic country like Canada could do so little to protect him.

DECADES AGO, OBVIOUS LOGISTICAL impediments made it difficult for governments to send agents abroad to surveil, intimidate, or harass ordinary people. Now, authorities only need an internet connection and some technological know-how — not a problem when so many talented hackers are available for hire.

The problem, says Ronald Deibert, is that democracies tend to focus their counter-espionage efforts on combating the theft of intellectual property and industrial trade secrets. The harassment of students and mothers and ordinary workers goes virtually unchecked. Deibert is the director of the University of Toronto's Citizen Lab, a team that does groundbreaking research on international censorship and digital espionage techniques.

"It's an unfortunate trend where despots and authoritarian regimes are able to reach across borders much more effectively than they could in the past," he told me in a telephone interview. "It's something that's been overlooked. We assume the connections we make across borders are benign, but these are the same tools autocrats use to track their targets, including journalists, researchers, and immigrants. Moving abroad doesn't give people the same degree of protection it once had."

The cases I reported on in Canada drove home to me that Beijing leaders truly feel anyone of Chinese descent is fair game and they have a right to curtail their freedom of speech years or even generations after they settled abroad.

I spoke with Brad West, mayor of Port Coquitlam, a small city near Vancouver, who was shocked to learn that dozens of his constituents had received threatening phone calls and even in-person visits from Chinese government officials. None of the targets were public figures; they were mostly first- or second-generation immigrants from China in a variety of ordinary professions.

His constituents said the Chinese officials expressed anger over "little things, like a post on social media or an attendance at a certain event," West told me, adding that he had alerted police and federal agencies to the threats, because the individuals themselves were too scared to file reports.

"It's so unsettling to know these people — who are our people, who live in our communities — are subject to surveillance and harassment by a foreign government on Canadian soil," he said with a grave expression. "What's equally shocking is how fearful they are. When we meet in my office, they want the blinds closed. They're that fearful."

Mayor West assumes this kind of harassment occurs across the country, and federal intelligence officials have said as much, but he worries that many targeted people are suffering in silence because they're too afraid to seek help, or they think Canadian politicians wouldn't care if they did speak up.

Cherie Wong, an Ottawa-based Canadian activist and graduate student involved in supporting Hong Kong's pro-democracy movement, is among the few who have spoken openly about being a target of harassment.

On a trip to Vancouver in January 2019, Wong, the executive director of the Alliance Canada Hong Kong advocacy group, received a call to her hotel room demanding that she leave immediately and that "people" were coming to collect her. Wong reported the anonymous threat to police, but a year later she told me police hadn't given her updates on the case.

This is a shame. For democracies to function, Ronald Deibert argues, people need to feel safe enough to express themselves, online or otherwise. Deibert believes Canada could pass legislation to make cross-border digital harassment illegal, which might encourage more people to come forward and report such behaviour. But there is little political will to find solutions, he thinks.

A spokesperson for Canadian Heritage, the federal government department supporting "Canadian identity and values, cultural development, and heritage," told me in an email that it was working with the departments of justice and other government agencies on a strategy to better safeguard Canadians' privacy and rights. But, she said, "Given the significant scope of this major undertaking, we cannot provide a specific timeline at this time."

Though Beijing's targets in Canada tend to be people of Chinese origin, this is far from a fringe issue affecting a small population. Metro Vancouver has nearly 500,000 people of Chinese descent, about 20 percent of the region. The Greater Toronto Area has more than 630,000.

"There's a conflict here," Deibert says. "Canada is a country of immigrants and trumpets the fact we're accepting and multicultural. But when push comes to shove, are we going to stand up and protect those people from the threats they're escaping from?"

PERHAPS IN ACCORDANCE with the United Front's new directives on cultivating overseas assets, the Chinese embassy in Ottawa has been recruiting people of Chinese descent to harass and collect information on anyone who is critical of Beijing.

As mentioned in chapter 2, screenshots leaked to the *Washington Post* in February 2019 showed Chinese embassy officials in Ottawa instructing students of Chinese descent to gain information about a talk on rights of Uyghur minorities in China and to inform the embassy whether any Chinese nationals were involved in organizing a talk by advocate Rukiye Turdush at McMaster University in Hamilton, Ontario. Turdush, who is a Canadian citizen of Uyghur descent, told me she later discovered someone had shared a video of her talk on a WeChat group for the university's Chinese Students and Scholars Association (CSSA). A concerned member of the CSSA had turned the information over to her, showing that the Chinese embassy was not completely successful in co-opting the students.

The McMaster student union soon voted to strip the school's CSSA of its official club status. But Turdush told me that no government or university official had reached out to her to investigate the possible collusion between students and Chinese government representatives. "I thought that if I spoke with media, the government would take actions to deal with the Chinese government extending their influence to suppress freedom of speech here in Canada," she said. "This is United Front work. I've called for an investigation...but I've heard nothing."

WHILE UNITED FRONT ACTIVITIES are perhaps most obvious in a country like Canada, with its large ethnic Chinese population, this is happening in a number of countries. Canada is an example of what is going on internationally in China's treatment of middle powers. It is also a case study of what happens when a government fails to protect its citizens.

If Canadian leaders had paid heed to testimonies about Beijing's harassment and meddling in Chinese diaspora communities decades ago, vulnerable people might now feel safer to express their views in Canada, advocates say.

Veteran publisher, activist, and documentary filmmaker Cheuk Kwan is now in his early sixties. I met him at a Cantonese seafood restaurant overlooking Toronto's harbourfront. Kwan walked in looking like an artist, in a practically all-black ensemble with his greying hair partly shrouding his eyes. He gave me a firm handshake and politely asked if my colleagues at the *Toronto Star* were doing well.

Unlike the elders in Beijing who deflected my questioning, Kwan was eager to talk about the past. In 1980, he co-founded the Chinese Canadian National Council (CCNC), an organization with a mandate to monitor racial discrimination and educate youth about the contributions of Chinese Canadians. In the wake of the 1989 Tiananmen Square massacre, the group took a stand and called on Ottawa to accept more refugees and help political dissidents.

What happened next left him utterly bewildered.

"That pissed off the Chinese consulate, so they started their own group to counter our work, the National Congress of Chinese Canadians [NCCC]," Kwan said. In my notebook, he wrote out, side by side, the Chinese names of the two organizations—his and the one the embassy started—and pointed out the similarities in both languages.

The rival group organized yearly celebrations of the establishment of the People's Republic of China. To Kwan's consternation, many Canadian politicians accepted invitations to join in such celebrations, which granted them legitimacy.

The NCCC became bolder, issuing statements that were the opposite of statements from Kwan's group. For example, when the CCNC asked Canadian leaders to officially apologize for the racist "head tax" Canada placed on Chinese immigrants between 1885 and 1923 and provide significant financial compensation to affected families, the NCCC issued statements saying no compensation would be necessary, actually.

The new group's activities successfully confused the public and watered down his group's advocacy work, Kwan said. Canadian journalists interviewed representatives from the NCCC by mistake when they meant to reach out to the CCNC.

Kwan clarified that he had no proof that the Chinese embassy directly founded the NCCC, but plenty of photographs show embassy officials attending the group's events as guests of honour. Today, "astroturfing" — the practice of masking an organization's sponsors to make it appear like a grassroots group — is a popular stratagem of the United Front. The tactic emerged in the 1980s in cities with large Chinese immigrant populations.

As the years passed, Kwan said, more pro-Beijing groups sprang up in the guise of benign-sounding Chinese cultural associations. He thought it was obvious that these were "shell" groups, purporting to be non-partisan and non-political while aggressively spreading pro-Beijing propaganda. But it was not as clear in their English-language materials.

Kwan said the tactics proved very successful in sowing confusion. But some activists reacted by speaking more loudly.

In 2006, Kwan testified before a Canadian parliamentary subcommittee, imploring Ottawa to help build an international coalition among liberal democracies to push for meaningful action on China's human rights abuses. Even in the transcript of his remarks, his passion shines through: "Canada needs to adopt a consistent and principled stance when dealing with China. Only then will we earn their respect and not wrath. Canada need not fear any adverse outcomes for trade relations. There is no substance to the claim that a decline in trade will result."

More than fifteen years later, Canada still doesn't have a comprehensive counter-interference strategy. Its efforts to guard against foreign bribery and money laundering are also "shockingly low," especially when compared to similar-sized countries like the United Kingdom and France, according to a 2020 review from Transparency International Canada.

"We tried to warn about Beijing's activities in Canada for decades," Kwan said with a sigh.

SPY CHIEF RICHARD FADDEN may have been one of the few in power in Canada who did take such warnings seriously, but his comments in 2010 on foreign interference in Canada proved so unpopular in the Canadian government that he almost lost his job. The director of the Canadian Security Intelligence Service had revealed in a televised interview with broadcaster CBC that foreign countries were performing extensive espionage in Canada and trying to influence Canadian politicians. He strongly hinted that China was a key player and had successfully co-opted key figures in the province of British Columbia in particular. "In a couple of provinces . . . we have an indication that there's some political figures who have developed quite an attachment to foreign countries," he said.

Furious parliamentarians swiftly demanded Fadden's resignation. Making allegations without providing details cast aspersions on foreign nationals in Canada as well as all elected officials, they said. The uproar ultimately forced Fadden to walk back his comments, saying that none of the actions he referred to were illegal in Canada.

So the status quo was maintained. Politicians later supported the Canadian launch of *China Daily*, a state-run propaganda newspaper, and Prime Minister Justin Trudeau attended several cash-for-access fundraisers with pro-Beijing entrepreneurs. Guests at one dinner included a businessman who subsequently donated C$1 million to the Pierre Elliott Trudeau Foundation and the University of Montreal Faculty of Law—including $50,000 to fund a statue of Pierre Trudeau—according to a *Globe and Mail* report.

One such dinner, in late 2016, at the home of a Vancouver property developer, saw attendees lobby Trudeau to approve the bid of Vancouver-based Cedar Tree Investment, an affiliate of China's Anbang Insurance Group, to purchase a large chain of Canadian retirement homes. (Later, Cedar Tree Investment's retirement properties were beset with a string of complaints about elder abuse, and the company was hit with a class-action lawsuit.) The controversial deal was approved later that month, and the federal ethics commissioner found Trudeau violated no rules.

Many domestic critics have accused Canadian leaders of making concessions and avoiding political confrontation in return for more trade with China. In 2003, China surpassed the U.K. and Japan to become Canada's third-largest trading partner, after the United States and a group of twenty-seven EU members. China's share of Canada's trade has risen dramatically in the last twenty years, from about 1 percent in 2000 to nearly 6 percent in 2019. While China still represents quite a low proportion of Canada's international trade overall, some agriculture industries have found great success in recent years in the Chinese market. According to the Canola Council of Canada, 40 percent of the canola produced by Canadian farmers is exported to China each year. Exports of meat products to China surged between 2018 and 2019, and a record forty million cubic metres of logs from Canadian forests reached Chinese ports in 2018.

And while Canada's trade with China pales in comparison with its trade with the United States, China is still an important trade partner at a time when Ottawa is eager to address its over-reliance on the U.S. market.

Canadian leaders from different political parties have, however, consistently spoken out to criticize China's human rights record. Even as Trudeau pursued a free trade agreement with China, the talks reached an impasse in April 2018 after Beijing firmly rejected Canada's insistence on entrenching labour, gender, environment, and governance standards as part of the framework.

Trudeau's father, Prime Minister Pierre Elliott Trudeau, successfully established diplomatic and trade relations with Communist China in 1970, when the country was still recovering from the Cultural Revolution. The elder Trudeau has since been criticized for pursuing economic ties at the expense of speaking truthfully on China's human rights situation at the time. In 1961, seven years before starting his first term as prime minister, Trudeau co-published a book with a Canadian journalist on their travels to China in 1960 at the height of Chairman Mao's disastrous "Great Leap Forward," which resulted in the worst famine in history with an estimated thirty million deaths. Their book, titled *Two Innocents in Red China*, engaged an often humorous tone, such as in passages discussing Trudeau's flirtation with an attractive Chinese translator, and did not investigate the famine that lasted from 1959 to 1961.

The younger Trudeau hoped to continue his father's legacy and expand economic ties with China, while also standing firm on human rights, several government sources and consultants have told me. While his senior China advisers were executives from the business world, Justin Trudeau also crafted a foreign policy emphasizing feminism and human security. He thought he could make it all work.

In recent decades, Canada had routinely employed a kind of dual-track diplomatic approach with Beijing. The two sides discussed trade and business matters more or less independently from any other issue. On the one hand, Canadian leaders would publicly condemn the CCP's ongoing human rights abuses and advocate for the rule of law—and Ottawa also sent aid packages to China, including funds earmarked to support civil society groups and legal reform, totalling nearly a billion dollars from 2001 to 2013. On the other hand, as China's wealth grew, Canadian leaders would go on trade missions, attend economic summits, and arrange bilateral state visits in hopes of striking trade or investment deals. Often, when trade was the focus, human rights and the rule of law wouldn't come up at all.

UNTIL ONE DAY, when Canada-China relations went off the rails.

On December 1, 2018, Canadian police arrested Huawei Technologies executive Meng Wanzhou at Vancouver International Airport. She hadn't committed a crime in Canada; the arrest was a surprise extradition request from the U.S. Department of Justice. Meng was accused by the United States of lying to HSBC Bank about her company's relationship with an Iran-based affiliate, putting the bank at risk of violating American sanctions.

It's unclear whether Meng knew that fraud charges were being prepared in the U.S. or that she risked getting arrested in Canada, which has an extradition treaty with the States. If proven guilty, she could face up to ten years' imprisonment in the States—but first, she would get a chance to fight her extradition in Canadian courts.

The significance of the arrest can't be overstated. Huawei is China's largest nominally private company and the world's largest supplier of network equipment for telecommunications firms. However, Huawei has received as much as US$75 billion from Chinese government tax breaks, financing, subsidized land, and state grants since 2008, according to the *Wall Street Journal*. Its ownership system is complex, and analysts have argued that since trade unions possess a majority of Huawei shares and Chinese unions are under the monitoring of the CCP, the Party has significant sway over the company. Meng is the eldest daughter of the company's billionaire CEO, Ren Zhengfei. She rose from a position as a secretary in her twenties to become Huawei's chief financial officer, and she is often the face of the company at international forums.

Ren served in the People's Liberation Army for many years as an engineer before joining the Chinese Communist Party and founding Huawei in 1987. Back then, and to some extent to this day, entrepreneurs who weren't Party members couldn't get very far.

Prior to the arrest, experts had raised concerns about Huawei's opaque relationship with China's government and military. Yet former Canadian justice minister Martin Cauchon endorsed the company's move into a sprawling new operations centre in Ottawa in 2013.

"If you can't beat them, join them," Cauchon said at the time, arguing that Canadian companies wouldn't be able to rival Huawei's affordable 5G technology. The Ontario government even provided the Chinese firm with a C$6.5 million grant for the expansion, in part because Huawei promised to employ hundreds of Canadian researchers.

Many countries around the world, with the notable exceptions of the U.S. and Australia, were ignoring analysts' warnings about the security of Huawei technology. Dozens of countries installed Huawei hardware in the global race to create the next generation of 5G wireless networks.

Huawei's cutting-edge products are simply more affordable than those of its Western competitors—and achieving lightning-speed connectivity to enable a leap in technological advancement is not a cheap proposition. With 5G deployment, self-driving cars could be linked to traffic control infrastructure, and countless digital devices could be seamlessly connected to create futuristic "smart homes" and "smart cities."

The Americans' request for Meng's arrest was made very suddenly, on November 30, 2018, with no prior discussion between U.S. and Canadian officials, according to David MacNaughton, Canada's former ambassador to Washington. In an interview with the *Globe and Mail*, MacNaughton speculated that the U.S. might have some underlying motivations for targeting Meng, perhaps because it hoped to convince more allies to follow suit in banning Huawei. But President Donald Trump's office said the U.S. leader wasn't aware of the extradition request either.

When news of Meng's arrest broke, President Xi flew into a rage directed squarely at Canada, not the United States, according to Chinese media reports. Xi was apparently furious that he'd learned about the arrest from Beijing officials rather than from the Canadians. The Chinese foreign ministry issued a demand for Canada to "immediately correct the mistake."

Ottawa's stance from the beginning was that it was obliged to honour its extradition treaty with the U.S. and respect the independent legal process of Canadian courts. "The appropriate authorities took the decisions in this case without any political involvement or interference.... We were advised by them with a few days' notice that this was in the works," Trudeau told reporters, looking stressed. His country's relationship with China was about to hit a historic low.

In the years that followed, it was Canadians and not Americans who would bear the brunt of Beijing's vengeance.

IN INTERNATIONAL RELATIONS THEORY, the term "middle power" describes a sovereign state that is not a global giant but still has significant influence. Although Canada has a sparse population of 37.6 million—fewer people than the state of California—the Great White North punches above its weight in the international community.

Canada is rich in natural resources, has a seat among the G7 group of advanced economies, and is a key member of NATO (the North Atlantic Treaty Organization). The strength of Canada's military and counter-espionage defences is of particular interest to America, since the two countries share the world's longest international border, and a potential attack on Canada would endanger the States as well. U.S. defence arrangements with Canada are more extensive than with any other country, including various mutual defence obligations.

Canada's middle power status may have lent its leaders a false sense of comfort regarding China; they did not anticipate becoming involved in a serious conflict.

Wendy Dobson, co-director of the Rotman Institute for

International Business at the University of Toronto, argued in her book *Living with China: A Middle Power Finds Its Way* that for many years Canada simply had no intention of rocking the boat with China. "Canada...long used to a unipolar world dominated by the United States, lacks a China strategy," Dobson wrote. "As a middle power, its diplomatic relations have stressed engagement and accommodation with China, but living with China has meant being pulled into the orbit of the deteriorating relationship between China and the United States."

Other critics have rejected the idea that Canada should think that, as a middle power, it is a powerless third party that could get caught in the middle of a fight between the U.S. and China. They argue that policymakers had ample time to see potential troubles ahead, with Beijing having established a strategy of trying to divide liberal democracies against one another, often by using promises of deepening trade to gain leverage.

Terry Glavin, a veteran journalist and political columnist focused on Canada-China relations, noted that Canada has benefited in the past from disputes between the U.S. and China, such as gaining lucrative joint research deals with Huawei over a decade ago when the U.S. State Department was already warning its scientists against working with Huawei on security grounds. And in the maritime province of Nova Scotia, Canadian lobster exports to China have grown tenfold since 2013 at the expense of the Maine lobster fishery, which was hurt by the U.S.-dollar exchange rate and then directly by Chinese tariffs.

"This is not about being 'stuck between' the U.S. and China. It is about allowing ourselves to be pitted against the U.S., encouraging Beijing to further play us off against the U.S., and when it becomes untenable [such as the Meng extradition request], Beijing punishes us for not playing along," Glavin told me.

"The idea that Canada is stuck between Beijing and Washington also casts Canada as some sort of innocent bystander without any agency of its own," he argued.

ON DECEMBER 7, 2018, I found myself in the back of a large courtroom, waiting for the first day of Meng's bail hearing to begin. In this specially built courtroom, where notorious gangsters stood trial, onlookers were kept behind a pane of bulletproof glass so thick that audio of the proceedings had to be broadcast through speakers.

The spectator gallery was packed, and not just with local and international journalists. Notable Vancouver lawyers were also jostling for a seat, with one telling me this could be the highest-profile case in decades and might set precedent in extradition law.

I was on the edge of my seat, fingers poised over my laptop, ready to send out live updates on the *Toronto Star*'s social media feeds. But when Meng strolled in, she bore an almost serene expression. Her shoulders were relaxed. She wore a casual dark-green sweatsuit and kept her silky hair loose. As she smiled and chatted with her lawyer David Martin, one of the most experienced in the country, it looked almost as if she was relishing the break from her busy job.

When Martin spoke, he denounced his client's arrest as politically motivated. Gesturing dramatically, he told the judge that Meng couldn't possibly be a flight risk because fleeing would dishonour her prestigious family, Huawei, and China itself. A few observers around me snickered, but I thought he had a point about Meng's unusual significance.

In mainland China, Meng is practically royalty. Not only are her company's success and her personal business prowess widely respected, her father is part of the revolutionary cohort that established Communist Party power. She is also well connected to the Chinese government on her mother's side: her grandfather was the former deputy governor of Sichuan province.

Soon enough, the forty-six-year-old was out on bail and back in her multimillion-dollar home in Vancouver's elite west side. Though an ankle bracelet tracked her location, she was free to move around the city and enjoy the company of visitors while living with her husband and children.

The executive's arrest was all anyone following the news wanted to talk about. People were asking deep questions about the motivations of the U.S. and Chinese governments and fretting about how Canada would fare in the middle of the escalating conflict.

Huawei is a national champion and the pride of China, and Canadians wondered whether such a large company could truly be independent. After all, Chinese law obliges firms to "support, cooperate with and collaborate in national intelligence work." The company says it has never been asked to engage in intelligence work on behalf of any government, and Ren has insisted he'd sooner shut Huawei down than allow it to be used for spying.

But what some get wrong in the debate about Huawei, experts argue, is that there's no need for evidence that the company is *currently* facilitating spying by the Chinese government; the possibility remains that this could happen in the future.

"This is how I would do my calculus," Christopher Parsons, a senior researcher with Citizen Lab, told me. "Is it highly

likely that my government will come into an adversarial or
contested relationship with that country? If the answer is
yes, there has to be reflection and care taken when considering whether to buy critical infrastructure from them."
Parsons thinks countries shouldn't craft policy with only one
foreign technology company in mind; by making sure that
their future 5G networks are as secure as possible, they can
prevent a number of possibilities when it comes to potential
cyberattacks or espionage.

Such nuanced conversations have been quite a change from
the endless debates in Canadian media about whether Chinese
foreign buyers and recent immigrants hoovering up Canadian
real estate were driving up housing costs in cities. While a few
journalists like Sam Cooper and Ian Young were reporting on
the specific role that corrupt Chinese officials and organized
crime groups played in laundering money through Vancouver
real estate, the conversations I heard in public and on social
media tended to be xenophobic—about how "Chinese money"
was ruining Canadian cities.

So, admittedly, I was excited that, with Meng's arrest, a
huge international story had landed in our backyard. It was an
opportunity to get more people engaged in broader issues of
political interference, digital surveillance, and the hazy status
of China's nominally private companies.

I didn't know then that a terrible toll for Canada was yet
to come.

NINE DAYS AFTER MENG'S ARREST, Michael Kovrig, a former
Canadian diplomat living in Beijing, was apprehended by the
Chinese authorities without charge. It was past midnight in

China, and none of our mutual contacts were getting back to me. I started to panic.

Finally, I reached the previous Canadian ambassador to China, Guy Saint-Jacques. He was Kovrig's boss when Kovrig worked as a senior diplomat of the Beijing embassy from 2014 to 2016. Our conversation was grim. Saint-Jacques said he feared authorities would charge Kovrig with espionage and use him to press for Meng's release. My heart sank.

That kind of brazen hostage-taking wasn't unheard of. In 2014, Julia and Kevin Garratt, Christian aid workers from Canada, were jailed by Chinese officials and accused of spying. Many believed it was retaliation for Canada's arrest that year of Chinese citizen Su Bin, who was accused of hacking U.S. military databases. Julia spent six months in a dank prison cell, and her husband was released only in 2016 — a week after Trudeau's first official visit to China.

Kovrig was one of the first people I met in Beijing when I moved there in late 2014. We were all new to working in the capital, though Kovrig had, like me, worked in Hong Kong since 2012. After attending a folk concert with mutual friends, we got together the next week. Over an Italian set lunch in the Sanlitun entertainment district, we talked about our shared experiences in Hong Kong and how exciting (if overwhelming) it was to cover politics in mainland China. Kovrig told me his job was to monitor highly sensitive topics in the country, such as the rights of ethnic minorities and religious groups.

He felt like a journalist too, but he was reporting to his government rather than to the public, he said with a laugh.

From then on, Kovrig always tried to make it to my gatherings and invited me to the parties he threw in his apartment — including one where he hired a swing band to mark his last days working as a China diplomat. The way he danced, exaggerating those old-fashioned flourishes, was completely innocent and full of joy.

In mid-2016, when his two-year post was winding down and he was due for reassignment back to Ottawa, he spoke openly about his decision to seek a leave of absence from Canada's Ministry of Foreign Affairs. He wanted to stay in China and keep learning more about the country he had grown to love.

Saint-Jacques gave Kovrig his blessing. "I told him, 'You can take a leave of absence from the government and try to find something, and good luck with your plans,'" the former ambassador told me. "And that's why he decided to stay and enjoy living and working in China."

Kovrig got a new job and started working as a senior adviser on Northeast Asia for International Crisis Group, a respected NGO that examines ways to prevent and resolve deadly conflict. And when police barged into his Beijing home and dragged him away, Kovrig didn't have diplomatic immunity to protect him.

We weren't close, but he was part of *my* group of people, and to many around the world who had never met him, he was one of *their* people too — someone who chose to live in China out of a mix of affection for and curiosity about the country, despite all its problems.

Days after Kovrig's arrest, we learned that a second Canadian, Michael Spavor, had also been arrested and accused of working with Kovrig to steal state secrets. Spavor is the director of an organization called Paektu Cultural Exchange, which organizes business and tourism trips to North Korea, and he has served as a consultant on North Korea for years. Many expatriates in Asia held jobs similar to Kovrig's and Spavor's.

To be frank, I think the news rattled so many people because, until that point, most of Beijing's political prisoners had been of Asian descent. Now, here were two middle-class white men sitting in jail cells, being interrogated for hours a day with no access to lawyers and no ability to speak with their families.

Canadians behind bars in China also include those of Asian origin, such as Sun Qian, a Falun Gong practitioner who was arrested in Beijing in 2017 for her involvement with "heretical religious organizations," and Huseyin Celil, a Uyghur Muslim, who was seized by local police in 2006 while visiting his wife's family in Uzbekistan and sent to China at the request of Chinese authorities. Even though Celil is Canadian, Chinese authorities have denied Canada consular access. Little is known about his case, including what crime, if any, he was charged with; officials have only said he will remain in jail until 2036. A family representative told me it has been gutting for Celil's loved ones to see the outpouring of global calls for the two Michaels' release when Celil has been all but forgotten.

Then came the death threat diplomacy.

On January 14, 2019, a court in Liaoning province, in the northeast of the country, summoned Canadian Robert Schellenberg to a hasty one-day retrial for drug trafficking charges. He was already serving a fifteen-year prison sentence, having been found guilty a year earlier of joining a methamphetamine smuggling operation. In an unusual move, authorities welcomed foreign journalists into the Dalian city courtroom to watch the retrial, which escalated his sentence to death. He has a chance to appeal, but Schellenberg's life had become another bargaining chip in the dispute over Meng and Huawei.

Almost overnight, people around the world seemed to awaken to the consequences of angering a technologically advanced and increasingly authoritarian world power. Not only were Kovrig and Spavor widely relatable victims, other medium-sized nations like Canada with close trade ties to Beijing, and therefore some dependency on it, recognized that they could find themselves in a similar position.

Middle powers do have global clout and strong alliances, but individually their militaries are not mighty. And if Canada threatened China with trade sanctions, Beijing probably wouldn't blink. In contrast, sanctions from the U.S. could cripple certain Chinese industries overnight.

Canada was in a vise, and the small cohort of journalists, activists, and academics who had earlier tried to warn Ottawa had their "I told you so" moment.

In a public debate in March 2019, Charles Burton—at the time an associate professor of political science at Brock University in Ontario, and a former diplomat at the Canadian embassy in Beijing—argued that Canada had been foolish for pursuing a "friendship of utility" with a country that would detain Canadians for no valid reason while imprisoning over a million Uyghur people in "re-education" camps. "Simply put, there is no reciprocated goodwill present in current Canada-China relations, because China does not respect Canada," Burton said.

Over several months, I reached out to contacts in Canadian government to find out why the dramatic shift in Beijing's attitude toward their Canadian "friends" had apparently come as such a surprise to decision-makers. Most government departments gave me canned, generic responses.

But one anecdote I heard was quite telling. According to a number of my sources, when Kovrig and Spavor were arrested, Ottawa tried to figure out how to push for their release without jeopardizing the independence of Canada's legal system. Senior officials held meetings that looked like collective panic attacks.

The government was in uncharted waters with Beijing, and it seemed they didn't feel they had the expertise on staff to handle the crisis. At a meeting of the Privy Council Office, the committee that advises the prime minister and cabinet, a frustrated senior official asked, "Where the fuck are the China people?"

KOVRIG AND SPAVOR HAD been suffering since their December 2018 arrest in extreme solitary confinement for months. The lights in their cells were on twenty-four hours a day. They could not speak on the phone with any lawyer or family member, and their only contact with the outside world consisted of sporadic visits from Canadian consulate officials. It was considered good news when, some months into the detentions, a mutual friend told me that Kovrig had received some reading material.

Like many Canadians, I struggled to contain my frustration over the situation. There is ample expertise in the country, so why hasn't this translated into smart policy to protect innocent people from falling victim to Beijing's authoritarian whims? In Vancouver alone, where I had taken an array of classes in Chinese and Asian studies from world-class professors at the University of British Columbia (UBC), there was no shortage of knowledge on China.

My former undergraduate thesis supervisor, Timothy Cheek, looked exhausted as we sat outside a university café on a mild winter day in early 2019. Cheek has considerable influence as a prolific academic researcher and director of the Institute of Asian Research at UBC. He said he didn't want to make excuses, but for a while it had been the consensus among scholars in North America that it was better to let their counterparts in China try to enact change from within. As Chinese citizens, they were better placed to foster academic freedom and freedom of expression, and—so the thinking went—the strident voices of foreigners might only anger decision-makers.

One by one, however, formerly outspoken Chinese scholars, artists, journalists, and public intellectuals were silenced, one way or another, be it through their employers threatening professional repercussions or through police intimidation and arbitrary arrest.

Still, Cheek said, he had remained among those who didn't think Beijing would brazenly take Canadians as hostages. And while Westerners were dithering about how to respond, the scale of human rights abuses against Chinese citizens and the terrorizing of the Chinese international diaspora had grown to staggering proportions with little resistance from democratic nations.

"China never made the bargain to become more liberal when they joined the World Trade Organization and agreed to diplomatic exchanges, but we had it in our head. We were hopeful. We kept thinking, it's a big country; there are some people working on it. We were hopeful our colleagues in China could do something.

"You compromise a bit, because you're hoping it's going to be better. But what's changed in the last few years is a loss of hope.

"We've been privileged. We've been stupid."

AND AFTER HOSTAGE-TAKING and death threat diplomacy came economic retaliation.

In June 2019, Trudeau accused Beijing of "inventing excuses" to ban imports of Canadian pork and canola products. This hit Canada's farmers hard; roughly 20 percent of their pork and 40 percent of their canola seed, oil, and meal was being exported to China. Mostly because of these trade measures, affecting canola, soybeans, meat, and other food products, Canadian exports to China declined 16 percent in 2019 after years of steady growth.

In this, Canada was far from alone. Other middle powers experienced similar problems that year, as U.S.-China feuding escalated. For various reasons, China has threatened Denmark, the Czech Republic, and Australia. In one particularly clear example, China's ambassador to Denmark threatened to withdraw a trade deal with Denmark's Faroe Islands if Huawei didn't get a 5G contract there. This didn't exactly bolster Beijing's claim that Huawei was independent from the Chinese government.

Similarly, in January 2020, China's ambassador to the Netherlands warned that trade relations between China and the Netherlands would suffer if Dutch semiconductor equipment supplier ASML was not allowed to ship its newest machines to China. According to Reuters, the Dutch government withheld the licence ASML needed to export its latest product to China following strong pressure from the U.S. government. The Dutch firm holds a near-monopolist speciality in lithography equipment, a key tool in the manufacture of advanced computer chips, and China needs ASML equipment if its chipmakers are to compete globally.

"We are concerned that the Netherlands is politicizing our trade relationship under American pressure," Chinese ambassador Xu Hong was quoted as saying in the *Het Financieele Dagblad* newspaper. "If this movement continues it will of course negatively affect bilateral relations."

Beijing's foreign policy playbook includes all kinds of economic coercion, such as investment restrictions, boycotts of goods and services, import and export controls, and the barring of Chinese students and tourists from visiting certain countries. While other countries, including the U.S., have certainly employed economic coercive techniques too, authoritarian China is better equipped to force companies and its citizens to halt doing business with certain countries or foreign companies.

Beijing has been using these tactics for years in the Asia-Pacific region. When South Korea dared to allow the U.S. to install the Terminal High Altitude Area Defense system southeast of Seoul in response to missile threats from North Korea, Beijing was livid. It thought the system's radar could snoop on China's military defences. The Chinese government ordered the closing of dozens of South Korean supermarkets in China, banned Chinese travel tours to South Korea, blocked concert tours of K-pop stars, and rejected game licences for South Korean game companies, among other measures. The economic hit amounted to billions of U.S. dollars for South Korea from 2017 to 2019, according to the *Asia Times* newspaper.

"Similar tactics have occurred for the last decade, and Beijing initially saw developing countries as easy targets. Now it's becoming more aggressive and less subtle," says Ashley Feng, an independent researcher who co-authored a 2020 report on coercive economic measures in the U.S.-China relationship for the Center for a New American Security think tank.

"In the past, governments in Europe, Canada, and the U.S. watched what was happening and thought it would be limited to other countries and 'not us,'" Feng told me. "Now it's apparent that no country is above reproach from China."

However, while Beijing has issued public threats and slapped tariffs on certain Canadian goods, trade volumes between

Canada and China rose throughout 2020, even with the challenges of the COVID-19 pandemic, with Canadian exports to
China increasing more than 4 percent in the first nine months
compared to 2019. In the two agricultural sectors hardest hit
by China's tariffs in 2019—pork and canola products—export
volumes recovered in 2020 and even exceeded 2018 levels. This
suggests that economic coercion in some cases disproportion-
ately impacts only some sectors, and the targeted sectors recover
rapidly once tariffs are lifted.

But meanwhile, Canada's international trade overall dropped
by around 8 percent for both imports and exports between 2019
and 2020, in large part because of the COVID-19 pandemic.
Critics say the continued importance of the Chinese market
can explain why the Trudeau government has dragged its feet
on making significant changes to its foreign policy approach
to China and why, many months after most major Western
countries had made a decision on whether to allow Huawei
into 5G infrastructure, Canada still hasn't said what it will do.
As of June 2021, Canada had made no decision.

When opposition parties in the Canadian Parliament
banded together in late 2019 to form a special House of
Commons committee to study and make recommendations
on "all aspects" of the relations between Canada and China,
Trudeau's Liberal Party members overwhelmingly voted against
the launch of that committee. Garnett Genuis, a member of
the special committee, told me that the Trudeau administration
has appeared to oppose the Canada-China committee's work,
such as by impeding efforts to convene digitally during the
COVID-19 pandemic. "That isn't so surprising when you see
how effective the committee has been in exposing problems
with the naive approach the Canadian government has taken

to responding to issues," Genuis argued, referring to committee reports such as one criticizing the federal government's slow response to Beijing's campaign of "intimidation" against Hong Kong democracy supporters in Canada.

In February 2021, Trudeau's cabinet abstained from a Parliament vote on whether the Chinese government's persecution against Uyghurs and minorities in Xinjiang amounted to genocide (the House of Commons vote was unanimous in affirmation).

Terry Glavin notes that more than two years since Meng Wanzhou's arrest touched off Canada's current crisis, Ottawa has yet to articulate a plan for addressing the challenges of dealing with an increasingly belligerent Beijing.

Despite the change in tone from many officials in Ottawa suggesting a tougher stance on China, Glavin says he sees no evidence of a concerted effort to reduce Canada's trade vulnerability vis-à-vis Beijing, and no concerted effort to shift exports to other markets. "Quite the opposite," Glavin told me in an email. "Canadian ambassador Dominic Barton says he remains very 'bullish' on China, and our official policy seems to be 'Don't do anything to upset Xi, and maybe he will be nice to us.'"

On September 24, 2021, American authorities approved a deal between Meng Wanzhou's lawyers and U.S. prosecutors that allowed the executive to avoid criminal liability. Within hours, Meng was on a plane leaving Vancouver.

Most observers expected Chinese authorities to wait at least several weeks to release the "two Michaels" to keep up their pretense that the two Canadians were not mere pawns. Instead, Kovrig and Spavor were able to board a plane home, too, the very same day.

4.

AUSTRALIA

Influence and Interference

In 2015, the government of the Northern Territory, in Australia, blithely announced that Chinese company Landbridge would take over Port Darwin for ninety-nine years. The A$500 million (more than US$357 million) deal was struck between the regional government and the private Chinese company without the oversight or say-so of federal authorities.

Landbridge Group's billionaire owner, Ye Cheng, like virtually all successful tycoons in mainland China, has close ties with the Chinese Communist Party. In an interview with Beijing media in 2016, Ye boasted that the acquisition of the strategically located port would serve China's goal of expanding global infrastructure holdings as part of the New Silk Road, China's mammoth global trade investment initiative, which Australia has not joined.

Australia's national government in Canberra was left red-faced, fielding questions from its strongest ally, the United States, about the security of American military bases near Port

Darwin, as well as from the general public about national security implications. The ninety-nine-year lease of the port gave the Chinese company control over a large body of water capable of harbouring large ships less than five thousand kilometres away from the contested South China Sea, where Beijing has continued to build artificial islands and military bases.

But the deal was signed and sealed; national authorities concluded they could do nothing to reverse it.

At a private meeting, U.S. president Barack Obama told Prime Minister Malcolm Turnbull he understood Australia's relationship with China and its role in the region, but that Washington should be given a "heads up about these sorts of things," sources told the *Australian Financial Review.*

"Let us know next time," Obama ribbed. In response, Turnbull joked that the president needed to subscribe to the Northern Territory tabloid *NT News* instead.

The Port Darwin sale was widely understood as a one-off gaffe, and the awkward joking seemed to forestall more serious conversation about whether Australia's laws were far too weak when it came to guarding against threats to national security and sovereignty. Should a foreign company be able to scoop up an important asset in a country without the knowledge of the federal government?

For decades, Australia's overarching goal in its relations with China had been to expand trade and economic ties in as many sectors as possible to take advantage of huge opportunities for Australia to attract more investment, tourists, and students from China. After all, Australia is located in the Asia-Pacific but has all the cultural and political trappings of an unmistakably "Western" country. A direct flight between Shanghai and Sydney takes ten hours, which is brief compared to the more than twenty-one hours it takes to trek from London to Sydney. The year-round warm climate is also attractive to wealthy Chinese looking to purchase investment properties or send their children to study abroad. And with China's growing middle class increasingly perturbed about food safety scandals in their own country, demand for Australian imports like infant milk formula, supplements, and skin-care products had surged.

"It was a relationship cast purely in economic terms," Andrew Hastie, Liberal Party member of the Australian House of Representatives, told me. "Neoliberalism [free-market capitalism] was the guiding orthodoxy for our approach to China. Twenty fifteen was the high-water mark of that approach to China with the lease of Port Darwin."

Hastie admits that when he was elected in late 2015, he was very much a political rookie and unfamiliar with everything to do with China. He had entered politics after a twelve-year military career, which he'd finished in an intelligence operations role in the Middle East, countering the Islamic State's terrorist activities. At the time, Australia's defence community was chiefly concerned about risks related to events in the Middle East, such as the Syrian civil war and the rise of the Islamic State.

Terms like "foreign influence operations" were not yet ubiquitous even in American policy circles. This may be surprising to those who have only more recently followed China news, because the topic (and phrase) has since become popular to the point of sounding overused. But back then, few journalists around the world covered the United Front's activities, and politicians received little pressure from the public to take action.

But Australia would soon make a dramatic shift in its approach to Beijing, which pushed other democracies toward a different direction too.

IT TOOK A SERIES of political scandals in Australia, often tied
to explosive media investigations, to draw public attention to
the ways in which Beijing's United Front system had laboured
for years to curry favour among the country's top politicians,
as well as stifle criticism within ethnic Chinese Australian
communities.

Perhaps the biggest driver of change was the "Sam Dastyari
incident." Labour senator Sam Dastyari, a rising political star,
was forced to resign in disgrace in December 2017. The year
before, he had exceeded his yearly travel budget by A\$1,670,
and instead of paying out of pocket, he asked the Chinese-
government-linked Top Education Institute to foot the bill. The
private school is run by Chinese businessman Zhu Minshen,
who in 2014 was a delegate to the Chinese People's Political
Consultative Conference, the CCP's prestigious advisory body
and highest-level United Front organ.

That was after Dastyari had already asked a company owned
by his party's major political donor, Huang Xiangmo, to help
him pay a A\$44,000 settlement for an undisclosed "outstand-
ing legal matter." And if that wasn't enough, Dastyari also
accepted a fifteen-day free trip to China from the Australian
Fellowship of China Guangdong Associations. Huang
Xiangmo is the founder of that group and served as chairman
before Australia rescinded his permanent residency and ousted
him from the country on being advised by intelligence officials
that Huang had aided Beijing's foreign interference activities
in the country.

Dastyari denied wrongdoing on the financial matters but
acknowledged he shouldn't have made public statements in

support of Beijing's positions on controversial topics. During a press conference, he had contradicted the Australian government's concern over the South China Sea territorial dispute, instead backing Beijing's position that foreign countries had no right to protest its claims to the resource-rich isles. "The Chinese integrity of its borders is a matter for China. The role that Australia should be playing as a friend is to know that we see... thousands of years of history where it is and isn't our place to be involved," Dastyari had said. "And as a supporter of China, and a friend of China, the Australian Labor Party is playing an important role in maintaining that relationship," he added.

Media reports also cited senior government sources alleging Dastyari provided counter-surveillance advice to Huang, such as telling him that his phone was likely being tapped by intelligence agencies, and in 2015 Dastyari tried to persuade the Labor Party's foreign-affairs spokesperson to cancel a meeting with a Hong Kong pro-democracy advocate.

The whole saga touched off a period of soul-searching among the Australian political elite. Much of what Dastyari did was within the realm of legal activities, since he dutifully reported the amounts he accepted from supporters linked to the Chinese government, and some colleagues defended him for doing so.

Environment minister Josh Frydenberg, however, said the "Dastyari itch" would become an outbreak "engulfing the whole of the Labor Party" unless he was fired. And as Prime Minister Turnbull asked Dastyari to leave for the good of the Labor Party, immigration minister Peter Dutton went even further, calling him a "double agent."

Yet it was painfully obvious to outside observers that Australia's lax political donation system deserved much of the blame. The rules allowed politicians to accept most kinds of financial assistance, as long as they reported them.

IN DECEMBER 2017, Prime Minister Turnbull unveiled sweeping legislation to overhaul Australia's espionage, counter-intelligence, and political donations laws. "Foreign powers are making unprecedented and increasingly sophisticated attempts to influence the political process, both here and abroad," he said in his announcement.

He specifically said he was concerned by reports of Chinese foreign influence, though the laws were not focused on one country alone. He also cited reports of Russia's meddling in the 2016 U.S. presidential election as a reason for Australia to be better prepared.

Representatives of rival parties banded together to support the legislation. In June 2018, Parliament passed the suite of laws, which made industrial espionage — the theft of trade secrets — one of a new set of criminal offences, and increased penalties for people who leak classified information. The legal definition of "espionage" was broadened to make it a crime for unauthorized persons to possess sensitive information, instead of merely to communicate it. Lobbyists in Australia working for foreign governments must also identify themselves on a new public register. In a separate piece of legislation passed later in the year, the government also completely banned foreign political donations.

The world took notice.

China's ambassador to Australia, Cheng Jingye, railed against the new legislation, warning that "bias and bigotry" were damaging bilateral ties. The embassy in Canberra repeatedly portrayed the policies as racist attacks on China as well as the "Chinese people." Randall Schriver, the former U.S. assistant secretary of defense for Indo-Pacific security affairs, said in a February 2018 interview that Australia had "woken up people in a lot of countries to take a look at Chinese activity within their own borders." He also said Australia had done a "great service" by publicizing much of this activity, and the U.S. would take inspiration and increase scrutiny of Chinese influence programs on its own university campuses, among other areas of concern.

The U.S. and other countries actually already had similar protocols in place. The Foreign Agents Registration Act is an American law passed in 1938 requiring that agents in the U.S. representing the interests of foreign powers in a "political or quasi-political capacity" disclose their relationship with the foreign government.

But there was a pointed message behind Australia's introduction of new laws: here was a Western country that was particularly economically reliant on China, but economic ties were not to pave the way for political manipulation.

THE AUSTRALIAN LEGISLATION WAS informed by the findings of a top-secret government probe, which was unknown even to most government officials and elected representatives.

Two years earlier, Malcolm Turnbull had quietly asked John Garnaut — Turnbull's security adviser and a former China-based foreign correspondent — to lead a report on Chinese influence on Australian politics. The report itself remains classified, but its conclusions were openly discussed within Parliament, with foreign governments, and with the press.

In the process, Australia sparked an overdue worldwide conversation about how a country can protect its sovereignty without stoking racism and xenophobia when China appears to be a major actor in foreign interference activities—a tension similarly present in Canada and other places with large ethnic Chinese populations.

As Turnbull put it while unveiling the counter-interference strategy in December 2017, "Our diaspora communities are part of the solution, not the problem."

Just days after the new laws were introduced, an opinion poll in the Sydney seat of Bennelong, home to one of the country's largest ethnic Chinese communities, found that two-thirds of voters supported the foreign interference legislation. This highlighted the diversity in political opinion among the Chinese diaspora. While some, like Huang Xiangmo, appeared to directly assist Beijing's foreign interference efforts, others were publicly critical of Beijing, and a large number seemed to be quietly supportive of Australia's efforts to strengthen basic national security safeguards.

It seemed extraordinary. Many countries were debating if and how to counter China's influence without endangering economic relations. Australia is a Western country with perhaps deeper ties to China than most others, and it's also a middle power, and yet it has stood up to Beijing's activities.

WHAT WERE THE CONSEQUENCES of Canberra's new foreign policies? While economic threats would come later, it has been Australia's ethnic Chinese minorities who have borne the brunt of Beijing's retaliation, and this started even before the new laws were introduced.

Covering the human rights beat in Beijing, I used to start my day by turning on my computer, which would already have about forty tabs open, each a different stream of news alerts and group chats. There were often reports of arrests of people branded "troublemakers" in China—political dissidents, government critics—but we didn't write about each case, since unfortunately they occurred too frequently. But on the morning of March 26, 2017, I saw that among the mysteriously disappeared was a prominent Australian university professor, Feng Chongyi.

Chinese officials had somehow found out about the secret inquiry in Australia led by John Garnaut into Chinese foreign influence, and to stymie it had detained Feng. Lawyers in China were sending panicked messages to each other about the rumoured detention on WhatsApp groups that included a few international journalists and human rights researchers. Feng was a friend to many of them.

Feng, the best-known Chinese-born scholar in Australia, was apparently trapped in his hotel room in the southern city of Guangzhou, with several secret police officers guarding his door. The Australian permanent resident had been visiting mainland China for field research.

The former head of the Chinese Studies department at the University of Technology Sydney, Feng was not only a leading expert on the crackdown on lawyers and democracy activists in his home country, but had also been vocal about Beijing's extensive intimidation of journalists, politicians, and other prominent community figures in Australia.

I noticed in one of the group chats that a Beijing lawyer called Liu Hao appeared to have made recent contact with Feng, so I fired Liu a message in Mandarin.

He quickly typed back: "On Friday, police blocked Feng from boarding a flight for Sydney from Guangzhou Baiyun International Airport. They told him he was suspected of harming national security and could not leave China."

Then my inbox pinged again. To my surprise, it was Feng himself, responding to an email I'd sent to his university address. He assured me he was safe but being held in Guangzhou.

"I don't know when I'll be able to leave," Feng wrote. He didn't elaborate.

After a little over a week cooped up in his hotel, Feng was released, and he boarded a flight back home. Experienced observers found it odd; it was an abnormally short detention in the strange, sad history of Chinese secret policing. Unlike the American CIA or the British MI6 spy agencies, the Chinese equivalent, the Ministry of State Security, has no public spokesperson and no appeal mechanism if an individual wants to complain about the behaviour of its agents.

What kind of clout did Professor Feng have? Hundreds of his fellow Chinese nationals have spent months in "residential surveillance in a designated place," a notorious kind of detention where psychological torture and complete isolation are used to extract confessions. Secret police are enabled by Chinese law to detain suspects for up to six months in an unknown location before they are charged with any crime, without giving them access to family or lawyers. Feng had escaped this fate. He had never opted to apply for an Australian passport, but did his Australian permanent residency protect him from being "disappeared" for longer?

Feng was tight-lipped with Australian reporters when he returned home. I chalked the detention up as an interrogation to get him to tone down his public criticism. I had no idea Feng was involved in the secret Australian investigation that would dramatically change the course of the country's relationship with China. But to the small circle of people involved in the top-secret government probe on the CCP's covert activities in Australia, Feng's detention—however brief—was a signal to move faster.

In March 2017, the same week police were holding Feng in a Guangzhou hotel room, other Chinese officials dangled the fate of three Australian prisoners, in the country for gambling-related crimes, to pressure the Turnbull government to ratify an extradition treaty, according to *The Australian* newspaper.

These were some of the issues on my mind when, two years later, I wrote to Feng to tell him I was heading to Sydney and ask if he had time to meet. At the time, he hadn't spoken at length to any journalist about what transpired during his detention.

I LANDED IN SYDNEY IN APRIL 2019, groggy from my sixteen-hour flight and disoriented, after a long Canadian winter, to feel the sun beating down on my skin. I checked into my hotel and was instantly struck by how much the Chinatown neighbourhood reminded me of Hong Kong. I took in the towering high-rises, snack kiosks, bakeries, dim sum restaurants, and lively street life.

It seemed like a place where many people lived and thrived, unlike other Chinatowns around the world that have shrunk into soulless tourist attractions. According to the 2016 census, 487,976 (or nearly 11 percent) of the inhabitants of Sydney reported being of mostly Chinese ancestry. This was a huge population, and it explained why the Chinatown area looked like a small city in China where you can find all the major Chinese regional cuisines. I also noted the businesses catering to younger people's tastes, such as bubble tea and dessert shops.

After grabbing some fried dumplings for lunch, I took an Uber out of the city to a nondescript suburb to meet Feng and his friend John Hu for tea.

Feng's house looked small and plain from the front entrance, but inside, the rosewood furniture, calligraphy scrolls on the walls, and view of the lush backyard made it feel like we were sitting in an aristocratic Chinese garden. The scholar was born in the tropical island province of Hainan, on China's southernmost point, where the people are warm and welcoming.

Two years after Feng's detention in Guangzhou, the Australian Parliament's inquiry into Beijing's meddling was no longer a secret. Feng, wearing a loose striped shirt and khakis, spoke freely as he boiled water in a kettle and assembled a plate of steamed chestnuts. He even made some jokes at his former police guards' expense.

"I tried to scare them. I banged my hands on the table and said, 'You dare yell at me? You're all my students' age. You should treat me like I'm your teacher. Your boss was my classmate.'"

He told me the three young officers sent to interrogate him put up their hands and said, "Whoa, whoa, whoa, don't bother your friend. We're just doing our job. This has nothing to do with your classmate."

Feng wasn't bluffing. He is indeed friends with their boss, the head of the provincial security bureau of Guangdong province. In the early 1980s, as an undergraduate and master's student at Sun Yat-sen University, Feng forged close friendships with future Chinese politicians and bureaucrats. It was a hopeful time, he said, when artists, workers, and students across the country were excited about the opportunities of their country's gradual opening up to the Western world.

The guards then asked about Feng's involvement with the Australian probe into CCP interference and his dealings with Garnaut. They did not hide their anger about Garnaut's role in the secret investigation.

Feng maintained his haughty, indignant act and did not admit to being close friends with Garnaut or helping with the inquiry. Luckily, the guards did not resort to physical force to try to get answers.

"What people don't understand is that there are still moderates and liberals within the Chinese Communist regime. They're trying to keep things from getting too bad," he said.

"There's nothing more to it. I was able to travel freely in China to research sensitive topics when others in my position couldn't for so long because of the protection of my connections."

"But not anymore!" his friend Hu interjected. "You better not try to go back to China again."

Hu, a former councillor of the City of Parramatta, in greater western Sydney, co-founded a group called the Australian Values Alliance in 2016, which brought together like-minded Australians of Chinese heritage to warn of attempts to infiltrate the government, community groups, the media, and the education system in Australia. Feng is one of their most prominent members and a frequent seminar speaker.

Now that Feng had conceded to avoid travel to China, he was open to talking about the government inquiry he aided. "I had been writing and teaching on the topics for years, but luck would have it that my close friend had the ear of the highest level of power, and I was able to help," Feng explained, referring to his connection with Turnbull's senior adviser Garnaut.

"Garnaut and I had frequent discussions, and we organized forums to educate the Australian bureaucrats about China's foreign interference activities. . . . Soon, there was a strong community within the government dedicated to formulating the new legislation and working with Parliament members in different parties to make sure the law would pass."

Feng marvelled at how quickly the parliamentarians achieved bipartisan support for the sweeping legal changes. "It was good luck, all those things falling into place," he concluded. He hadn't thought it would be possible in Australia.

When Feng first decided to move to Australia, he was in his early thirties and had a newly minted doctorate in contemporary Chinese history. While he was on a research exchange in the U.K. in 1989, he supported the pro-democracy movement from afar, so safety was a factor.

After he settled in Sydney in the early 1990s, he noticed that pro-democracy activists among Chinese immigrants were an ever-shrinking minority. It wasn't a problem that most people stayed out of politics, but Feng was distressed to watch Chinese consulates and their community allies become increasingly brazen in quashing the speech of dissenting voices.

He had felt rather isolated, but then he met people like Hu and Garnaut.

According to Feng, the CCP is not as strong as it appears to be, and in fact it acts out of a place of insecurity and fear.

"The United Front presence has been so successful in the last several decades simply because democracies around the world have not worked properly, practising a policy of appeasement and capitulation to the Chinese regime instead," he remarked at the end of our conversation. "When democracies around the world are able to form strong democratic alliances against the aggressive United Front operations, [they] are much, much stronger than the Chinese Communist regime."

I thought there was truth to what he was saying, and it's wrong to view the Chinese elite as a monolith to be sure, but Feng was also speaking from a position of privilege. His position as a well-known scholar in Australia, with good connections amongst the relatively moderate voices within the Chinese elite, had helped him escape a longer detention in China.

Many other Australian nationals of Chinese descent haven't been as lucky.

AT A MEMORIAL SERVICE at Parliament House in the wake of the 1989 Tiananmen massacre, Australian prime minister Bob Hawke gave a raw, emotional speech, telling his country that in Beijing, soldiers "went through the square, bayonetting or shooting anybody... who was still alive."

He announced, with tears rolling down his cheeks, that he was offering asylum to Chinese students residing in Australia. In the crowd, young people of Chinese descent holding white flowers and wearing black armbands—symbols of mourning—wept with him.

Hawke had not consulted his cabinet colleagues before making this offer. It was a heartfelt gesture that led to forty-two thousand people obtaining permanent residency. Some sponsored family members, so Australia gained about one hundred thousand new residents in total. Many later became citizens.

Australian officials did not, however, have a plan to protect this new population from the CCP's continued harassment, nor to guard against attempts to recruit susceptible immigrants as patriotic allies of the Chinese state. With so many new Chinese immigrants, many of whom lacked fluency in English, Australia was an ideal laboratory for Beijing to experiment with techniques to secure the loyalty of overseas Chinese.

It seemed that Australia also didn't anticipate that within a decade Beijing would rise from the shame of the Tiananmen massacre to become a global economic power. Following Deng Xiaoping's ambitious market reforms in China in the early 1990s, economic links between Australia and China deepened, and the Asian giant soon became Australia's largest trading partner, to the point where some Australian industries have become entirely reliant on the Chinese market. China now accounts for more than a third of global sales for most of Australia's top export products. Australia shipped more than eight hundred million tonnes of iron ore to China in 2020, and only about one hundred million tonnes to the rest of the world.

Furthermore, though many Chinese immigrants had settled in Australia, their businesses often remained dependent on connections back home, whether they worked in the retail sector, restaurants, media, or commodities. With Beijing's growing economic clout, it developed significant influence over both the general Australian business community and the members of the Chinese diaspora there.

Often, financial incentives and disincentives worked best in China's efforts to extend its influence to political matters in Australia. Other times, United Front agents would turn to direct harassment. If a Chinese-language media outlet became too critical, for example, officials would pressure Chinese companies to pull their ads to deprive the outlet of funds.

The *Vision China Times*, a newspaper founded by Chinese Australians, got on Beijing's radar because it ran in-depth stories and critical analysis related to political issues in China.

Meanwhile, most Chinese-language media in Australia were already toeing the line.

Attempts by the Chinese consulate to silence the independent *Vision China Times* started, as in many other documented cases, with intimidating advertisers in the Chinese-language newspaper to withdraw their ads. But then, in an unusual move, Chinese consular officials issued at least eight warnings between 2018 and 2019 to a Sydney-area government council to sever ties with the newspaper. The paper was a sponsor for the 2018 Chinese New Year celebrations in south Sydney, hosted by the Georges River Council, which oversees one of the country's largest populations of Chinese Australians.

In a joint investigation by the *Four Corners* documentary television program and newspaper chain Fairfax Media, reporters obtained multiple documents sent by Chinese consular officials to the council also protesting the newspaper's role in the 2019 New Year's celebrations.

"We have attached great importance to our cooperation with the Georges River City Council and hope there will be no change to the policy of the Georges River Council on supporting the development of the Australia-China relationship," one memo read.

The same day the memo was sent, the council voted to ban *Vision China Times*'s sponsorship. A council staff member later emailed the Chinese consulate to confirm its capitulation: "Council respects and values the relationship with the Consul General and also the development of the Australia-China relationship," stated the email, retrieved through freedom-of-information legislation.

It's not exactly clear why the council was so keen to stay in the good graces of the Chinese consulate. I posed the question to the general manager of the *Vision China Times*, Maree Ma. She was also puzzled—her newspaper sponsored celebrations in eight other jurisdictions throughout Sydney in 2018 without any problems—but she thought the large number of people of Chinese descent living in the Georges River Council areas might have something to do with it. The council might not have wanted to risk angering a sizeable proportion of their constituency. There were also economic opportunities at stake, since China's government has the ability to restrict tourism to Australia and the enrolment of Chinese students in Australian schools.

But as some observers pointed out, the Georges River Council area is only a small region, less than forty square kilometres within the sprawling Sydney area. Why would the Chinese consulate devote so much attention to a local-level council?

I had witnessed similar occurrences in Canada's small cities and towns. As one former prospective community-level Canadian politician, Alan Harris, told me, "I'm some nerd from a rural municipality where cows outnumber people, and even I was targeted by the CCP's foreign influence operations." He later wrote in an op-ed for my newspaper that during his campaign for a seat on a rural council in his hometown of Clarington, Ontario, he received an invitation for an expenses-paid "friendship" trip to Xining, China, which he declined. As an avid news reader, he was aware that United Front officials use techniques such as political donations, paid trips to China, and effusive flattery to attract the support of local politicians around the world.

"Municipal politicians are often the prime target," says Stephanie Carvin, an international relations professor at Carleton University in Ottawa and former national security analyst for the Canadian Security Intelligence Service. "They can often make decisions over land use and educational issues, so for foreign governments, in some cases, it's much easier to try to influence at the municipal level." And while top-level national politicians may receive regular security training and access to intelligence briefings, these are not available to municipal politicians.

Making local politicians further vulnerable, according to Canadian political scientist Stewart Prest, is that they see their role in relation to foreign countries as purely economic, allowing them to leave political concerns to more senior levels of government. But at a time of high diplomatic tensions, politicians cannot assume any level of government is below notice.

United Front strategies in Australia, however, have been noticeably more obvious, such as cash payments to a senator and hostile memos sent from the Chinese consulate to a Sydney-area city council. Yet Canada and Australia are very similar in terms of demographics, middle power status, close ties with the U.S., and history of migration of people of Chinese descent following the Tiananmen massacre.

I wondered if Beijing was being more brazen simply because Australia was located in its own backyard in the Asia-Pacific and was seen as a relatively weak Western middle power. Clive Hamilton, professor of public ethics at Charles Sturt University in Canberra, identified numerous cases of United Front officials targeting city councils in Australia in his 2018 book *Silent Invasion: China's Influence in Australia* and in a follow-up volume on international trends, *Hidden Hand*, with co-author Mareike Ohlberg.

Hamilton posited in a 2018 lecture that the CCP views Australia as a "weak link" among American allies, but as a

Western nation located in Asia, the country is also a "major prize in its push for strategic dominance across the Asia-Pacific region." Along with Australia's large Chinese population, which Beijing sees as a potential threat, the country has "accordingly been the target of the full force of the CCP's sophisticated influence and interference operations," Hamilton argued.

THE SAME EMOTIONAL BAGGAGE from the "century of humiliation" at the hands of Western imperial powers at a time of national vulnerability for China has a similar bearing on its United Front activities further afield. As discussed in chapter 2, Beijing views foreigners of ethnic Chinese descent as particularly influential if they express critical views about the Chinese government.

The story of one plucky Chinese international student in Australia illustrates the extent to which Beijing can go in trying to control global diaspora communities and recruit immigrants to woo foreign politicians on its behalf.

I arranged to meet the student, whose first name starts with H, in Canberra. To get my bearings of the city, with its orderly city streets nestled in rolling green hills, I first took a hike, then made my way to the perfectly manicured Australian National University campus.

Chinese students usually make up about a third of all international students in Australia but bring in a disproportionate amount in contributions to the domestic economy, since they gravitate toward prestigious universities and expensive accommodations. Overall, international students contribute A$35 billion a year to the Australian economy.

I haven't seen many articles in Australian media that fully

presented students' perspectives. The *Guardian* Australia has said it spent ten months trying to interview Chinese international students but that some respondents refused to talk because they found media coverage hostile to them, while others said they worried about consequences back home if they expressed honest opinions. The reluctance of people to speak, partly out of fear of repercussions, suggests that views among students are more varied and complex than what's implied by images of students fervently waving the Chinese flag at patriotic protests in Australia, or stories about them angrily calling for the sacking of Australian university lecturers for teaching about Taiwan.

H. and I sat outside at a small café across from the university bookshop. The fourth-year student, who is from Shanghai, was all smiles and showed no hint of the caution I was expecting. He looked younger than his age, like an earnest Asian version of Daniel Radcliffe in one of the earlier Harry Potter movies. With his messenger bag laden with textbooks, it was obvious he was taking his top-ranked liberal arts education very seriously.

"In the first year of my program, I went on exchange in Italy and learned the language. I thought, if I could speak Italian to my friends, why couldn't I speak my own language, Shanghainese? It gave me a reason to study Shanghainese and question why, when I was growing up, we were encouraged to only speak Mandarin and forget about our mother tongue," he said.

Back in May 2014, the Chinese national State Administration of Press, Publication, Radio, Film and Television issued a directive saying all TV and radio programs in the country must use Mandarin, the standard national language, and avoid all local dialects and foreign languages. The move was part of a general crackdown on minority groups under President Xi's leadership.

People in Shanghai, famously proud of their unique culture and language, risked repercussions to publicly express their outrage over the move, but many of their comments were scrubbed from social media networks. While Beijing had long been the political hub of the country, Shanghainese were proud of their city's reputation as China's most fashionable, cutting-edge, and cosmopolitan megacity. It was there, after all, that the first motor cars in the country appeared, and where famously influential writers and thinkers of the early twentieth century, like Lu Xun, pioneered modern realist ways of writing that fostered biting social commentary.

"The central government...is discouraging China's own rich array of regional dialects and customs out of concern that strong local identities could challenge Beijing's authority," an article in the *New York Times* cited critics as saying. The piece quoted several Shanghai commenters who likened the language restrictions to "news of a death" and called regional languages "endangered."

At the time, H. was finishing secondary school in Shanghai and didn't have access to Western publications. He didn't notice the hubbub around the state directives. But later that year, as a university student on exchange in Europe, he learned all about the situation in Spain as protesters pushed for an independent Catalan. Photographs of Spanish national police beating protesters stirred him deeply.

He wasn't sure whether he agreed with the protesters in Spain, but he wondered whether similar movements existed in China. So he conducted research on an unfettered internet, a novelty to him after growing up with the Great Firewall of China. There, he discovered Chinese writers who had long been banned in his homeland.

H. quoted the Berlin-based author and former political prisoner Liao Yiwu to me: "My dream is that China splits up into ten or so countries. Because China as it is today is a threat for the whole world," Liao said in an interview.

I stifled a gasp, shocked that he was speaking with a foreign journalist about these topics. As we talked, H. seemed more and more like the classic picture of an enthusiastic and idealistic student keen to debate all kinds of political theories. That would be unremarkable in a secure and open society, but since he is a Chinese citizen with family members in Shanghai, his idealism was alarming.

Even Liao Yiwu didn't seem to take the idea of separating China into ten different states seriously. His remarks, in an interview with Agence France-Presse, centred on the fact that he thought Xi's China was irredeemable, rather than going into detail on the hypothetical splitting up of the country.

By mid-2016, H.'s interest in exploring the potential of Shanghai independence had become a full-blown passion. He made an anonymous Facebook page to share his views, and it attracted several hundred followers. On a visit home that summer, he stood on the Bund boardwalk facing the futuristic Pudong skyline, pointed his camera at the tourist-heavy crowd, and spoke softly about why Beijing should consider allowing Shanghai to form a separate state, then shared the video to Facebook once he returned to Australia. It was a thrill to speak his mind on Chinese soil.

A few days later, he flew back to Canberra to resume classes. Nothing had happened to him, but, he later concluded, "They must've noticed the video and then monitored me to see if I would do something else."

In January 2018, he was back home again for winter break. This time, he went further and spray-painted some Shanghai independence slogans on two streets near his parents' apartment. "It was snowy and quite dark. I checked and didn't see cameras," he recalled. "I don't know how they found me. Maybe they knew I had done that video and knew I was back home and the graffiti was near my home."

Police officers appeared at his home that night, terrifying him and his parents. They hauled him away.

As H. told me this part of the story, he remained cheerful and starry-eyed, as if he were recounting a grand adventure.

"I spent a lot of effort to try to convince the officers to let me out," he said.

The local police station temporarily held people from all walks of life. None of them seemed dangerous. All looked bored.

"The officers spoke to me patiently, explaining like I was a child, that what I did wasn't just pro-democracy; it was pro-separatism. It's serious. I understood they were trying to warn me so. They are not bad people, just local police, and in a Communist country they have their political rules."

They let him go after ten days, making him promise to stop his troublemaking.

H. no longer posts on his Facebook group, but he hasn't changed his mind. "Talking about independence is reasonable. It's valid. Even if we cannot realize it in ten or even twenty years, it's okay to say that it is your goal or your dream to protect your culture."

At least he is circumspect with his classmates. He thinks some might understand his political viewpoints, particularly if they come from Shanghai or Guangdong (where Cantonese is spoken), but to him, many classmates seem truly appreciative of the Chinese Communist Party's leadership and proud of Beijing's growing strength as an economic power.

He is a member of a large WeChat group where students criticize Australian media exposés on United Front activities. When a campus restaurant displayed a sign supporting Tibetan independence, members of the group vowed to boycott the eatery.

He showed me the messages on his phone and shrugged. "I don't know why they're like that," he said. "Maybe they have different family backgrounds. In the environment they grew up in, they believe the CCP helped make them rich."

He hopes to find a job in Australia after graduation and remain there for as long as he can. He does want to return to Shanghai someday but plans to wait until China becomes more "stable and peaceful."

On bidding him goodbye, I broke the norms of journalistic neutrality to urge him to be more careful. In fact, when I asked if he wanted to withhold his name, he just shrugged and said he wasn't sure if there would be consequences. I said I would err on the safe side and only use his first initial.

As I had guessed, H. was an unusual case. I approached many students on his campus that day. None wanted to speak with me, even under the protection of anonymity.

His Facebook group had several hundred followers, which isn't nothing, but those who watched his videos did not necessarily agree with him. By holding such minority views, was H. a credible threat to the Chinese government? I suppose the revolutionary Sun Yat-sen must have looked as fresh-faced and idealistic in his youth, studying in Hawaii and dreaming improbable dreams about toppling the Qing dynasty. And he ended up realizing his goal.

DESPITE AUSTRALIA'S NEW LAWS to guard against foreign interference, continued harassment of people of Chinese descent and others in Australia shows that the work to counter the long arm of Beijing's influence in the country is far from complete.

"I feel like we failed to protect a lot of people who come to live in this country. Partly because of the freedoms we enjoy, we didn't understand the ways Beijing can pressure and coerce people here," said Andrew Hastie, the Liberal Party member of the Australian House of Representatives, when I interviewed him. He says the government should look carefully into how to disrupt existing avenues used by Beijing to harass Australian residents and spread misinformation and propaganda in the country, such as on the WeChat app.

Hastie also thinks Australia is still quite vulnerable. "We're so economically integrated with China, they have so many points of leverage they can use against us. This is the great challenge," he says.

Vicky Xu, a writer, researcher, and former journalist for the *New York Times* and the Australian Broadcasting Corporation, says she has received the kind of threats and intimidation that many people with her areas of specialty routinely experience. But she suspects she has attracted an unusual amount of vitriol from Chinese state media and swarms of online harassers—who call her a "female demon"—in part because she is a younger woman of Chinese origin. An editorial in the state-run *China Daily* newspaper said: "Even as a Chinese person, she insists on going against China; the doxing of [Xu] and trashing of her reputation are in no way undeserved." As a frequent media commentator and researcher on Xinjiang and Uyghur issues, she has also attracted the ire of Chinese state security organs. Intelligence officers have repeatedly pressured her parents and friends, who reside in China, to tell them to intervene and halt Xu's work.

But what many people don't understand, Xu told me in mid-2020, is that people of Chinese heritage in Australia also face discrimination from fellow Australians, which undermines both their safety and sense of belonging.

People like Xu with invaluable China-related expertise, including language skills, are underrepresented in the country's public service roles. While around 1.2 million Australians are of Chinese heritage (5.6 percent of the total population), and 3.7 percent of the population speak a Chinese language at home, only 2.6 percent of Australia's public service employees were of Chinese heritage in 2019, according to data analysis by the Lowy Institute.

"Our lived experiences or cultural knowledge are sometimes not valued, and even considered by people in power in Australian newsrooms and organizations as a disadvantage," Xu says. "If a white man addresses similar topics, they're considered more trustworthy and objective. This makes life hard — when you are dealing with pressure from China . . . at the same time as facing suspicion in Australia."

Xu says that racism in Australia, as in other Western countries, is deeply embedded and unlikely to go away anytime soon. Western governments could do a lot more to engage with ethnic Chinese communities, she says, such as supporting their career advancement in the public service as well as providing programs, with services available in different languages, to help people being personally targeted by China or whose family members are being harassed.

IN AUSTRALIA, AS ELSEWHERE, an increasing number of people who are *not* of Chinese descent feel it's unsafe for them to speak freely about Beijing's activities. One of them is John Garnaut.

I had already corresponded with Garnaut, leader of the Australian government's secret probe on foreign interference, before I met him for the first time. We were co-panelists at several think tank events, which took place in hotel ballrooms in Sydney and Canberra and in an airy co-working space in a Melbourne high-rise, and I was a little starstruck to be on stage with the former prominent journalist who had played such a critical role in shaping Australia's new policies toward Beijing.

While Garnaut gave composed and eloquent remarks at the panels, and even cracked a few jokes, everyone could see there was something weighing on him. His friend Feng Chongyi may have been able to leverage his connections to secure his freedom from Chinese custody, but another close friend of Garnaut's hasn't been as lucky.

Author Yang Hengjun, a former diplomat in China's Ministry of Foreign Affairs who later became an Australian citizen and a pro-democracy critic of the Chinese Communist Party, was arrested earlier that year, in January 2019, while on a visit to Guangzhou, the same city where Feng was briefly detained. While his distraught wife searched for answers about her husband's disappearance, Yang was charged with one count of espionage, with no other details released by Chinese police, and there was no indication if he would face trial.

Australian journalists reported that less than a year earlier, in 2018, Yang had been intercepted and questioned by Chinese officials in Sydney while on his way to meet Garnaut. The officials were intensely interested in what Yang knew about the Australian government inquiry into Chinese foreign influence, Garnaut told ABC News following his friend's arrest: "[They questioned Yang] about me, what was the nature of our relationship, what was I doing, what was I working on."

Yang's case was still in the news, but at the conference Garnaut did not seem to want to discuss it himself, so I brought it up instead. I wanted to remind participants that, for minorities in Australia, the consequences of speaking up are very real. Racism and xenophobia run deep in Australia and other countries, and, when combined with external United Front pressure, the result is a very difficult environment for people of Asian descent and a feeling of unsafety when participating in public conversations. After the workshop, Garnaut thanked me for the comments. He gave me advice on my book research but declined to give me a formal interview.

He had warned his friend not to go to China. Now, it was unclear what pressure Garnaut and his family were under as well.

I concluded my weeks of reporting in Australia with respect for the many people I met in the country who work hard to learn more about China, as well as disappointment and trepidation about the sidelining of minority perspectives and the harassment of researchers.

THROUGHOUT THE CORONAVIRUS PANDEMIC, Beijing has increased its economic threats and coercive tactics against Australia. As I observed the events from afar, I wondered how much longer the Australian political establishment would remain mostly unified in its China strategies.

In 2020, Beijing suspended beef and cotton imports, slapped an 80 percent tariff on Australian barley, and instructed Chinese students and tourists not to travel to Australia. Officials also opened an investigation into Australian wine, claiming wine-makers were "dumping" their products in China to undercut local competitors—claims that producers have vehemently denied.

China's foreign ministry even faced widespread criticism for tweeting a computer-generated image to criticize Australia's military. After Zhao Lijian, deputy director of the Chinese Ministry of Foreign Affairs Information Department, shared the digital image of an Australian soldier holding a knife to the throat of an Afghan child, Australia's current prime minister, Scott Morrison, called on Beijing to apologize for its "repug-nant tweet." Morrison had recently returned from Japan, where he signed an in-principle agreement with Japanese prime minis-ter Yoshihide Suga on a mutual defence pact.

In a fiery editorial, the state-run *China Daily* newspaper warned that "Canberra should realize it will get nothing from Washington in return for its collusion in its schemes, while Australia will pay tremendously for its misjudgment."

And a Chinese embassy official told Nine News reporter Jonathan Kearsley at a meeting in a Canberra hotel on November 17, 2020: "China is angry. If you make China the enemy, China will be the enemy." Kearsley wrote that the comment seemed like the strongest public indication from the embassy of how "toxic" the relationship had become.

Canberra has publicly stated its intention to diversify trade ties away from an over-reliance on China, but the COVID-19 pandemic stalled these efforts. In November 2020, Australia was among fifteen countries, including China, that signed a free trade deal for the Asia-Pacific region, the Regional Comprehensive Economic Partnership (RCEP). The agreement was first proposed in 2012 to create of one of the world's largest free trade zones, eliminating many tariffs on goods traded between members. It's not clear whether the partnership will bolster China's standing and influence in the region or smooth over conflicts such as South China Sea territorial disputes.

Within days of the conclusion of the RCEP deal, Beijing furiously lashed out at Australia after first airing a list of fourteen grievances, which included the fact that Canberra had called for an independent investigation into the origins of COVID-19, stopped Huawei from participating in Australia's 5G network, and spoke out against Beijing's human rights violations in Hong Kong and Xinjiang.

While observers like public policy economist Percy Allan, writing in the *Financial Review*, argued the Australian government has invited hostile reactions by repeatedly singling out Beijing for criticism, others, like Lowy Institute public opinion program director Natasha Kassam, pointed out that Canberra's actions on China tend to have widespread approval. These include a call for an independent inquiry into the origins of COVID-19, which was later endorsed by a record 137 countries at the World Health Assembly in May 2020.

I wrote to *Silent Invasion* author Clive Hamilton to see if his thoughts on how Beijing perceives Canberra's position have changed in light of recent events. Does the CCP still view Australia as a "weak link" in the West?

"Beijing believed it could exploit Australia's trade dependence on China and its network of sympathizers among Australia's elites to shift Australia away from its alliance with the

U.S. and turn it into a compliant state," Hamilton replied in an email. "Its extraordinary campaign of economic punishment of Australia in 2020 was a decision to ramp up the pressure, to prove China's strength and willingness to use it. But Beijing misjudged Australia. . . . Australian people reacted strongly against Beijing's bullying. Now the Western world is swinging behind Australia and speaking of it as a model for how to resist Beijing's intimidatory tactics."

Other observers aren't as optimistic. "I think we are all waiting to see which way [U.S. president] Biden heads," Geoff Wade, a Canberra-based historian and political analyst, told me. He points out that amid economic uncertainty, Australian officials are facing pushback from business groups advocating for a return to friendlier relations with Beijing to safeguard their economic opportunities. Others agree it is important to resist attempts by Beijing to bully Australians into submission but want more support from the government to diversify their export markets. "Farmers want to partner with government to look for opportunities to develop long-standing markets like South Korea and Japan, and new, growing markets like Indonesia and India," National Farmers' Federation president Fiona Simson said in a January 2021 statement.

An analysis from Bloomberg News has asserted that China's volley of attacks against Australia was meant to deter others, such as Canada, the European Union, and Japan, from siding with America to counter China's rise. "Communist Party officials see Morrison's government as one of their most vocal critics, and an easy target: China accounts for about 35% of Australia's total trade, three times more than the next highest country, Japan. Australia accounts for less than 4% of China's commerce," Bloomberg noted.

On September 15, 2021, Australia entered into a trilateral pact with the U.K. and the U.S., called Aukus, that gave Australia access to nuclear-powered U.S. submarine technology for the first time. While the three countries' leaders did not mention China, analysts widely viewed the initiative as a move to challenge China's naval power in the region. It also signalled that Canberra would unequivocally side with Washington over Beijing if war were to break out.

At this point, however, it is still too soon to predict what concrete supports America would lend its ally if Beijing continued to try to intimidate Australians to send a message to other middle power countries.

The increased diplomatic tensions, coupled with scapegoating for the COVID-19 outbreak, has impacted Australians of Chinese heritage the most. This is a disturbing trend that government leaders must address. A 2021 Lowy Institute survey found that nearly one in five Chinese Australians had been physically threatened or attacked because of their Chinese background in the previous year. The majority thought the COVID-19 pandemic and the state of Australia-China relations had contributed to that experience.

5.

ITALY

The New Silk Road: Part 1

Marco Polo was a merchant in Venice before he left with his father and uncle and travelled the ancient Silk Road from Europe to China. There, he met the emperor Kublai Khan, and apparently the travellers made such an impression in Khan's court that the Yuan dynasty emperor asked the Venetians to act as his ambassadors to the West.

Historians have since questioned whether Polo made it as far as China or merely retold stories he had heard from other travellers. Nevertheless, to this day, people in China read *The Travels of Marco Polo* in translation and watch epic movies about the thirteenth-century explorer's illustrious years of service to Kublai Khan.

Seven centuries after these disputed events, in March 2019, China's president, Xi Jinping, and Italy's president, Sergio Mattarella, took the stage at the Quirinal Palace in Rome. They announced to a business forum assembled there that Italy would be the first major European country and first G7 member to join Xi's titanic trade infrastructure investment project, the New Silk Road. The initiative calls for the expansion of international land and maritime networks to increase trade and stimulate economic growth. This was a far more ambitious version of the dusty ancient route, which merchants had traversed on the backs of camels. Along with the signing of a memorandum of understanding came a twenty-nine-part trade package worth €2.5 billion.

But the unexpected deal rankled Italy's traditional allies. The announcement came in the thick of the ongoing U.S.-China trade war. By that point, both sides had imposed tariffs on hundreds of billions of dollars' worth of one another's goods, and tensions were high. Washington was accusing Beijing of following unfair trading practices (such as "dumping" an oversupply of steel or aluminum) and providing state subsidies for Chinese companies that created an uneven playing field for foreign companies, as well as engaging in intellectual property theft and forced technology transfers (compelling foreign companies to share their tech in exchange for market access). In China, there was a widespread perception that the trade war stemmed from American jealousy of China's rapid economic growth and other achievements.

The European Commission in Brussels soon hardened its stance on China, chastising Italy for signing up to the New Silk Road. In a strategy paper outlining ten proposals for dealing with Beijing, it called China "an economic competitor in pursuit of technological leadership and a systemic rival promoting alternative models of governance." The commission—the EU's executive branch responsible for managing day-to-day business of the bloc—also moved to restrict Chinese investment in public projects in Europe, such as railways and telecommunications networks.

Unfazed, Chinese government entities like the Port of Shenzhen continued to pursue investments in Italy's large ports of Trieste and Genoa so that they could become designated New Silk Road trade routes. This would help Beijing solidify trade networks and seek better customs conditions in the heart of the continent. It would also create a steady flow of international business for bloated Chinese state-owned enterprises.

As discussed in chapter 1, Mao Zedong's hardline Communist "iron bowl" system, where the state steered the economy and provided benefits to workers, was replaced from around 1978 onwards with Deng Xiaoping's partially state-controlled "socialism with Chinese characteristics" philosophy, which said capitalism was compatible with Marxism–Leninism. In the ensuing decades, the Chinese economy integrated with the international market economy, and many Chinese companies were encouraged to "go out" to invest and set up business operations abroad.

China is now one of the top sources of foreign direct investment around the world. With foreign direct investment, a company has controlling ownership in a business outside its home country, whether it's through a controlling stake or complete management responsibilities over that business. Overseas investments offer countries an opportunity not only to boost their own domestic economy, but also to increase their economic clout and influence abroad.

In 2019, the value of outward foreign direct investment (FDI) from China totalled approximately US$117 billion, after declining from a historic high in 2016, and major recipients have included Hong Kong, the U.S., Singapore, and Australia.

In ancient times, Chinese traders rarely ventured as far as Europe. It was Westerners who journeyed the original route in search of coveted silks, teas, and ceramics from China. With its stated goals of transitioning to a more modern and high-tech economy, and to help build a world order where the U.S. is no longer the sole superpower, Beijing now plays a much more active role.

THE NEW SILK ROAD is the most ambitious endeavour of President Xi's foreign policy. His vision, announced in 2013, was for an expansive network that would link China with most of the world through new or refurbished ports, roads, airports, pipelines, and other infrastructure.

The project now spans more than 125 countries that have signed cooperation documents, according to Chinese state media, representing most of the world's population and world economy. While "New Silk Road" is the more recognizable name to foreigners, Chinese officials prefer to call it the Belt and Road Initiative in official communications. Admittedly, the name is catchier in Mandarin (*Yi dai yi lu*) than it is in English.

In 2017, the project even became enshrined as part of the Chinese constitution. The new amendment pronounced that the Party would, for the indefinite future, follow "the principle of achieving shared growth through discussion and collaboration, and pursuing the Belt and Road Initiative."

Former Portuguese secretary of state for European affairs Bruno Maçães wrote in his book *Belt and Road: A Chinese World Order* that the project reflects a "change towards a more active foreign policy strategy, one aimed at shaping China's external environment rather than merely adapting to it. ... The Belt and Road is the Chinese plan to build a new world order replacing the US-led international system."

Maçães predicted that American hegemonic power would recede due to this new world order—and while Japan, Australia, and nations in Western Europe may want to preserve a "privileged" relationship with America, China may build enough leverage over the majority of the world through the New Silk Road that even ties between the U.S. and its strongest allies could weaken.

I HAVE REPORTED ON CHINA'S economic policies since Xi came to power, and to me the New Silk Road has for years seemed like a vague proposition without clear metrics—a large umbrella framework under which past and present global investment projects have been lumped together. It is difficult to estimate the total value of investments since the definitions are so broad. But there is no question that acting as a bankroller for infrastructure projects has been integral to Beijing's plans to expand its world influence. This has been happening while Beijing has also been growing its presence within established international institutions like the UN, including gaining a seat at the UN's Human Rights Council and creating its own alternative to the World Bank, the Asian Infrastructure Investment Bank (AIIB).

However, the project had a publicity problem in its first few years, because as much as foreign correspondents in China duly covered significant developments, the New Silk Road initiative was not widely known outside of the country. So in the spring of 2017, in the run-up to an extravagant global summit to discuss the mammoth infrastructure framework, Chinese state media bombarded international social media sites with video clips. *China Daily* posted short English-language videos featuring a white American journalist who works for the newspaper telling bedtime stories about the global infrastructure project to his daughter. In the first instalment, he uses a map and Lego blocks to explain how the multibillion-dollar plan would help move goods around the world more easily.

"It's China's idea, but it belongs to the world," the father tells his daughter before turning the bedroom light off. The clips were clearly aimed at a foreign audience: they appeared in English on Facebook, Twitter, and YouTube—all of which are blocked in China.

Another video was a cartoon called "Bon Voyage, Whisky!" which followed the twenty-day journey of a bottle of whisky (named Whisky) riding a newly opened freight train service linking London to China's eastern trade hub city of Yiwu, which was launched in January 2017 as part of a costly expansion of the China Railway Express. Facing a likely downturn in trade volume from the looming Brexit deal, the U.K. had been supportive of the New Silk Road but hadn't formally signed on as a member. (It still hasn't.) Whisky falls in love when he meets a vitamin bottle in a pink dress also being shipped to China. They end up together on a shelf in a Chinese family's dining room.

On a beautiful day under clear blue skies in May 2017, I covered the hotly anticipated (if you read Chinese state media) international "Belt and Road Forum" (regrettably abbreviated BARF). But there wasn't much to report on, since journalists weren't allowed to observe any of the conversations. Instead, we were on the sidelines of what looked like a prom for world leaders interested in the economic opportunities of the extremely well-resourced initiative. There were a lot of group photographs and shuffling along red carpets. Myanmar's Aung San Suu Kyi looked elegant in her bright-blue flowing dress, while Xi accessorized with a gold Belt and Road pin on his suit lapel.

It was more interesting to see who didn't show up. India skipped the summit because Prime Minister Narendra Modi angrily objected to the proposed China-Pakistan Economic Corridor, a New Silk Road project that would cut through Pakistan-administered Kashmir, disputed territory that India claims is illegally occupied. The German and French governments had also spoken out against the project's allegedly hegemonic intentions.

Others said the massive funding available for a seemingly unlimited number of projects was simply too good to be true. Sri Lanka's experience weighed on many politicians' minds. The impoverished country, having received funding from multiple countries including Beijing to finance an ambitious port project, struggled to pay instalments for the roughly US$1 billion debt. China asked Sri Lanka to hand over the port entirely, according to media reports. For a lease of ninety-nine years, China now controlled the Hambantota port, situated just several hundred kilometres from the shores of its most powerful Asian rival, India.

World politicians and experts at the time warned that other projects in the New Silk Road could similarly function as "debt traps" for struggling countries, although China's ambitions were unclear. (The narrative around Sri Lanka's experience has since been disputed. In a 2019 interview, the Sri Lankan ambassador to China stated that it was the Sri Lankan government that sought out China to lease the port, and research from the Chatham House in 2020 concluded that Chinese lending was not a major source of Sri Lanka's debt distress.)

In response to growing criticism of the project, Xi insisted that it was open to everybody and implied that suspicion of it had more to do with Western insecurities than actual malicious intentions on Beijing's part. "In a world of growth, interdependence, and challenges, no country can tackle the challenges or solve the world's problems on its own," Xi said at the forum, as Putin sat next to him and nodded.

This echoed Xi's numerous other speeches, such as at an economic conference in Papua New Guinea a year earlier, where he said, "The [Belt and Road Initiative] is not designed to serve any hidden geopolitical agenda. . . . It is not an exclusive club that is closed to non-members, nor is it a 'trap' as some people have labelled it."

FROM BRITAIN'S EMBRACE of New Silk Road projects in the wake of the Brexit vote to Italy signing up to become the first major European member, the initiative seemed to appeal most to countries with shaky economies. Outside of Europe, projects are primarily located in developing economies in Central Asia and in countries like Pakistan, which are less attractive to most foreign investors because of higher investment risks.

Italy's populist coalition government, made up of the anti-establishment Five Star Movement and the right-wing League party, came to power in May 2018 at a time when public debt had reached 132 percent of the country's GDP. Italy was in a state of technical recession after months of negative growth, the third time Italy had entered into a recession since the 2008 financial crisis.

In order to have a chance of future economic growth, infrastructure investment was crucial but costly. The new government needed to spend in order to boost job growth and enhance key sectors like tourism. The coalition government also solemnly promised to slash taxes and give poor families a basic monthly income. Their plan did not, however, explain *how* all the extra benefits would be financed.

With austerity measures and dwindling public coffers across the continent, Chinese state-owned companies filled the void. Compared to North America, Europe has been relatively open to Chinese investment, with 362 completed deals between 1988 and 2015.

Despite the generally extensive economic ties between most EU members and China, Rome's decision to join the Belt and Road Initiative still struck other Western powers as rogue. Aside from the memorandum of agreement with Beijing, the Italian government said early on that it was open to cooperating with Huawei to build Italy's 5G networks. The Trump administration railed against the decision, and many Italian media editorials dubbed it a diplomatic disaster. French president Emmanuel Macron chastised Rome, saying EU countries should present a united front and "coordinated approach" to China.

The *Washington Post*'s Rome bureau chief wrote that "in pursuing the Belt and Road deal, Italy's populist government is breaking ranks with the most powerful countries of the West, defying the wishes of the Trump administration, and highlighting the unsettled debate within Europe on how to deal with China's globally expanding ambitions."

Italy's interior minister, Matteo Salvini, was the most outspoken domestic politician in opposition. His party successfully lobbied for a watered-down version of the agreement that limited Chinese involvement in telecommunications and other potentially sensitive areas, including 5G development. Two defence ministry officials described the tense behind-the-scenes deliberations to *Politico* magazine, saying that some officials thought economic and trade ties could have been "stepped up" without signing an agreement that "effectively compromises Italy's international position," including its relations with the U.S. The Italian government hoped the watered-down language of the deal would strike a balance and avoid further angering any allies.

However, an architect of the deal, Michele Geraci, undersecretary of state at the Italian economy ministry and long-time expatriate in Beijing, soon fanned the flames further by telling the *South China Morning Post* that critics were just envious that Italy had got an edge over other European nations by being first to sign up for the Belt and Road project. "It's a competition, so I understand their jealousy," he said. Before his appointment in 2018 as undersecretary, Geraci held no previous political positions. He had worked as a finance professor at Zhejiang University in Hangzhou, China, and at New York University's Shanghai campus. Once in government, he worked closely with Deputy Prime Minister Luigi Di Maio, a leader of the Five Star Movement. Di Maio was also minister of economic development at the time, and the two were at the forefront of reaching out to Beijing to improve state relations. Both men went to Shanghai for initial talks to negotiate the Belt and Road deal in September 2018.

Beijing didn't stay out of the debate either. Foreign minister Wang Yi called on Europe to stay "independent" in its dealings with China in the face of Washington's warning that joining the scheme would damage Italy's international reputation.

The week following Xi's tour of Italy, President Macron, German chancellor Angela Merkel, and president of the European Commission Jean-Claude Juncker banded together to meet as a trio with President Xi in Paris. There, Macron urged Xi to "respect the unity of the European Union." Xi said in response that a prosperous Europe corresponded with China's "vision for a multipolar world," adding that the EU and China were "advancing together" despite "suspicions."

The comment was part of a pattern of Chinese leaders increasingly challenging what they consider a "unipolar" world, where America alone is the dominant and unchallenged super-power. It was also consistent with Beijing's professed view that a stronger China that can challenge the U.S. will benefit all its economic partners and help create a more balanced world system in which the U.S. needn't always have its way.

Xi's pronouncement, in a way, raised the stakes further. It implied that supporting the Belt and Road project wasn't merely about working together to improve global trade infra-structure. By signing on, countries could be seen as siding with Beijing in its goal of countering American hegemony, even if they would rather not take a side in geopolitical power strug-gles. Even if Xi's counter-American messaging was subtle, it was clear that Washington saw the Belt and Road project as a threat. In a March 9, 2019, tweet, the U.S. National Security Council stated, "Endorsing BRI lends legitimacy to China's predatory approach to investment and will bring no benefits to the Italian people."

THE SUDDEN INTERNATIONAL SCRUTINY of Italy's actions and the heated debates — which concerned the very future of the balance of world power — took many Italians by surprise. Before Italy's Belt and Road deal, China relations rarely made front-page news, and many of Rome's TV stations and news-papers turned to a vivacious community figure for insight, a restaurateur who speaks fluent Italian and goes by only one name: Sonia.

Sonia is the glamorous proprietor of Rome's Hang Zhou

restaurant, established in 1981 by her uncle, who abandoned his tumultuous country in search of a better life. She joined him in 1991 and took over the restaurant in 2001. After her first few appearances on Italian TV to talk about Chinese culture and cuisine, Sonia discovered to her delight that she was a natural in front of the camera. With so few people of Chinese descent in the public eye in Italy, she was happy to give interviews on any subject matter.

Her restaurant, on a corner across the street from a large gelato shop in the neighbourhood of Esquilino, Rome's unofficial Chinatown, is nondescript on the outside and tricky to find. Inside, a collage of laminated clippings on the walls displays Sonia's portraits in media outlets through the years, usually in her signature pose: hands on hips, eyes coquettishly peeking from behind her heavy black fringe of hair. Other walls display cheerful Chinese Communist revolution propaganda posters and memorabilia.

Sonia told me she was proud to act as a spokesperson in Italy for all things China. "*Zhi you hao chu, meiyou huaichu,*" she said confidently as we sipped tea after lunch. "The Belt and Road will only bring good things. No bad things."

Did that mean more Chinese tourists and entrepreneurs would come to Italy?

Sonia laughed at the idea. "Rich Chinese nowadays don't want to come to Rome! It's too dirty."

Italians were better off trying to sell more goods to China, she said, as she summoned a waiter bearing a plate of prickly cactus fruits. She deftly peeled one and handed over some slices so we could sample the kind of export she thinks could be popular in China. I bit into the fruit and smiled politely while struggling to swallow the hard seeds.

In 2018, more Chinese goods came to Italy (US$36 billion) than Italian goods went to China ($15.5 billion). Overall, however, trade is quite modest both ways. Poland, with a fraction of Italy's population, imports more Italian goods from Italy than are imported by the Chinese.

Hang Zhou was full, but outside its doors, the Chinatown of Rome was disappearing. When I visited the city five years earlier, stalls around the Piazza Vittorio Emanuele II bustled with vendors from all parts of China selling bulk quantities of affordable clothes, bedding, and home accessories. Now, many of those storefronts were covered in graffiti or replaced with businesses staffed by Bangladeshi, Nepalese, and other newcomers. Only faded red lanterns reminded locals of Chinese restaurants that used to cater to large tour groups from mainland China. But it wasn't the case that fewer people of Chinese descent were living in Italy. In the past ten years, the number of migrants from China had swelled to more than 320,000 people, and this number doesn't include former Chinese citizens who have acquired Italian nationality.

Xi's visit provided a glimmer of hope for ethnic Chinese entrepreneurs in Rome who, like all entrepreneurs in Italy, were coping with a seriously sluggish economy. Yang Hong, an electronics supply shop owner who had moved to Rome in 2006 from the Chinese industrial hub of Shenyang, told me that Xi's visit made his family "feel elevated." "It seems like Italians respect us more now," he told me, as his younger associate greeted a customer in fluent Italian. "Even though we haven't seen economic benefits yet, people seem more impressed by us Chinese and what we can offer." Their shop exclusively sells Huawei phones, which are popular during tough times because of their low prices and competitive features, Yang explained.

That afternoon, I talked with dozens of Chinese migrants and was surprised to find that quite a few thought, like Yang, that the honour of Xi's visit and the Belt and Road deal improved their status in Rome.

It struck me as very odd. How could a single state visit make such a noticeable impact? Why were television networks interviewing a restaurateur about geopolitics?

Before the trip, I had worked with an Italian-speaking journalist, Catarina Martins, to pore over domestic media coverage in Italy of recent Chinese investments — or, in some cases, mere *hope* that Chinese investors would swoop in to save the day.

Factory closing down? The Chinese could buy it! Harbour infrastructure on its last legs? Never fear, Beijing was here! There were various thinly sourced media stories suggesting the Port of Palermo in Sicily would soon become a Belt and Road project. Undersecretary of State Michele Geraci often fed the press nuggets of hopeful conjecture: a Chinese company might even come to the rescue of Alitalia, Italy's struggling national airline, he mused in a Facebook video.

We noticed that the optimism mostly had to do with Chinese investment in Italy. When it comes to increased trade, the mood was more wary. Thirty-four percent of Italians "fear the possibility of an invasion of Chinese products" that would hurt local businesses, according to a 2019 survey by EMG Acqua, a market research association.

Despite those concerns about uneven trade, the general attitude in Italy toward China appeared to be very different than it is in places like the U.S., Canada, and Australia, countries that are part of the "Five Eyes" intelligence alliance. Few thoughts were spared, it seemed, for national sovereignty and cybersecurity or human rights issues. Such topics rarely appeared in media stories. Ordinary Italians as well as their governments sounded genuinely hopeful that the Belt and Road deal would make China a much bigger economic partner for Italy, and maybe even a saviour.

IT WAS RAINING TORRENTS the week I reported in Rome. Side streets in the Eternal City became rivers, while Venice suffered from the worst flood in fifty years. More than one person told me the weather reflected the grim mood in their country.

Not many Rome-based institutions did research on China-Italy relations, but Catarina Martins introduced me to the work of Lorenzo Mariani, a prolific researcher at the Istituto Affari Internazionali who has had several articles translated into English. His tone became increasingly exasperated during the course of our conversation.

"[The Italian government] had promised all these things but had no money to pay for it. The Five Star Movement began to champion the idea of turning to China as a way to finance itself out of a deep hole," Mariani said, as rain hammered down outside his dimly lit office near the Trevi Fountain. "But they were not China-savvy and mostly relied on Geraci to reach out to Beijing and make the deals."

According to Mariani, the inexperienced new government wagered that the promise of more Chinese investment in Italy and more Italian businesses entering the huge China market would outweigh the cost of temporarily upsetting Washington and EU partners. "It's the myth of the China market: a false belief that if you manage to go to China, then you will sell to 1.4 billion people," he said, shaking his head. "That's just not how it works.... It doesn't recognize the problems that

European companies face in China. It's not just a matter of red tape and bureaucratic procedures, it's also an issue of patents and other ways that China doesn't always abide by the rules of the free market.... We in the West are reacting badly. It's hard to compete for Chinese investment and at the same time abide by our own rules."

Mariani didn't advocate for avoiding Chinese investment entirely, but he thinks Italy would be better served if it cooperated with its EU partners in pushing China to adopt its long-promised market reforms so that international firms can compete with their Chinese counterparts in accordance with international trade rules and intellectual property treaties.

Mariani acknowledged that parliaments and companies are not the only European organizations lacking China savvy. In universities and think tanks, East Asia has never been a priority. He personally only stumbled into the field of China research out of an initial interest in North and South Korea. Since 2014, he has been one of the researchers for the European Think-tank Network on China, which meets in a different capital city every six months to try to improve the quality of research on European-China relations.

He hopes that with time and experience, Italians will become more strategic and realistic when pursuing economic opportunities with China.

NOT EVERYONE IN THE ITALIAN MEDIA had been looking the other way. Giulia Pompili, a reporter for the newspaper *Il Foglio*, has earned a reputation for asking tough questions of Italian politicians and publishing scoops on China-related news.

A month before my visit to her newspaper's sleek office in

Rome's fashionable downtown core, Pompili had acquired a set of confidential documents showing Huawei has tightened its employees' freedom of expression internationally. The updated corporate business conduct code forbids its global employees from voicing *any* political opinions, putting a Facebook post on par with attending a political rally.

When we sat down in *Il Foglio*'s boardroom to talk, Pompili told me that Huawei's activities in Italy, like elsewhere in Europe, were enthusiastically welcomed as a source of research funding and job creation. The company has even sponsored a popular annual half marathon: the Huawei Roma-Ostia. But once the company settled in and established a new Rome head-quarters, it fired many Italian employees and started to bring in staff from China.

"They promised jobs in Rome but actually ended up doing quite the opposite and encountered no opposition," she said, rolling up her shirtsleeves as she showed me a news article about the marathon.

We spoke about how this single incident reflected a broader pattern where China-related opportunities end up having a smaller positive impact than Italians initially expected.

Pompili has also written on the strange behaviour of some politicians when confronted with China's civil rights issues. When Hong Kong pro-democracy activist Joshua Wong visited Italy, she told me, "few people were willing to even say his name on record. They would change the subject." She added that she'd noticed people becoming more careful to not offend Beijing in the last five years. Even as a reporter at an established newspaper with access to senior politicians, she has found it increasingly difficult to engage officials in frank conversation about China's politics and human rights situation.

She hadn't heard of United Front agents harassing or intimidating Chinese immigrants in Italy, but Chinese dissidents looking to seek asylum overseas have told her they have ruled out fleeing to Italy because they wouldn't feel safe.

Pompili is grateful to work for a company that allows her to take reporting trips to East Asia and write occasional analysis pieces. In one of those columns, she profiled Undersecretary of State Geraci and commented on his outsized role in shaping Italy's evolving China strategy.

She pulled no punches. Under the headline "Who Put China in Government," she quoted unnamed Italian government sources describing Geraci as "obsessed" with getting Italy closer to Beijing and "ready to do anything to please the Chinese." Geraci's methods, and the expenses he incurred from frequent trips to China, have frustrated more than one of his colleagues, Pompili wrote. She also raised questions about his qualifications to teach finance at Nottingham University's business school in Ningbo, China, when his training and most of his work experience was as an engineer. He had worked only short stints with two investment banks, but nonetheless had "managed to gain accreditation as an economist…and in fact between 2015 and 2018 he did everything to secure his reputation as a credible Chinese business analyst, first in the Italian community in China and then especially in Italy, where competent people on China are few." In 2018, newly installed as undersecretary of state at the Ministry of Economic Development, he became responsible for Italy's international trade and foreign direct investments.

Pompili's profile then examined Geraci's alleged insistence on getting ministry staff to drop WhatsApp as a communication method and download WeChat, the Chinese app notorious for surveillance and censorship, instead. Pompili said she did not want to speculate about Geraci's motivations and, rather than accuse him of acting like an agent of the Chinese state, only presented information confirmed by her government sources.

Soon after the piece was published, Rome's Chinese embassy spokesman, Yang Han, confronted Pompili in front of a group of other Italian journalists before the press conference outside the Quirinal Palace where President Xi and Italian President Sergio Mattarella were about to formally announce Italy's participation in the New Silk Road. He demanded that she stop writing critical articles about China. When she told Yang, whom she had never met before, that it was her job to write critically, he told her, "Anyway, I know who you are." Later, after the exchange was reported in the Italian press and drew public criticism, an official from the Italian interior ministry contacted Pompili to warn her to avoid flying to China or stopping over in China for a while, out of safety concerns.

The embassy's defensive response to Pompili's article only seemed to bolster people's suspicions about Geraci's relationship with the CCP. (I emailed Geraci asking for his comments. He responded once, but I didn't receive replies to my follow-up requests.) Although the embassy's mild threat to Pompili was downright friendly compared to Beijing's treatment of other journalists, it also raised questions about how Beijing might respond if the friendly stance of the Italian government toward China were to change.

A swift transformation in tone had happened elsewhere in Europe. After the Swedish chapter of PEN International, which works to defend writers' freedom of expression, announced that Swedish bookseller Gui Minhai, kidnapped by China, would receive the 2019 Tucholsky Prize for writers and publicists living under threat or in exile, the Chinese embassy in Stockholm called the nomination a "farce." In a statement on its website, the embassy demanded that Swedish PEN withdraw the prize or "face consequences." But it didn't stop there.

Speaking to a Swedish public broadcaster, Chinese ambassador Gui Congyou said, "We treat our friends with fine wine." Sitting back in his armchair, he added, "But for our enemies we got shotguns." *The Diplomat* magazine remarked that it seemed more like a scene from a gangster movie than real life.

Some European politicians have stood strong against such threats, like Prague's mayor, Zdeněk Hřib, who first drew Beijing's ire for refusing to expel a Taiwanese diplomat from a political meeting he hosted. Beijing responded by cancelling Prague music groups' tours to mainland China.

Later, Hřib rejected a sister city agreement with Beijing because of a clause that supported China's claim to Taiwan. In response to a renewed avalanche of verbal threats from the furious Chinese ambassador, Czech Republic Senate chairman Jaroslav Kubera came to Prague's support, warning Beijing that it must respect the Central European country's sovereignty.

Seeing what was happening internationally, Pompili felt downright uneasy about the whole situation, but along with Lorenzo Mariani, she was part of a small minority of public China skeptics in Italy at the time.

ALSO UNDER-EXAMINED IN EUROPE — in addition to Chinese human rights issues and potential United Front activities — is the question of whether educational institutions are prepared for the kind of pressure from Chinese embassies, Confucius

Institutes, and patriotic international students that schools in North America and Australia have encountered.

Since 2004, China's Ministry of Education has supervised and funded the Confucius Institutes to partner with schools around the world to make Chinese language and culture education more accessible. The program, which provides teachers and textbooks and helps to cover other costs, was widely embraced initially, with more than sixty institutions in the U.S. hosting Confucius Institutes on campuses. But this number has been dropping across North America as students, faculty, government representatives, and members of the public have complained about bias and censorship in teaching, which either avoids or advocates Beijing's controversial positions on issues like Taiwan's independence, the Tiananmen Square massacre, and Tibetan sovereignty.

It was still pouring when I took a taxi past the ruins of Palatine Hill on my way to Sapienza University. I was going to meet Professor Federico Masini, a sinologist who started his career in China at the Italian embassy in Beijing after becoming, in 1982, one of the first Italians to study in a Beijing university. My newly acquired Italian loafers got drenched as I made my way up the stairs to the university's Italian Institute of Oriental Studies.

Masini's office was filled with Chinese paintings and Chinese-language books, some of which Masini had written himself. The sixty-year-old Chinese language and literature professor absentmindedly shuffled through papers on his desk as he recalled the June 4 Tiananmen massacre. In 1989, he was working at Italy's embassy in media relations.

"It was very tense," he said. "Italians responded as other European countries did at the time. There were demonstrations outside the Chinese embassy in Rome. We were in charge of getting Italian students and expatriates at the time evacuated on a special plane."

But soon, Italy was one of the first countries to normalize relations with Beijing. The prime minister, Giulio Andreotti, was the first European leader to visit China after Tiananmen — to talk about trade relations. "In a way, the Chinese remember that Italy was very early in feeling that the old history has to be overcome. Relations have been going quite well since then," Masini said, referring to the relatively conflict-free interactions between the two countries.

Later, Masini became a champion for language-learning and cultural exchanges between Italians and Chinese, telling the Xinhua state news agency that "the best way to avoid any kind of fears by Italians or by any other Westerners about China and the other way around is to increase mutual knowledge."

Returning to Rome, he became the founding director of the first Confucius Institute in Italy. He told me about how the institute helped design university curricula and now offers high school students Chinese-language courses in history and geography.

He paused to greet a colleague who had dropped by to pick up some papers. They chatted about work in rapid Italian, and then we shared some Vietnamese chocolates.

After we were alone again, I asked Masini whether he was worried at all, given the scandals involving Confucius Institutes in other places, that inviting teachers from China to teach on potentially sensitive subjects could help spread Beijing's world view among students. Masini remained good-natured but took exception to my suggestion that Italian academic institutions could be vulnerable to influence campaigns. "From our view, imagining what has happened abroad in England and the U.S. is very strange. Here, it's absolutely impossible. Freedom of teaching is a key tenet of our system."

But what about indirect influence, I asked him, or the possibility of Chinese students organizing protests against free speech?

"No, never here," Masini insisted.

I left his office feeling stumped. I had asked some pretty pointed questions, even referred to the United Front by name, and asked Masini directly if he felt the Confucius Institutes were part of Beijing's plans to gain political influence in his country.

While those things did happen in other countries, he acknowledged, Italy was, according to him, somehow inoculated from the risks.

The next month, in December 2019, Vrije Universiteit Brussel, one of Belgium's leading universities, had to shut down its Confucius Institute after Belgian security services found information leading them to suspect that Song Xinning, former head of the institute at the university, was a Chinese spy and recruiter for Chinese intelligence.

RETRACING XI'S STEPS EARLIER that spring in Italy, I hopped on a flight going south. After Rome, Xi had flown to the island of Sicily to visit its biggest city, Palermo. It was an unusual choice of location for the second stop of a state visit, and many observers saw it as a sign of respect for President Mattarella and perhaps also for Geraci, both of whom hail from Palermo. Xi and his folk singer wife, Peng Liyuan, had descended the steps of their Air China plane and walked past a military honour guard standing at attention before riding in a large motorcade toward the city.

They arrived at a place chock full of history and tragedy— probably the most conquered place in the world. Palermo was founded by Phoenician traders in 734 BC, then became a colony of the Greeks, Romans, Spanish, Arabs, Ostrogoths, Normans, Germans, and French before Sicily finally became a part of Italy in 1860 after a revolt led by general Giuseppe Garibaldi during the period of Italian unification.

For the second half of the twentieth century, Palermo was terrorized by the Mafia. Until recently, many people didn't dare venture into the downtown area, and businesses languished. The Cosa Nostra syndicate had infiltrated the construction and cement industries in the 1950s, then smuggled and manufactured illicit drugs, including heroin, destroying whoever stood in their way. Between 1978 and 1983, the Mafia killed more than one thousand people. When magistrate Giovanni Falcone was killed in a car bombing, Rome dispatched five thousand soldiers to the city to restore order, leading to the gradual demise of the crime empire.

In September 2019, Rome's former chief prosecutor declared that the Sicilian Mafia had finally been defeated. Palermo was in a veritable state of rebirth, the populous city free to dream about a prosperous future. With Xi's visit, local commentators waxed poetic about the symbolism of China's president choosing to come to Sicily. The subtropical island was located near the historical beginning of the original Silk Road, after all, at the heart of the Mediterranean, connecting Europe, Africa, and the Middle East. Surely, Xi was coming with his chequebook at the ready.

Many speculated that China would buy a stake in or lease the Port of Palermo, despite how far-fetched the idea seemed;

Sicily has been an important military base for the U.S. Army for decades, and Chinese control of major infrastructure would surely alarm the Americans, making the prospect highly unlikely.

Nonetheless, the president of the Palermo Chamber of Commerce, Alessandro Albanese, told Chinese state broadcaster CCTV that the Port of Palermo was in need of a €5 billion investment. This would cover the building of a hotel, residences, office spaces, and beach facilities. Albanese pitched it as a fruitful investment opportunity: "The Mediterranean Sea represents 0.6 percent of the seas around the world, but in reality, 20 percent of sea traffic from around the world passes through the Mediterranean."

I was hoping to take a break to enjoy a seaside stroll in the dramatic natural soundings, with the crashing sea ahead and jagged mountains to the sides. But a quick walk to the beach confirmed that the port was indeed barren of basic infrastructure. Only a dilapidated concrete walkway looked out to piles of rocks serving as a breakwater. There was no beachfront and no businesses along the shore.

The city core, meanwhile, its ancient architecture reflecting the mixture of colonial influences, was very busy despite the off-peak season. The daily storm of activity overwhelmed the senses. Walking through one of the open-air markets, I felt transported to the crowded back-alley markets of southern Chinese cities. Instead of crouching on stools over mahjong tiles, the men of this market were playing cards. Fishmongers, butchers, and metalsmiths set up next to fruit sellers and knick-knack hawkers. Groups of people shouted conversations on every street corner, effortlessly dodging vehicles barrelling down the narrow cobblestone alleyways. But this heady atmosphere had not drawn many Chinese migrants to the area. More than half of the Chinese citizens residing in Italy live in the northern part of the country, with less than 2 percent residing in Sicily.

I stopped to buy some herbs for dinner. A man sitting on a stool nearby said *ni hao* in greeting, and then, in slow English, offered advice on how to prepare spaghetti *aglio e olio*. A shopkeeper hurried over to scold the man for apparently talking down to me. "Chinese are smart," he said. "She understands!" As I was leaving the market, another man murmured, "*Cina*," then smiled and nodded at me.

Normally, when someone says "China" to me in public, it's some kind of taunt, but the tone felt respectful. Overall, I felt in Italy that the average person's opinions about the country and people of China appeared freshly formed. This differed from countries like Canada, the U.S., and Australia, where there has been a long history of sizeable Chinese migration, and many diplomatic ups and downs with Beijing.

IN THE MORNING, I had coffee with Roberta Pellegrino, the tall and willowy cofounder of the tech startup Ludwig. She was one of several ambitious entrepreneurs I met in the city who had an eye toward China. It was fascinating to see how they were starting to grapple with how much they were willing to compromise their personal values in order to do business in the authoritarian state.

While working toward her Ph.D. in economics and quantitative methods, Pellegrino collaborated with friends to design a search engine that helps non-native English speakers figure out if their English sentences make sense. The search engine then provides examples from respected English-language publications.

To their surprise, the team noticed a surge in app down-loads from mainland China. Students and academics there were finding the tool useful. Sensing a massive opportunity, the team applied for a small-business travel grant from the Italian government and got funding to spend three months doing market research in Beijing and Shanghai.

As soon as Pellegrino arrived in China and switched on her phone, she was shocked to find that the internet was slower and even more cumbersome than she could've imagined. "Even with VPN on, it was terrible!" she told me.

But she soon "fell in love" with China, Beijing in particular, thrilled by the capital's long history and the heady atmosphere of the ancient *hutongs*. She developed a deep respect for the hardworking people she met who seemed to have one foot in the past while lurching toward a version of hyper-modernity that surpassed anything she had encountered in Europe.

Pellegrino realized that attracting more Chinese customers would be a difficult process, requiring permits to register a business in China and establish servers in the country, and her team would have to find a way to market their app that would resonate with locals.

Another hurdle was that Ludwig's search engine algorithm drew from publications, such as the *New York Times*, that are banned in China.

Pellegrino took a sip of her coffee and continued her account. Her company was willing, she said, to self-censor in order to do business in China. Her team was already working on it.

"We have our ideas, but who am I to judge?" she said. "There are no good guys and bad guys. Italians like to try to remain neutral."

She recognized, however, that her view of China was

influenced by growing anti-Americanism in Italian society. This included a common distaste for Donald Trump and the way he talked about Italians, such as calling an Italian American journalist "Fredo," a slur that is very negative in Italy, referencing a Mafia character in the *Godfather* movies. Sicilians also resent the presence of U.S. army and naval bases, with protesters clashing with police and effectively halting projects in the past out of health and environmental concerns.

"It's hard to not respect how China isn't bowing to the U.S. They're fighting," Pellegrino said.

On our way down the stone steps outside her bohemian studio office overlooking a grand cathedral, Pellegrino wondered aloud whether speaking to me could lead to any consequences from Chinese authorities. She knew it would be impossible to tell.

THE FOLLOWING MORNING, having misread my appointment schedule, I rushed out the door and sprinted to the nearest train station to hail a cab, which then had to navigate gridlock traffic. My first interview of the day was with Enrico Fardella, and as I would find out, he was not the kind of man to be kept waiting.

A Sicilian who has spent two decades working and teaching in Beijing and who was part of the welcoming party for Xi's visit in Palermo, his indignation was clear at first, but soon he dissolved into apologies when he realized I'd made an honest mistake.

Well-built and exuding confidence, he was waiting at the atelier of Mauro and Carmelo Crimi, an expert father-son team of bespoke tailors. Fardella is a professor at the History Department of Peking University, where he is also the founder and director of the school's Centre for Mediterranean Area Studies. In Beijing, he is part of the same influential Italian expatriate circle as Michele Geraci, a group of people the Italian government has relied on to help facilitate high-level dialogue between the two countries.

As a proud Sicilian, Fardella is passionate about helping talented countrymen like the Crimis make inroads in China. The year before, he had arranged for them to travel to Beijing to create bespoke suits for the affluent artists and businesspeople in his large Chinese network. The pair worked alongside local seamstresses and were impressed by the refined tastes of their new customers.

After a tour of the atelier, I hopped on the back of Fardella's Vespa and we cruised toward the waterfront to tour a sprawl-ing palace once owned by Bulgarian princes and now being converted into an art gallery and creative hub by millionaire art collector and philanthropist Massimo Valsecchi. Renovating such a beautiful building and filling it with priceless artifacts in the middle of the former base of the Sicilian Mafia was the most convincing sign of renewed optimism I had seen in Palermo so far.

At a café outside, after ordering a smorgasbord of Sicilian street food specialties, Fardella told me he wants to help however he can with cultural and trade ties. China is one of the great loves of his life, he said, and he thinks Italians have a lot to learn from the efficient and pragmatic way that many Chinese do business.

His country's unbridled enthusiasm for bringing all kinds of Chinese investment and companies to Italy does worry him, however. It's important to stay "sane," think independently, and make decisions accordingly, he said. "We talk about whether or not to accept Huawei, but would the Chinese let a foreign company be in charge of developing its 5G networks? No! Because the Chinese aren't stupid. So why should we?"

Fardella thinks people in the political class in Europe either exaggerate or underestimate the CCP's ability to interfere in other countries. Such simplified debates only serve the people who benefit from the polarization and obfuscation, according to him. While he passionately believes that citizens and companies in Italy and China have a lot to learn from each other, he currently has more faith in private entrepreneurs than in Western governments' capacity to translate knowledge into action.

"I see fewer and fewer people in Italy's leadership who know what they're talking about. I think what people like to see generally in the world is a state that's based on competence, not incompetence.

"Five percent of our exports go to China. I ask them, 'Why are you so obsessed with China? Think about other rising economies, like Vietnam and Indonesia.'"

INSIDE THE VILLA NISCEMI, a building that looks nondescript on the outside but inside is ridiculously spectacular, the mayor of Palermo was spending his weekend in back-to-back meetings with eager entrepreneurs and women's rights advocates.

In his lifetime, Mayor Leoluca Orlando, seventy-two years old when we met, has seen the Mafia rise and fall. Now, in his second long stint as mayor since the 1980s, he feels very close to seeing the soul of Palermo restored as a multicultural meeting point where nationalities are only arbitrary borders drawn on a map.

But from the decor of his study, at least, it seemed the mayor was mainly looking East. On his desk was a hefty copy of Xi Jinping's book of speeches, *The Governance of China*. Resting against a bookcase, a large framed photograph showed Orlando with his "old friend" the Dalai Lama leaning on his shoulder. And on the fireplace mantel, a trio of symbols: the American flag, a Lunar New Year banner with the Chinese character for "fortune," and Palermo's crest.

It all looked so neatly metaphorical for Italy's diplomatic balancing act, I couldn't help but ask whether it was arranged for my benefit. Orlando just chortled.

"It's the dog, the cat, and the mouse! Italy is caught between the EU and the U.S. and everyone else. It is too weak to stand on its own. We have no foreign policy when it comes to interacting with the EU. We can't even stop the Americans from having their bases here.... I've protested all my life against it."

Orlando confirmed that talk of Chinese investment in his city's port was all hot air. But despite his reservations about the CCP's human rights record, he would be willing to work with Beijing on ventures like the New Silk Road, saying that he was initially skeptical but impressed by Xi when they met. "Palermo is not for sale to anyone.... But we need to have an open attitude."

But even as Orlando grudgingly praised Xi, I thought he had a sparkle in his eye. He must have known that publicly calling himself a friend of the Dalai Lama was as obvious an affront as any to the CCP.

I wondered if there were more politicians like Orlando in Italy, likely inwardly skeptical about China but biding their time to see how the political winds might blow, since Italy's national government is so notoriously unstable.

The Economist Intelligence Unit reported in 2019 that it had rated Italy a "flawed democracy," citing a high degree of fragmentation that led to short-lived coalition governments. Since the end of the Second World War, Italy has changed governments at an average rate of once every 1.14 years.

In January 2021, amid weeks of infighting over the government's coronavirus response, Italian prime minister Giuseppe Conte resigned. Even before the resignation, the Five Star Movement political party, which had championed closer ties to Beijing, had lost popularity. In June 2020, prominent Italian senators joined the Inter-Parliamentary Alliance on China, an international cross-party group of legislators working to reform the approach of democratic countries to China. The alliance has been outspoken on issues such as Beijing's human rights abuses against Uyghurs and ethnic minorities.

Italy's new prime minister is former president of the European Central Bank Mario Draghi. While Draghi has been credited with saving the euro currency from collapse, it's unclear what his strategy for China relations will be. He has, however, repeatedly emphasized his pro-NATO stance and commitment to working with the European Union, which makes sense given his background. Geraci is no longer in government, and those who remain in leadership from the previous administration, such as Luigi Di Maio, now minister of foreign affairs, are no longer emphasizing partnerships with China. With the sombre mood of the COVID-19 pandemic prevailing, it seems the optimism I witnessed about China's ability to save the country's economy was short-lived too.

6.

GREECE

The New Silk Road: Part 2

I stepped out of the Piraeus metro station and caught a whiff of sea air before a mob of tourists rushed past on their way to one of the many island ferries. Besides being one of the busiest container ports, Piraeus is also the largest passenger port in Europe. Located in a natural harbour in the Saronic Gulf, on the western coast of the Aegean Sea, it once hosted the mighty Athenian fleet of early antiquity.

The skies were uncharacteristically overcast, and most of the stores selling tourist kitsch and housewares were empty. But quite a few of the simple sidewalk cafés were filled with older men sipping coffee or playing cards at tables. I wandered from café to café asking if people knew what the Chinese state-owned shipping giant COSCO had in store for the working-class neighbourhood.

Since 2009, Greece has enthusiastically accepted Chinese foreign direct investment and even agreed to lease two docks and surrounding land in its historic Port of Piraeus to COSCO in exchange for €100 million a year for thirty-five years. Subsequently, Athens has voted in line with Beijing's interests at the United Nations and other global institutions.

"Ah, the Master Plan," a barista said, in answer to my question. "I don't know. We don't have much information. It will be that way, though. See those big towers? Those will be replaced with shopping malls and offices, but I don't know officially, just rumours. Whatever happens, it will bring more people. More people will come, yes."

It was November 2019, and President Xi had just wrapped up a state visit. Greece had been an official member of the Belt and Road project since August 2018, and regulators were busily working on the final approvals for COSCO's US$670 million "Master Plan" to upgrade the Piraeus waterfront with luxury hotels, a shopping mall, warehouses, and a world-class cruise-ship terminal. Beijing is now on track to make Piraeus the main Mediterranean gateway for the New Silk Road between Asia and Europe. Currently, most sea traffic between Asia and Europe goes through ports in Western Europe.

Meanwhile, other Chinese state-owned companies have been working on upgrades to the railway line connecting Budapest to Belgrade after Beijing struck New Silk Road deals with Hungary and Serbia respectively. Beijing and Athens are now working together to continue this line to Piraeus — creating a transportation corridor linking Europe's hinterland with the Mediterranean and beyond.

Inside one of the empty homeware shops, owner Harris Papoulias, a stocky silver-haired man, was fed up with his country's embrace of Chinese investment. He had never heard of the New Silk Road project but thought COSCO's takeover of the port could only hurt small businesses like his, facilitating greater flow of Chinese goods into the country that included counterfeit items.

"It's not good for Europe. Chinese have a different way of doing business," Papoulias said, leading me to the glass cabinets in his shop that displayed more-expensive products. "I have Casio watches. China shops also have Casio, but not original. They sell for €1.5. Real Casio is €100. Tourists choose the cheaper one," he said, looking dejectedly at his well-stocked shelves.

Greece does score sixth in the world for trafficking of counterfeit or pirated goods. It serves as a key entry point for fake handbags, watches, clothes, and other products that then make their way to other parts of Europe, according to a report from the European Union Intellectual Property Office and the Organisation for Economic Cooperation and Development based on 2011–13 figures.

To be fair, counterfeit goods are also produced in places like India and Thailand, and there is no evidence that a Chinese company's takeover at the Port of Piraeus would affect the rate at which counterfeit goods make it through customs. But critical voices like Papoulias's have not been prominent in conversations about the impact of Chinese investment and foreign management in Greece. Rather, the Athens and Beijing governments both point to the Piraeus success story as proof that Chinese investment could bring huge benefits.

The takeover happened in two stages. In 2009, COSCO won a thirty-five-year concession to upgrade and run container cargo piers in Piraeus, potentially pumping in over US$1 billion. Then, in 2016, COSCO bought a majority 51 percent stake in the entire port and started working on plans to overhaul the area.

The transformation has been dramatic. In 2008, the year before the first deal, the rundown port—frequently shuttered by worker strikes—moved only 433,582 containers. By 2013 that number had grown more than sevenfold, to 3.16 million containers.

The *Wall Street Journal* called it a "rare public-relations victory for Beijing," noting that critics have accused China-backed firms of overpaying for high-profile investments elsewhere, from oil fields in Canada to mines in Australia, and "bungling their management."

At first, some Piraeus dock workers continued to protest, unfurling banners saying "COSCO go home," but the two sides have since engaged in rounds of negotiations. COSCO has allowed unionization to continue while providing competitive salaries with promises of creating more jobs for locals.

When I visited in late 2019, I spoke with the president of the dockworkers' union, Nikos Georgiou, who worked with a few other men out of an office building that had definitely seen better days. He told me older workers were largely dissatisfied with COSCO's initial compensation packages—many retired early—but the latest negotiations have led to better conditions. People had feared that COSCO would fire Greek workers and bring in Chinese replacements, but so far that hadn't come to pass, he said, and only senior managers had come from China. "We were against privatization from the beginning…but the political will in this country is different," Georgiou told me with an air of acceptance.

ORANGE AND LEMON TREES lined the sidewalk outside my surprisingly affordable Athens Airbnb apartment, steps away from a wooded path that led directly to the Acropolis. It was a stark contrast to the dusty construction zones of Piraeus and its empty buildings slated for demolition. Looking over the hill toward the parks that surrounded the temples, I could see the ruins of an ancient stone path with remnants of carriage tracks from before the time of Alexander the Great.

The idyllic neighbourhood buzzed with people—not only tourists but fashionable locals on relaxed afternoon dates, chain-smoking and sipping cups of strong Greek coffee with sandy grounds settled on the bottom. Boutiques sold handmade ceramics, jewellery, and home decor. Well-fed cats roamed the streets and preened themselves atop parked motorbikes.

I was expecting a bleaker atmosphere. Just a few years earlier, citizens had been rushing to empty ATMs and the country's economy was on the brink of collapse.

Greece has a population of only 10.7 million, comparable to Tokyo's, but the country's government managed to rack up €300 billion in debt in the aftermath of the 2007–08 global financial crisis. By 2019, this amount had risen to around €366 billion.

The European Union issued three rounds of rescue packages totalling €289 billion, requiring in return controversial austerity measures to help avert a disaster for the Greek economy that also threatened to ruin the euro currency, shared by nineteen countries. After Athens slashed public wages and pensions in order to receive the first bailout, suicide rates spiked along with extreme poverty. Small businesses shut down, and young people left the country in droves in search of work. Resentment against the EU's bailout conditions became widespread among Greek citizens.

Even though the bailouts and the toughest austerity measures are now over, Greece doesn't expect a full economic comeback anytime soon, if ever. The government continues to struggle to create jobs and get people to pay their taxes. Corruption is entrenched in a large shadow economy, as professionals in elite fields such as medicine, law, engineering, and the media continue to under-report their yearly incomes. A study in 2012 by three economists at the University of Chicago and Virginia Tech found that self-employed people evaded €28 billion in tax in 2009 alone. Greece continues to lag behind other EU countries in tax collection efforts, according to a 2019 International Monetary Fund report. The country's future membership in the EU has been in limbo, as Greek politicians debate the merits of leaving the EU and eurozone.

Amid this precarious climate, China's president made regular visits, bearing gifts of much-needed investment funding as well as assurances that Beijing and Athens will face economic challenges as allies—and equals.

DURING PRESIDENT XI'S STATE VISIT in 2019, he and Greek president Prokopis Pavlopoulos toured the Acropolis museum together. As the pair strolled through the halls of artifacts, Pavlopoulos appealed to Xi for Beijing's support in a long-standing diplomatic dispute with Britain.

It was a matter of national pride. Two centuries ago, Britain's ambassador to the Ottoman Empire, the 7th Earl of Elgin, Thomas Bruce, had pillaged the Parthenon temple of intricate marble sculptures depicting Greek gods. Lord Elgin's men used ropes and pulleys to extract the large stonework from the temple on the Acropolis for transport to London, and most of the surviving sculptures are now displayed in the British

Museum. They're known as the "Parthenon Marbles" or the "Elgin Marbles," depending on who you ask.

Not only did Xi immediately agree to help, he also proposed that the two countries work together to get national treasures back. China had lost priceless relics to European colonialists too, he explained. In 1860, during the Second Opium War, Anglo-French forces launched a wave of brutal attacks on Chinese forts as well as on the populous southern city of Guangzhou. Later, the Chinese were in no mood to speak with the men in a negotiating party sent by the enemy, and tortured and murdered them.

On October 18, 1860, the British high commissioner to China retaliated by ordering the sacking of Beijing's Old Summer Palace. These were culturally revered palace grounds known as the "Garden of Perfect Brightness," which successive Chinese emperors had stocked with countless treasures. After a meticulous looting of the Summer Palace, thousands of British and French troops set the complex ablaze, unknowingly killing some three hundred eunuch servants and maids who had hidden inside locked rooms. The looters carted away a three-thousand-year-old bronze artifact and delicate porcelain vessels that were hundreds of years old. The palace's destruction was ordered by the 8th Earl of Elgin, father of the man who took the Parthenon Marbles.

China would lend its support, Xi told Pavlopoulos, "because we have a lot of our own relics abroad, and we are trying as much as we can to bring these items back to their home country as soon as possible."

This kind of diplomacy, though highly unusual, proved very effective. China was approaching Greece not as an economic superpower offering assistance to a heavily indebted and weakened country, but as a fellow ancient civilization choosing to engage with another ancient civilization based on mutual interests.

IT'S A SMART STRATEGY: treat the "black sheep" of Europe with respect and invoke a history Greeks are proud of in order to forge a sense of solidarity between two aggrieved countries that otherwise could not be more different. After all, Athens is literally where democracy began, and it's still a city of protests, where tens of thousands exercise their right to free speech in public squares to challenge government decisions.

Yet the government of Greece has used its vote in international organizations like the United Nations to stand with Beijing. In the summer of 2016, Athens stopped the European Union from issuing a unified statement against Beijing's aggression in the South China Sea. In 2017, Athens surprised the world again by vetoing a high-profile EU criticism of human rights abuses in China. It was the first time the bloc, which prides itself on defending human rights and supporting minority groups like the international LGBTQ+ community, tabled and failed to pass such a statement to the Human Rights Council.

Greece denied that the veto was a sign of its gratitude to China. But COSCO's majority ownership of the Port of Piraeus had quickly turned a decrepit facility into one of Europe's most productive ports, and a year before the veto, China's state-owned electric utility, State Grid, had purchased a minority stake in Greece's struggling publicly owned power grid operator.

As the *New York Times* reported in 2017, Greece's actions at the UN hardly went unnoticed by its European allies or by the U.S., "all of which had previously worried that the country's economic vulnerability might make it a ripe target for Russia, always eager to divide the bloc." Instead, it is the Chinese who have become an increasingly powerful foreign influence, appearing to use "chequebook diplomacy" for political leverage.

Marietje Schaake, at the time a prominent Dutch member of the EU Parliament, said in a public statement that "the Greek government needs to choose where its alliances lie and realize the EU is not only a market, but first and foremost a community of values." German chancellor Angela Merkel also commented on Athens's veto of the human rights statement, saying Europe "has to speak with China in one voice." She warned that China's economic influence allows it to pressure weaker European nations.

Xi, for his part, piled on the praise. "When drinking with a bosom friend, a thousand cups will still be too little," he told Pavlopoulos, quoting a Chinese proverb. China and Greece, said Xi, two countries born of ancient civilizations, had both toiled to achieve modernization, making the duo well suited to work together for a "more just and rational international order."

By the end of President Xi's late-2019 visit, Pavlopoulos had signed a joint statement committing to support China within multilateral world organizations such as the United Nations. He also agreed to back China's core interests, such as the "One-China" principle, referring to China's claim over Taiwan. Local media paid little attention to the signing of the agreement, even though it contained the same kind of wording that the mayor of Prague had balked at, earning furious threats and retaliation from Beijing.

Since mid-2019, Greece has also been a member of the China-led coalition of nations known as "17+1," a complement to the New Silk Road initiative, where the "17" are Central and Eastern European countries, including Poland and the Czech Republic, and the "1" is China. The move further triggered unease among major Western European governments about Beijing's growing influence over smaller and economically weaker European states.

GREECE HAS A PARLIAMENTARY democratic republic system, where the president—a position held by Prokopis Pavlopoulos from 2015 to 2020—is the head of state, and the prime minister is the head of the multi-party government. Before Prime Minister Alexis Tsipras came to power in 2015 (his party lost the national election in 2019), the left-wing Tsipras had campaigned passionately against the parcelling and selling off of Greek public resources and infrastructure to foreign investors. His stance set him up to be at odds with Pavlopoulos.

Leaping onto a stage during one of his campaign stops in front of a banner reading, "We have the power," Tsipras bellowed to a crowd, "This is a battle between two worlds, the elites against the many!...Electricity, health, education, water, energy—they are not for sale!"

After he won, he announced that all privatization deals, especially the concession of the Port of Piraeus to the Chinese state-owned company, would be halted and reviewed. But COSCO executives in Athens did not take lightly the possibility of changes to its majority stake in the port. The company accused the new government of reneging on a signed-and-sealed deal, and senior opposition politicians called the potential dispute a "fiasco" that would further damage Greece's international standing as a viable economy.

The government quickly backtracked on its privatization reviews, and Tsipras jetted off to Beijing on a state visit to try to repair any damage to the country's relationship with China.

Though he had won the election, which suggested a majority of the public shared his trepidation about foreign investment, Tsipras still made a dramatic U-turn in his stance on COSCO. He may not have had a personal change of heart, but as prime minister he seemed to accept that his government was in no position to fund the urgently needed revival of a rundown and poorly functioning port.

To learn more, I met with Polyxeni Davarinou, an affable researcher at the Athens think tank Institute of International Economic Relations. She has coordinated some of the best local research projects I was able to find on topics such as the Belt and Road project and Chinese investment and soft power in Greece. Since Davarinou couldn't find opportunities to focus on Asia studies at Athens universities, she had gone to the U.K. to get her master's degree at Durham University in international relations.

"Why did the U-turn happen?" I asked her.

"Tsipras seemed to have no choice but to accept the offer," Davarinou told me, referring to the huge foreign direct investment deficit in her country, as well as the colossal amounts of debt. "When you have a country like China coming to invest in a country that is hungry for investment, it is a big thing."

Despite assurances from Beijing that China saw Greece as an equal, Greece was in a vulnerable position because it needed help so badly.

"Absolutely, our government has been too eager, and we

could have avoided some of the backlash from traditional allies," Davarinou told me. "In the EU and in America, it's not being viewed very positively that we have such warm relations with China nowadays, and this could've been avoided if the government moderated its political statements."

As to Athens's new propensity to veto criticisms of Beijing's human rights record at the UN, Davarinou says the consensus among Greek analysts is that doing so was never a blatant stipulation from Beijing as a condition for investment funding. "We have just been too eager to please," she concluded.

In Davarinou's estimation, it doesn't help that Athens is a "small town," with a culture where politicians closely consult with local business leaders. This dynamic is also common in many other countries, such as Italy, but when it comes to China policy, Greek politicians have little to counterbalance the influence of business owners with vested interests, since there is such a dearth of China-focused researchers and academics in the country.

IN ATHENS, I CONDUCTED several interviews with translation help from Alexandros Kottis, a former colleague at Agence France-Presse, whose mother is French and father is Greek. When Kottis moved from Paris to Athens two years ago, locals were shocked by his choice. "You were living in a world-class city," they'd say. "Why would you want to come here?"

At an inexpensive eatery near Metaxourgeio, the city's unofficial Chinatown, Kottis told me about the inferiority complex that many in Athens seem to harbour from the humiliation of the debt crisis. Costs had been rising in Athens while good jobs remained scarce, making people frustrated and leading the young to question whether they should leave to start their lives elsewhere.

All around the city centre, I spotted graffiti blaming Airbnb and tourists for driving up rents. The proliferation of short-term rental accommodation has caused a lack of affordable housing, some locals contend, and earlier that summer, in July 2019, youthful protesters had clashed with riot police. While police said they were responding to violence from protesters wielding sticks and stones, video footage captured police initiating attacks on groups of unarmed protesters.

In the past, locals were generally curious about and welcoming of Chinese migrants who arrived to set up small businesses in the city centre, according to Chinese shop owners I spoke with in Metaxourgeio. But as more migrants and more busloads of tourists arrived, the Chinese presence in Athens became associated with the city's rising unaffordability. Business owners like Maria Xu, who started her electronics store twenty years ago, have noticed that fewer Greeks are frequenting their shops, and much fewer greet them warmly on the streets. "There is an atmosphere of distrust," Xu told me.

The first Greek entrepreneur I interviewed with Kottis showed no sign of anger toward Chinese in Greece, however, nor was he young and financially struggling. He did have some peculiar ideas around survival of the fittest, suggesting it was natural to view Beijing as a modern-day colonizer and that this wasn't necessarily a bad thing.

Nicolas Vernicos, vigorous at the age of seventy-four and with an imposing air, is a fourth-generation ship owner as well as the president of the Greek chapter of the International Chamber of Commerce. He sits on the boards of the Hellenic Chamber of Shipping, the Piraeus Chamber of Commerce and

Industry, and the Athens-based Public Power Corporation.

When we sat down at a spacious restaurant on the grounds of the palatial National Garden of Athens, we exchanged business cards. Vernicos seemed familiar with the custom in China of making small talk inspired by what you see on the other person's card. He peered down at mine and criticized the paper quality. I agreed it wasn't very impressive and complimented him on the Chinese version of his name on his business card, printed on the reverse side of his chamber card.

The back of the card also identified him as the vice-chairman of the Silk Road Chamber of International Commerce, a trade group headquartered in China and chaired by Lu Jianzhong, a member of the Chinese government's highest political consultative body, the CPPCC, linked with the United Front Work Department.

"They honoured me by naming me vice-chairman, so I go every year to the executive board meetings, which are held either in Xi'an, which is where the chamber is based, or in Hong Kong," Vernicos said, adjusting the cuff of his three-piece suit. We were speaking mostly in English, but Vernicos sprinkled in words of French and Greek.

I asked what he thought the benefits were of involvement in the Belt and Road project, and he said "involved" wasn't the right word: "You can say Greece is one of the countries that are taking advantage of the materialization of the Chinese president's dream: to become the Marco Polo of the twenty-first century." Greece was fortunate to be the gateway between Asia and Europe in the New Silk Road, he added. "In a period when Greece was under financial strain difficulties and needing investment, this was like a gift from God!"

As for what China gains by providing all these countries with millions in infrastructure investment, Vernicos put it plainly:

"The Chinese found out that by financing the infrastructure of the countries you conquer them."

Kottis and I exchanged surprised glances. Kottis asked Vernicos if he'd meant to use the English word "conquer." Vernicos acknowledged it sounded a bit aggressive, but, yes, that's what he meant. He saw no downside for Greece in the arrangement, however. He challenged us to present him with critiques we had heard so he could comment on them: "Are there any?" he asked.

I responded that perceptions of the COSCO deal seemed generally positive, but that I'd heard from the dockworkers' union that they were concerned about future salary decreases and generally opposed the idea of foreign management of critical public infrastructure.

Vernicos guffawed at the word "union," informing us that Greece was in a crisis *because* people like the dockworkers were too lazy to fulfill their basic duties to work. Local managers had no power to force them to complete eight-hour shifts without taking long breaks to go fishing or shower. He admired the Chinese managers, he said, for coming in and restoring order.

Large Greek cargo ships like the ones Vernicos owned often carried Chinese goods around the world, and local ship owners have enthusiastically backed the COSCO deal since the early stages of negotiation. But it occurred to me that it was strange to hear Vernicos, a ship owner with a clear stake in the success of the Port of Piraeus, speak so freely in his capacity as international chamber president. When I had spoken with other chamber leaders in the past, they usually tried to keep their personal businesses and their chamber duties separate, lest they be accused of favouring their own industries.

But Vernicos dismissed my questions about his personal

interests. He suggested ship owners were *already* rich, since they do business internationally, and it was inconvenient that the sad state of affairs in his country meant he had to avoid flaunting his wealth.

"I cannot sit in a Ferrari or my Maserati when my neighbours are starving, so my interest is to have Greeks rich and healthy so I can buy a better car. Now I cannot go to my island with a Porsche. No, because Greece is still suffering. I hope I can do this before my expiry date," he said with a laugh.

It was a shame, he told me, that the Chinese government was also "conquering" Africa through investments in infrastructure like airports and railways; he would prefer that Europeans were still the colonizers in Africa so when he visited there he could feel more comfortable. He didn't mind if Chinese were the ones in charge in Africa now, but if it were the French, he would enjoy the food better and get around more easily.

I blinked a few times to process everything he'd just said. I imagined the public reaction in Canada or America if an influential business leader espoused such an argument, which seemed to glorify colonialism. Then again, it's possible that global dialogue on Beijing's world ambitions would benefit from perspectives as blunt as his.

It wasn't surprising that China appeared to lack soft power in Greece and mostly seemed to possess only economic power. My conversations so far reflected the findings of public opinion surveys, where most Greeks viewed relations with China as having a positive economic impact while holding negative views of the country overall.

It reminded me of my conversation with Lorenzo Mariani in Rome, when he criticized the myth of the China market bestowing riches on all those that welcomed Beijing's embrace.

Certainly, some people have benefited handsomely, but they are a distinct minority.

IN BOTH ITALY AND GREECE, I wondered if I was witnessing a stage in a process that other Western countries had already progressed through in their interactions with Beijing. Middle powers such as Canada and Australia had also appeared overly optimistic at first but later adjusted their expectations after seeing only moderate benefits from Chinese investment—and after suffering the blows of Beijing's economic coercion, including trade tariffs, or the threat of tariffs, in response to criticism over human rights cases.

I was keen to speak with a government representative in Greece. Kottis helped me submit requests to the Greek foreign ministry and economic ministry, but both refused to grant an interview. So I prepared instead to meet Vaggelis Kteniadis, another business figure who has been heavily influential in the development of the Greek government's economic policies toward China, which include a "golden visa" investor immigration program aimed at the ascendant Chinese middle class.

On the way to see Kteniadis at the headquarters of his company, V2 Development, which bills itself as the country's leading real estate firm, I spotted one of its ads emblazoned across a tram station in the middle of a busy thoroughfare. It wasn't in Greek, and it wasn't in English either. Large simplified Chinese characters declared, "Invest in Greece, change your life!"

Since 2013, non-EU citizens can get a Greek residency permit by investing a minimum of €250,000 in Greek real estate. It's one of the most affordable residence-by-investment programs in the world, and successful applicants are eligible for visa-free travel within the Schengen Area, the twenty-six European countries that function as a single jurisdiction for travellers crossing their mutual borders. Out of the more than 5,300 residency permits that have been issued since the scheme's launch, about 65 percent have gone to mainland Chinese investors, official data shows. These investors can't take jobs as employees in Greece, but they are welcome to start their own enterprises. The easy attainability of Greece's golden visa raises questions about whether a pathway to EU residency ought to be so accessible and whether the scheme unfairly disadvantages lower-income locals trying to gain a foothold in the country's real estate market.

Across the street from the billboard, a huge crowd of Chinese tourists with matching hats and buttons gathered outside Syntagma Square, in front of the Old Royal Palace, which houses the Greek Parliament. But many weren't looking at the architecture; they were playing delightedly with a flock of pigeons. Families fed them snacks and let the birds jump onto their shoulders for photos. I thought it was sweet—they clearly didn't have much experience visiting places where pigeons are considered pests—but most passersby shook their heads in disgust or averted their eyes as they walked by.

Despite the cozy rapport between President Xi and President Pavlopoulos, the average Greek citizen appears to be of two minds when it comes to China. More than half believe that China's growing economy is good for their country, and nearly four out of five think Chinese enterprises could create new jobs in Greece. (Out of seven EU member states surveyed in July 2016 by the Institute of International Economic Relations, only British people held a more positive attitude toward China.)

But when it comes to non-economic characteristics, Greeks hold roundly negative views of China, with the majority stating they do not believe Chinese authorities respect their citizens' personal freedoms. A significant number misunderstand the basic nature of China's one-party authoritarian state, however. In April 2017, when Greek research agency Dianeosis asked Greeks to describe China's political system, more than 20 percent identified it as a "parliamentary democracy" or a "federal republic."

I hurried across the busy Syntagma Square and entered V2's ultra-high-ceilinged lobby, where every surface gleamed. I sank into one of the velvet chairs, and a public relations officer served us cups of espresso off a mirrored tray.

Vaggelis Kteniadis's office was surprisingly small, filled with stark white furniture and no personal effects or decorations. He was younger than I expected, and with his gelled dark-brown hair and slim-cut blue shirt, he looked like he could have gone straight from work to a nightclub.

I told him I'd noticed their ad outside and was wondering if Chinese tourists like the ones we'd seen in the square were among his firm's target clients.

"They're not rich now, but they could get rich later. We want to plant the seed."

Speaking in a deep voice at an intense staccato pace, his hands folded in front of him on the table, he explained that his company conducted research during the middle of the debt crisis and was largely responsible for designing the investment residency scheme and advising the Greek government on how to promote it.

The firm now has offices in several Chinese "first-tier" cities, including Beijing, Shanghai, and Guangzhou. The teams help

Chinese clients with every step of the application process, including the purchase, maintenance, and management of the properties. Kteniadis estimates about 5 percent of his clients live in Greece full-time and the rest of the homes stand empty or are rented out.

"Our country is bankrupt. Europe in general is an old, developed continent, and an old continent needs fresh new money from the developing countries to maintain its quality of life. Otherwise Europe will go down in flames. Even Germany, the steam engine of Europe... you're dying and you don't even know it."

He slammed his fists on the table to emphasize his point. "India, China, Brazil, wherever on the planet. Antarctica. I don't care. I'll make the *penguins* permanent residents of Greece. I don't care at all as long as fresh new money is coming into the continent."

Kteniadis said he "can't stand" detractors who question whether investor residency schemes allow too many foreigners to travel freely in Europe. He would much rather have wealthy investors coming to his country than immigrants from poor places.

Like Vernicos, he also found it appropriate to bring up his negative views about Africa: "I have to be honest, we don't like Blacks in Greece. We have all these African immigrants coming to our shores and we are not comfortable with them and we don't want them. Chinese, of course, are totally different. China is the second-strongest economy in the world, and people aren't coming because they want to work here. They don't care. They just want to travel freely and do whatever they want in Europe without going through the humiliating process of screening to get a visa in a *bankrupt country.*"

I straightened up in my seat and cleared my throat, bracing for his response to my next question. How about the young Greeks who struggled to pay rent or couldn't afford to buy a home, who worried that investor migrants had driven up real estate prices?

Kteniadis calmed. He had some advice for them: "Go to school, get ready to be a productive citizen of tomorrow. Make money and suck it up. Prepare yourselves for globalization and forget about social security and the state helping you retire early. Athens is going to become a metropolis and global force in real estate.

"They're not going to drag us back. We're going to drag them forward."

He showed me a photo of himself as a three-year-old with his father, touring a housing development. He said he'd named his company V2 and had worked to build it up in honour of his father, a pioneer in the business, whose first name was also Vaggelis. Kteniadis, who was so upfront with me about the lavish benefits his company enjoys from the policy he had urged the government to create, appeared to see no problem with business owners being the ones pulling strings and influencing policy on China.

I gathered up my notebook and camera, feeling numbed by the back-to-back interviews. They had both contained some pretty shocking moments, and neither of the men I'd spoken to had shown much genuine interest in Chinese culture or society. To them, China might as well be a cash machine.

BOTH NICOLAS VERNICOS and Vaggelis Kteniadis spoke about China's actions in Africa as if they were completely different from China's interactions with Greece. They seemed to share the view that Greece, as a Western civilization, was somehow protected from any negative consequences of outsized foreign investment and political influence. But while China's efforts to stamp a major economic and geopolitical footprint in the African continent predate the New Silk Road initiative, the strategies are very similar.

Trade between China and Africa increased by 700 percent in the 1990s, and China is currently the continent's overall largest trading partner. In 2000, the Forum on China–Africa Cooperation was established as an official structure involving Beijing and all states of Africa, except for Eswatini (formerly known as Swaziland), to strengthen the relationship through regular summits.

In exchange for access to Africa's abundance of natural resources — fuels and minerals that China generally lacks — Beijing has mostly provided funding for infrastructure projects, including highways, railways, seaports, and airports. According to financial advisory firm Deloitte, China is the largest single-country funder and builder of infrastructure projects in Africa, spending on average about US$11.5 billion a year from 2012 to 2016.

But controversies have bubbled up through the decades, such as when Chinese companies either eschew hiring local labour and bring in Chinese labour, or exploit or abuse African workers. Back in 1998, Zambians initially welcomed business dealings with Chinese companies, but as veteran Africa- and China-focused journalist Howard W. French detailed in a story in *The Atlantic* magazine, things went sour when the new Chinese managers of a copper mining company banned union activity and paid Zambian employees less than minimum wage. In 2005, more than fifty Zambians were killed in a blast at an explosives factory serving the mine, and witnesses said Chinese staff members fled the scene without warning African employees. A year later, a Chinese supervisor at the same copper mine opened fire on workers protesting work conditions and delayed back pay, wounding several.

As a result of various such incidents, Africans' attitudes toward Chinese investment have become "inevitably riddled with ambivalence," French wrote. Some have questioned whether African companies and governments have been too eager to trade access to finite natural resources in exchange for infrastructure that, while much needed in many places, will ultimately degrade and need replacing. How the continent can "overcome a pattern of extractive foreign engagement," as French put it, remains to be seen.

Furthermore, Beijing contravened its own principle of non-interference in other countries' domestic affairs by opening its first overseas military base in Djibouti, in the Horn of Africa, in 2017. Beijing said the base was necessary to protect its investments in the region, but political scientists saw it as a shift in China's willingness to expand its military power and intervene in other countries' affairs when it deems necessary.

IS CHINA'S SPENDING SPREE in Europe a modern form of geopolitical power grabbing, or even a new colonialism, in which Beijing targets weaker European states in the aftermath of financial crises? Is it a "win-win" arrangement for all, as President Xi likes to say?

And what are Beijing's grander geopolitical ambitions? Even as China becomes an alternative power to America and large Western European nations, it remains unclear what it wants to do with this growing influence. (It's important not to include in this calculation the small-scale entrepreneurism of individual Chinese migrants in Europe providing for their families.) At this point, most predictions are based on Beijing's previous actions in other regions, such as Africa, where it has had a slightly longer history of providing major loans and infrastructure investment.

As discussed in chapter 5, analysts have voiced concerns that economically weaker European countries that received large Chinese loans would not support efforts to challenge Beijing's human rights abuses. Global Risk Insights, a publication affiliated with the London School of Economics, has raised other areas of potential concern: "China's investment model in developing countries is likely to tolerate corruption and a lack of transparency, which has a range of destabilising impacts. Moreover, the risk of the institutionalisation of [Belt and Road] investments in developing countries has increased fears that it could increase the likelihood of the authoritarian model being adapted, whilst undermining the political and economic independence of developing countries in the long term."

Indeed, one of the main criticisms of the Beijing-headquartered Asian Infrastructure Investment Bank (AIIB), which China founded in 2016, is that the bank fails to monitor human rights and environmental standards in the projects it funds. While there is no evidence Beijing aspires to export its authoritarian model overseas, its financial institutions can enable authoritarian or unscrupulous governments to access alternative sources of financial backing.

Throughout, China's foreign ministry has continued to use buzzwords like "multipolar world" to argue that China's growing economic power is advantageous globally because it is a better alternative to American hegemony. In some countries where the New Silk Road is particularly popular, local commentators have championed this theory. An editorial by Seymur Mammadov, editor-in-chief of Azerbaijan's news agency Vzglyad.az, published by Chinese state-owned broadcaster CGTN, tackled the question "Why should Europe be friends with China?" The "Middle Corridor" of the New Silk Road goes from China to Azerbaijan via Kazakhstan before meandering on to Europe.

"Perhaps," Mammadov wrote, "some countries believe that regional leadership may 'grow' into regional domination in the future, but this is not the case, since the concept of 'mutually beneficial cooperation' and 'raising the level of economy of the participating countries' are at the core of the Belt and Road Initiative."

Mammadov's is an overly rosy view, but is it fair to call Beijing a colonizer when countries willingly sign up to investment deals with China that are not in their own best interests? In the summer of 2018, Montenegro became the first country in Europe to accept a massive loan from China, to build a sprawling highway linking the port of Bar, on Montenegro's Adriatic coast, to neighbouring Serbia. The Montenegro government had earlier failed twice to secure funding from the European Investment Bank to complete a forty-one-kilometre stretch of the highway after studies found that projected traffic volumes did not justify the cost. In early 2021, the highway still hasn't been finished. A massive loan of €1.3 billion, mostly from the state-funded Export-Import Bank of China, has sent the country's debt soaring from 63 percent of its gross domestic product in 2012 to nearly 80 percent in 2019. The disastrous infrastructure project has symbolic resonance to people in Montenegro as a reminder of bygone days of grand socialist projects. Milka Tadić Mijović, director of the Podgorica-based Center for Investigative Reporting, told the *Financial Times* that the loan from China "could be really dangerous for Montenegro and nobody is thinking that much about that in our country." Framing situations like these as a reflection of China's imperialistic motivations seems unfitting when economically struggling countries are willingly entering into deals with Beijing that don't make any prudent sense.

THE REALITY OF THE CHALLENGES of doing business with China just isn't fully appreciated by Europeans who have not lived in the country, Jörg Wuttke, Beijing-based president of the EU Chamber of Commerce in China, told me in an interview. "I've been here more than thirty years, and this is the most oppressive and depressing time since the summer of 1989. There's a gathering storm, including diplomatic tensions leading to U.S. sanctions [of Chinese-made software and components], that is making it harder and harder for European companies to function in China."

While some sectors are less affected, new Chinese laws that compromise international customers' digital and data privacy mean that 19 percent of European companies recently abandoned or postponed new China-based projects, goods, or services, the chamber found in a 2021 survey.

Even when it comes to Beijing's relations with relatively more powerful countries in Europe that have more leverage to negotiate fair economic deals, Wuttke sees years of friction ahead, as well as uncertainty over how German chancellor Angela Merkel's successor will steer the relationship.

"Germany has balanced trade with China," he says, "and there are strong investment flows in both directions, but at the same time, Germans have negative experiences with Communism and authoritarianism. Our country went through two periods of authoritarian rule, but Beijing doesn't understand that Germans genuinely care about human rights for that reason."

However, Mareike Ohlberg, a senior fellow in the Asia Program of the German Marshall Fund, says that even in Germany, leaders have an inconsistent record on speaking up about China's human rights.

"The German engagement policy with China is through the tagline 'change through trade,'" Ohlberg told me in an interview. "Most of this is about protecting business. Not that Germany is highly dependent on China among European countries, but we have key sectors, including automotive, technology, and chemical industries, where their businesses do depend on the Chinese market, and these big companies have an outsized influence on the German government. Larger countries in the EU want to maximize benefits for their economy while feeling voter-imposed and moral obligations to raise human rights with China, which a lot of politicians still do. But they go back and forth on this."

PART III

A NEW COLD WAR?

7.

TURKEY

Uyghurs in Exile

Police arrived at Jalilova Gulkbahar's hotel room in Xinjiang the morning after the Kazakh businesswoman checked in. Several officers confiscated her phone and passport, then dragged her in handcuffs to a station for questioning.

Bewildered, the fifty-three-year-old Gulkbahar, a new grandmother, kept asking for a lawyer.

"No lawyer for you," the Kazakh translator for the Chinese police said.

At the end of the night, they issued Gulkbahar a slip of paper confirming her arrest, but it did not say what she was suspected of doing. The guards then drove her in a van to a detention facility and dragged her inside to a small, windowless, pitch-dark room on the ground floor.

From the dim light of the hallway, she could see dozens of other women of all ages hunched over, their wrists shackled to their feet. They were waiting their turn to sleep, because there wasn't enough room for everyone to lie down on the cold concrete floor.

The Kazakh woman screamed.

A young female camp worker rushed over to beg her to stay quiet. But Gulkbahar couldn't stop wailing.

"Please don't! Breaking rules will be punished," the worker whispered in the Uyghur language. It was around eleven o'clock at night. After that, Gulkbahar lost track of time.

GULKBAHAR, A KAZAKH CITIZEN of Uyghur heritage, was detained on May 22, 2017, during one of her routine trips to Urumqi, the capital of Xinjiang, where she'd come to buy women's clothing and accessories in bulk from Uyghur wholesalers. As a single mother, she had been supporting her children with her retail store back home in Kazakhstan. She favoured flowing robes with colourful headscarves made of textiles from her shop and never wore makeup to accentuate her brown, almond-shaped eyes.

She spent the next fifteen months in several identical rooms that each housed about forty other women. The detention facility for women near Urumqi had a sprawling ground level, where all prisoners had to sleep on the floor; a separate medical centre; and a maze-like basement, where interrogations took place. There was no access to outdoor recreation areas. Gulkbahar didn't get to know anyone well, because guards kept rotating the prisoners from room to room. A squat toilet was located near the front of each crowded room, and a television was affixed to the wall above it. Some of her cellmates were feeble and in their eighties; some were only in their early twenties. Shackles were kept on the prisoners the entire time. Gulkbahar tried to stay as quiet as possible so as not to draw the attention of guards.

Gulkbahar silently endured long days of hunger and sleep deprivation punctuated with lengthy interrogations in an underground cell. She was afraid of what would happen to her if she resisted. When the camp assigned her a Chinese name and a camp ID number, she lost any hope of ever being found again.

At one point, during one of the basement interrogation sessions, a guard threatened to shove his penis in her mouth if she refused to sign a piece of paper printed in Chinese that she could not read. She fainted several times and had to be taken repeatedly to the camp hospital.

Hoping that good behaviour would lead to her release, Gulkbahar dutifully watched propaganda videos, sang patriotic hymns, and every week wrote letters on the floor praising Xi Jinping and the Chinese Communist Party.

The women had no access to showers. Because they weren't able to bathe, a lice infestation broke out, and the guards shaved their heads completely bald. They were able to exercise indoors once every ten days, doing group calisthenics, but were made to do so naked so that they wouldn't dirty their already filthy clothes.

They mostly only had *mantou* (plain white buns) and vegetable broth to drink.

In August 2018, more than a year after Gulkbahar was first detained, camp workers whisked her away from her cell. She assumed she was about to face another interrogation or maybe a beating. Instead, they brought her to the camp hospital, and as she lay weakly in bed, staff tried to take the shackles off her feet. But the shackles had dug so deep for so long that the metal had become stuck to her skin.

"Don't cry," a nurse whispered. "They are releasing you. Keep quiet. You can cry after."

After examining and weighing her, the camp doctor concluded Gulkbahar wasn't fit to fly. Having subsisted on steamed bread and watery soup for fifteen months, she had shrunk from fifty kilograms to just thirty-five, and after being deprived of sunlight for over a year, her skin was sallow and covered in a painful pink rash.

Workers were eventually able to ease the shackles off her ankles, and two police officers escorted her to a motel, where they stayed in an adjoining room. Each day, they forced her to eat small meals of rice and vegetables and yelled at her if she didn't finish everything in her bowl.

Gulkbahar slowly became stronger, and one day the officers brought her to a beauty salon. The women at the salon dyed her hair black and put makeup on her face. Gulkbahar had trouble processing what was happening. She submissively went along with it but was unable to believe she could be close to freedom.

To her astonishment, in mid-August 2018, police returned her passport and some of her belongings and drove her to the airport. She flew alone, and in the arrivals hall at Almaty Airport, she had to borrow a stranger's phone to call her children to pick her up.

They couldn't believe they were hearing from their mother.

GULKBAHAR AND I WERE speaking through a translator in her new home in a working-class suburb on the outskirts of Istanbul, where she moved in September 2018 to live with her oldest daughter's family. Kazakhstan's long shared border with China made her uneasy, and Turkey, as a strong regional power that might stand up better to Beijing, seemed safer.

By 2018, the United Nations Committee on the Elimination

of Racial Discrimination estimated that Chinese authorities had forced more than one million Uyghurs and other ethnic minorities into secretive "prison-like" complexes in Xinjiang. Officials imprisoned people without trial in a network of specially constructed compounds and repurposed school buildings while continuing other forms of persecution, such as the demolition of mosques and Muslim graveyards, restricting births, and the separation of children from their parents.

Gulkbahar chased her two young grandchildren out of the carpeted living room and barked at them to stay in their bedroom to play during our meeting. She was sweating lightly and her hair scarf was coming loose. I wondered if she would ask us to leave; she had already told her story many times to Turkish journalists over the past year, and I felt as if we were invading her privacy. But she regained her composure, secured her bright blue hijab around her oval face, and told me she was glad a Canadian journalist was interested in what was happening in the camps. Through the hours we spent with her, her eyes, ringed with dark circles, remained mostly clouded over, as if she had to maintain a trance-like state in order to speak of what happened.

Our conversation, conducted through the translator, proceeded slowly. Because she never lived long-term in mainland China, Gulkbahar knows few words of Mandarin, and Uyghur rights advocates had warned me that speaking Mandarin with camp survivors could re-traumatize them.

"I worry no one will believe me," she said, pushing a stack of original and photocopied documents and letters toward me to support her testimony. "It doesn't sound real. People don't even treat animals like that."

"You can read this," she said urgently, pointing to her arrest documents in Chinese characters and the letters her children had written to the Kazakh and Chinese governments and the UN seeking help for their missing mother.

While she was absorbed in her memories, describing interrogations where she would be confined to an iron "tiger chair" with bars immobilizing her legs and arms, her four-year-old granddaughter sneaked back into the living room and perched cross-legged beside her. Giggling, the child gleefully mimicked Gulkbahar's hand gestures, oblivious to what her grandmother was saying. I could only watch in astonishment at the juxtaposition between such innocence and such horror.

To this day, Gulkbahar struggles to understand why she was set free. Her adult children had written many letters to the United Nations and the Kazakh government, it was true, but no UN or government official ever made contact with her or her family.

At the time Gulkbahar was released, members of the UN hadn't even issued a joint statement to China to halt the mass detentions in Xinjiang. A formal statement from twenty-two ambassadors at the United Nations' Human Rights Council wouldn't come until July 2019. No Western delegation was willing to take the lead and appear to be a "ringleader," a diplomat told Al Jazeera in an interview.

Gulkbahar hesitated when I asked what she thought about her government's lack of action on her case, or about the radio silence from the UN in response to her desperate family members. She told me she just wanted to inform people around the world about what was happening in the camps and preferred to avoid talking about politics.

"I got to be free, but the other women are still there. It's not fair at all," she said, with a hardness in her voice.

I thanked Gulkbahar for her openness, and told her I admired her bravery.

"I'm not brave," she said with a steady voice. "Every day in the camp, I thought I would die."

UYGHURS ARE A MOSTLY MUSLIM group who speak a Turkic language. The history of their people in the region now known as Xinjiang, in far western China, is characterized by brief periods of autonomy punctuated by long civil wars and conquests by rulers from Central Asia, Mongolia, Manchuria, and imperial China. The region, while remote and mostly arid, was prized by many empires for its wealth of resources and strategic location between Central Asia and the region that is now mainland China.

Since the eighth century, the majority of Uyghur people have lived in the south of Xinjiang, in farming communities in the Tarim Basin. The Uyghurs, previously nomadic, settled there after they allied with and acted as mercenary fighters for the Tang dynasty in putting down a rebellion. In exchange, the Tang dynasty paid the Uyghurs an enormous sum in silk, and the Uyghurs claimed as their own an area around the Tarim Basin that had been left by the Tang dynasty after it had suffered a string of military defeats in the region.

The Uyghurs established self-rule in the area, but it was destined to be short-lived. Over the next several centuries, they would be conquered and ruled over by various Central Asian and Mongol kingdoms and were given various degrees of autonomy. During this time, the Uyghurs migrated to every town and city within the Tarim Basin and, not yet calling themselves Uyghurs as a collective ethnic group, integrated with existing inhabitants, merging their culture, language, and genetics.

The region benefited from its location along the ancient Silk Road trade routes through Central Asia to Europe, and under the rule of the Qing dynasty, the last in China, the Tarim Basin experienced a period of relative prosperity. But the discovery of ocean shipping routes eventually made the old Silk Road obsolete, reducing trade and commerce through Xinjiang and bringing steady economic decline.

In the late 1800s, the Qing implemented a policy of intense resettlement, encouraging poor and displaced Han who had lost their homes and land in the southeast of China during decades of civil unrest to relocate to Xinjiang. This period of rapid settlement led to an increase in ethnic tension and local resentment from the Uyghurs, who saw that more infrastructural and economic investments were happening in the increasingly Han Chinese–dominated Dzungar Basin while the southern Tarim Basin suffered from economic neglect.

To this day, roughly 80 percent of Xinjiang's Uyghur people still live in the Tarim Basin, while the rest mostly live in the modern-day capital of Urumqi, in northern Xinjiang, which has become much wealthier than the south.

During the early twentieth century, the Uyghurs of Xinjiang were affected by some of the major political ideas of that time. The Young Turks in Turkey, and their ideologies of progressive pan-Turkism and Turkish nationalism, took root in Xinjiang. The Turkic peoples are an informal collection of populations spanning Europe, Asia, and North Africa who speak languages in the Turkic language family.

In 1931, simmering nationalism exploded into rebellion. The Uyghurs located around the city of Hotan and the south rim of the Tarim Basin launched a bid for independence with help from the Kyrgyz minority people, and in 1933 the Khotanlik Uyghurs, as they are known, declared the formation of the First East Turkestan Republic. It was the first time the Uyghur people had established self-rule since the start of the tenth century. But just eleven months later they were defeated by the Hui Muslim armies of the Nationalist Chinese government, and the entire Tarim Basin was brought under direct Republic of China rule.

Even after the Chinese Communist Party declared victory over the Nationalists in the Chinese Civil War and in 1949 established the People's Republic of China to include the territory of Xinjiang, rebellions continued and were violently suppressed by CCP forces. Then, in 1955, to try to tamp down the ethnic tensions in the region, the Xinjiang Uyghur Autonomous Region was established, giving the Uyghur more autonomy and some degree of self-rule.

The discord did not die down completely, however, and a localized revolt in 1962 led to national forces opening fire on a crowd of demonstrators, killing dozens. This led to a mass exodus of Uyghurs to neighbouring Soviet Union states.

Today, some Uyghurs support calling Xinjiang "East Turkestan" to emphasize their connection with Turkic groups. Some also use the term to express the hope of someday becoming an independent nation. Uyghurs are divided on the matter, however, and other Muslim minority groups in Xinjiang, such as ethnic Kazakhs, tend to have no affinity for the East Turkestan idea. It's much more common for people of Uyghur descent to generally identify as Turkic, which is "quite like saying one is European or East Asian and not explicitly political at all," David Tobin, a research fellow at the University of Manchester, told me. His 2019 book *Securing China's Northwest Frontier: Identity and Insecurity in Xinjiang* is a detailed study of both China's majority Han ethnic group and minority Uyghur contemporary perspectives on ethnic relations in Xinjiang.

There is no formal movement behind the broad idea that Uyghurs are part of a collection of Turkic peoples living in Asia, Europe, and North Africa, though Uyghurs use such vocabulary partly as a subtle way "to resist [CCP] nation-building... to assimilate minorities and eradicate parallel civilisations," Tobin wrote in his book. Meanwhile, the Chinese state's "East Turkestan" narrative articulates Uyghur-ness as an external Turkic threat. The Party views any discussion of "East Turkestan" as suspect, Tobin noted, citing a 2002 State Council document that asserted only "imperialists" and "separatists" could possibly use the term outside quotation marks.

Now, Uyghurs who dare to openly use the term "East Turkestan" mostly live outside of China, since those who do so within China's borders would likely be immediately imprisoned.

IN RECENT DECADES BEIJING has repeated the policies of the last imperial Chinese dynasty by encouraging the majority Han Chinese ethnic group to move to the resource-rich but remote territory of Xinjiang. Promotional material promised an abundance of economic opportunities in the region, thanks to generous flows of central government investment and stimulus measures. The Chinese government launched the so-called "Great Leap West" in 1999 to increase population density in the western frontier in the hope that the influx of newcomers and government-aided spikes in economic activity would promote assimilation of minority groups. A Xinjiang government document at the time said the "mission" was to "reclaim land and garrison the frontier, populate the...borders of Xinjiang...

with a Han population engaged in economic activities in times of peace." As happened in the late nineteenth century, the influx of Han migrants angered many Uyghurs, who believed their presence in the region they had called home since the eighth century was intentionally being undermined.

In 1949, Uyghurs made up over 75 percent of the total population in Xinjiang, while Han Chinese accounted for only 7 percent. In 2020, the two populations were nearly equal, with about ten million Uyghurs and nine million Han people. Meanwhile, aggregate income for all ethnic groups in Xinjiang had indeed risen since the central government followed through on its plans to increase investment and stimulus programs in the region.

But the perks to attract Han to venture westward included blatant favouritism, such as priority access to some universities, property sales, apartment rentals, and jobs. Employment listings stated that positions were reserved exclusively for Han Chinese, including positions in the government, in state-owned enterprises, and in the private sector. In 2006, out of 840 civil service jobs offered by the Xinjiang Production and Construction Corps, Han Chinese received the vast majority of placements, while ethnic minorities got only thirty-eight jobs. Han people have settled mostly in the north of Xinjiang, where the capital, Urumqi, is located, while Uyghurs live mostly in the much poorer south.

In 2009, at the apex of mounting ethnic tensions, extremely violent street clashes broke out between Uyghurs and Han Chinese over several days in Urumqi, a modern city of high-rises and shopping malls. Hundreds died, and most of the casualties were reportedly Han, according to Chinese state media. It was impossible for journalists and researchers to check the data independently, but photographic and video footage showed that Han Chinese were killed in the clashes.

The conflict had initially started as a peaceful solidarity protest by Uyghurs after a brawl in Shaoguan, in the southern province of Guangdong. The brawl was sparked by a rumour, later debunked, that two Han Chinese women were raped by six Uyghur men at a factory employing a mix of migrant workers from all over the country.

Many Uyghurs were arrested as instigators of the Urumqi clashes and given very long prison sentences. Since then, all Uyghurs in Xinjiang—the majority of whom had nothing to do with the violence—have faced even more surveillance and restrictions. Meanwhile, the inequality that fuelled Uyghurs' discontent worsened. By 2011, the average income for Uyghurs in Urumqi was ¥892 per month, while the average Han Chinese worker earned ¥1,141.

An Urumqi storeowner told me in 2019 that even as a Uyghur who had nothing to do with the clashes, it was impossible to escape scrutiny from the massive number of police and soldiers that descended on the capital to monitor all Uyghurs in the city for signs of insurrection. Even in smaller cities, like Turpan, witnesses told me it seemed as if police had set up stations at every major intersection, while police vans seemed to circle city blocks non-stop. After the riots, distrust between Han and Uyghurs soared to unprecedented levels, and neighbours who used to be courteous to each other stopped talking.

CHINA BANNED OR RESTRICTED forms of religious observance in Xinjiang following the conflict, such as the wearing of veils by women, long beards on men, and fasting by civil servants, teachers, and students during the Muslim holy month of Ramadan. Although police surveillance and curbs on religious freedoms ramped up across the region under the leadership of Xinjiang's new Communist Party chief Zhang Chunxian, the period between the 2009 riots and 2014 was relatively quiet. Some Uyghurs with sufficient means were even able to acquire passports and move overseas. Hu Jintao, who was president of China at the time, portrayed himself as a technocrat and focused his tenure, from 2003 to 2013, on economic growth to secure China's status as a major world power, while promoting conservative social ideologies and tightening control over the media and online expression.

When Xi Jinping—a leader demonstrably more concerned about national "unity" and stability—became president in 2013, he scaled up military presence in both Tibet and Xinjiang and cracked down on civil liberties across the country.

At 9:20 p.m. on March 1, 2014, a group of eight assailants dressed in black rushed into the ticketing lobby of the main railway station in Kunming, the capital city of China's southern Yunnan province. Attacking crowds at random with knives and cleavers, the group killed 31 people and injured another 143 before a SWAT team arrived to stop the attack, killing four assailants and arresting the others, according to state media. The Kunming city government later blamed Uyghur separatists from Xinjiang for the attack, but authorities provided few details and international experts were unable to verify the attackers' identities. About five months earlier, authorities had said that Uyghur separatists from Xinjiang had driven a car into a crowd in Beijing's Tiananmen Square, killing five.

In response to the attacks, authorities swiftly launched the "Strike-Hard" campaign, using the global "war on terror" rhetoric championed by the United States to frame the 9/11 incidents as Islamist terrorism and jihad. As a reporter based in Beijing at the time, I worked with colleagues to verify information on the attacks by calling local police stations and trying to find witnesses, but the only reports that Chinese authorities approved were brief police statements and articles on state-run media outlets.

President Xi instructed senior officials to "show absolutely no mercy" to stamp out "terrorism, infiltration, and separatism," according to a trove of internal documents a senior Chinese government official leaked to the *New York Times*. This campaign was the basis of the development of internment camps, which began operation around 2016, according to researchers. The Chinese government at first denied the existence of the camps, but as evidence of them accumulated, including satellite images, the Party defended them as "vocational training centres" whose purpose was to improve economic standards and aid in the fight against Islamist "extremism."

The reference to extremism is noteworthy, since someone can hold what the Chinese government judges to be extremist views without being a terrorist or having broken any law. The approach has been to pre-empt criminal activity by interning Muslim minorities and attempting to purge them of their religious beliefs, an extraordinarily heavy-handed kind of preventive repression. While the actual threat level is virtually impossible for independent observers to determine, the shift in strategy was "likely catalyzed by changing [Chinese state] perceptions of Uyghur involvement in transnational Islamic militancy in Southeast Asia and the Middle East, heightening perceived domestic vulnerability to terrorism," according to research published in Harvard University's *International Security* journal, "Counterterrorism and Preventive Repression: China's Changing Strategy in Xinjiang." The proliferation of the camps, like the one Gulkbahar spent fifteen months in, coupled with ongoing criminalization of ordinary religious practices led government groups worldwide, including the Canadian Subcommittee on International Human Rights, to call what was happening in Xinjiang a "genocide." The committee stated in its 2020 report that there is compelling evidence that China's measures were "a clear attempt to eradicate Uyghur culture and religion."

Some local Xinjiang officials pushed back against the atrocities they were asked to commit, and thousands were disciplined for allegedly dragging their feet, according to the *Times*'s leaked documents. The records show that at least one Han Chinese official was thrown in jail as punishment for trying to slow down the rate of detentions to protect his Uyghur colleagues. I thought of Gulkbahar's account: from her telling, the low-level workers at the camps were often Uyghur women themselves, and Han Chinese nurses showed subtle compassion. The horrors truly seemed to be dictated from the very top of the Chinese leadership.

BEIJING'S RUTHLESS TREATMENT of minority groups should deeply worry leaders and citizens of democratic countries that support universal human rights. With China on the rise, what kind of global leader would it make if it became the world's most powerful economy?

If its treatment of Uyghurs is any indication, China is willing to criminalize religious practices, wrench children away from their parents, torture and harass camp inmates, sexually abuse detainees, and illegally harass Uyghurs around the world. But the international community has been slow to respond to the growing humanitarian crisis, raising the troubling question of what the CCP might get away with in the future.

In June 2020, the United States became the first country in the world to enact legislation to punish Chinese officials deemed responsible for the human rights abuses in Xinjiang. The Uyghur Human Rights Policy Act condemned the CCP for the internment camps and authorized economic sanctions against specific Chinese officials responsible for carrying out torture; prolonged detention without charges or a trial; abduction; cruel, inhumane, or degrading treatment; and other denials of the "right to life, liberty, or the security of persons" in Xinjiang. But the legislation came about five years after the camps were already in place, and the measures are largely symbolic, since none of the officials sanctioned so far have significant assets outside of China.

I am guilty of trying to look away too. When I lived in Beijing, I could have boarded a plane or train to Xinjiang but was never able to bring myself to do it. Instead, I left the grim work to colleagues like Agence France-Presse's Benjamin Dooley who risked police harassment, invasive searches of their equipment, and physical obstruction to produce reports that painted a harrowing picture of a dystopian high-tech police state.

I didn't trust myself to be careful enough to protect my sources. Uyghurs in Xinjiang were being detained for anything from praying to growing beards to owning religious books and corresponding with friends and family who lived abroad. Officials went so far as to argue that mere contact with outsiders was proof of a Uyghur person supporting separatism or terrorism. Entire families would disappear overnight as local officials sought to reach their quotas for camp internment.

More and more information came out about mass detentions happening in plain sight, but officials stuck to the party line that these camps were primarily for vocational training.

"Anyone infected with an ideological 'virus' must be swiftly sent for the 'residential care' of transformation-through-education classes before illness arises," said a document issued by party authorities in Hotan, a town in southwestern Xinjiang, and published in state media in 2017.

According to a report from Megha Rajagopalan for Buzzfeed News in 2017, armed police officers at checkpoints around Kashgar, in the Tarim Basin, seized Uyghurs' phones to search them for banned apps like Twitter and Facebook and scrolled through private text messages to see if they had discussed any religious topics. Rajagopalan was one of the first correspondents to travel extensively around Xinjiang in the post-2016 period of increased repression to describe the omnipresent surveillance apparatus and abuses of power there, and her work for Buzzfeed would go on to win a Pulitzer Prize.

After she published a number of other excellent reports on the persecution of Uyghurs, the Chinese foreign ministry refused to renew her journalist visa in August 2018 and effectively kicked her out of her home of six years in Beijing. Outside of China at the time, she wasn't even able to retrieve her belongings, and a friend had to convince a locksmith to break into her apartment so a moving company could box up her possessions and ship them to her.

Steven Butler, Asia Program coordinator of the Committee to Protect Journalists, told CNN that Rajagopalan's situation was a "transparent attempt to stifle news coverage" of how China treats the Uyghur population in Xinjiang.

Rajagopalan said on Twitter that although she couldn't report from inside China anymore, she wasn't going to stop writing about state surveillance, repression, and incarceration of millions of Muslim ethnic minorities in Xinjiang.

Over a year later, Rajagopalan told me that her work hasn't changed much, because a great deal of information has come out through interviews with Uyghurs living in exile in Turkey and other countries. "Because Uyghurs and other ethnic minorities in Xinjiang are under so much pressure, it's really difficult to interview them in Xinjiang without concern of repercussions for them. It's a trade-off, because of course people in the region are closer to new developments, but it's much easier to have a sustained, honest conversation with exiles, because the risks to them are lower. Additionally, our team used satellite imagery as well as interviews with recent exiles and government and company records to uncover new information about the internment camp system, forced labor, and what life is like for detainees. Obviously, it was not optimal that we could not get credentials to visit."

IN DECEMBER 2019, I flew to Istanbul to meet some of the Uyghurs who had recently fled from China to settle there. An estimated thirty-five thousand Uyghurs have successfully sought a safe haven in Turkey. Many have to live in legal limbo there, with no work permits or refugee status and no ability to renew their Chinese passports. Chinese officials will only issue them single-use passports that can only be used to travel home, at which point the traveller would presumably be detained.

The situation struck me as odd. Turkey's censorship and crackdowns on civil society mirror Beijing's approach in many ways. So why has it become an attractive place for so many Uyghurs to flee?

The storied former capital of the Roman, Byzantine, and Ottoman empires straddles the Bosporus strait, which separates Europe and Asia and which passengers traverse effortlessly on ferries and underground on the intercontinental train. The Blue Mosque, the Hagia Sophia, and other magnificent mosques, with their large central domes and spiralling minarets, dominate the old city on the European side.

I was staying in an apartment near the Galata Tower, a romantic Byzantine-era structure that resembles Rapunzel's lodgings. Vivacious young couples crowded the surrounding cobblestone streets to pose for endless pictures in front of the ancient tower. Bakeries did brisk business selling savoury Turkish cheese pies and pistachio baklava, along with expertly crafted croissants and macaroons.

Down the steep hill, facing the bustling bridge over the Bosporus, there was a white cube-shaped building completely plastered with a Huawei cellphone ad. The company is a major supplier of mobile phones and wireless hardware in the country. Underneath, on the walls of a dimly lit underpass, large Turkish flags and red banners showed tanks and portraits of soldiers with the slogans "Martyrs die to live in the homeland" and "Open yourselves to the Prophet."

I tried a Google search to learn more about the neighbourhood where I was going to interview Uyghur community leaders that evening. But my research was hampered by the fact that the Wikipedia, Twitter, and YouTube websites (and about 245,800 others, according to the Istanbul Freedom of

Expression Association) were blocked. Internet speed was also very slow. It was my first time navigating a heavily censored internet since I'd lived in Beijing.

In my part-time job with the Committee to Protect Journalists, from 2012 to 2014, I had tracked the staggering number of Turkish journalists jailed annually. Many years, the figure would overtake the number of journalists imprisoned in China. This reality on the ground clashed with what I knew about the founding principles of the modern Turkish state.

Founded in 1923, the new Republic of Turkey—the successor nation of the Ottoman Empire—championed secularism and opposed the dominant influence of religious groups and Islamic law. It has been a NATO member since 1952. Islam continued to be the dominant religion in Turkey, but by the twenty-first century, surveys showed that faith was waning, and more women were deciding to remove their headscarves. The majority of people seemed to embrace secularism and openness to different faiths and cultures, while some became staunch nationalists. At best, these groups had trouble relating to each other, and at worst, the rifts caused violent disputes. The emerging form of nationalism centred around the glorification of the Turkish people as both a national and ethnic group, and opposed foreign influences.

But still, even if modern Turks were becoming less devout, more than 98 percent of the population still identified as Muslim. It made sense that Uyghurs, who were persecuted in Xinjiang for their Muslim faith, would flee to the country. The rise of Turkic nationalism would also not necessarily negatively affect Uyghurs, since Uyghurs are considered a Turkic ethnic group.

In his ascent to power, President Recep Tayyip Erdoğan portrayed himself as a pragmatic, modern, and diplomatic leader in the mould of modern Turkey's founding president, Mustafa Kemal Atatürk, who would bridge Europe and the Middle East. In 2010, U.S. president Barack Obama praised Erdoğan's Turkey as a "vibrant, secular democracy." It was clear that Erdoğan's administration hoped Ankara would take leadership and act as a stabilizing force in the tumultuous region. Washington thus protested little when the Turkish government arrested thousands of journalists on charges of criticizing Erdoğan after the Arab Spring in the early 2010s. When pro-democracy protests and uprisings toppled authoritarian leaders in majority Muslim countries, including Egyptian president Hosni Mubarak and Libyan leader Muammar Gaddafi, Erdoğan doubled down on draconian tactics to stifle dissent. Turkey had been petitioning to join the European Union since 1987, and the talks seemed to be heading toward accession, but in 2016, EU members voted to suspend negotiations with Ankara over human rights and rule-of-law concerns.

With his hopes of joining the EU dashed, Erdoğan moved away from Atatürk's secularism, and in 2017 he formed an alliance with the far-right Nationalist Movement Party. That year, the government excluded the teaching of evolution from school curriculums and mandated the introduction of more religious education.

Erdoğan had dangled the promise of turning his country into a "potential beacon of democracy for a region rife with religious conflict," the *New York Times* wrote in a 2018 analysis piece. "But that was before Mr. Erdoğan began amassing supreme powers, and before his brutal crackdown on dissent following an attempted coup two years ago. It was before Turkey descended into a financial crisis delivered in no small measure by his authoritarian proclivities.... Whatever was left of the notion that Mr. Erdoğan was a liberalizing force has been wholly extinguished."

Turkey has its own dark human rights record with its treatment of minority groups, including the Ottoman Empire's systematic mass murder and expulsion of about 1.5 million ethnic Armenians between 1915 and 1923. Many historians call it the Armenian Holocaust, and yet the current Turkish government refuses to recognize the mass killings as a genocide.

To this day, Ankara officially accepts only three non-Muslim groups as minorities living in the country: Armenians, Greeks, and Jews. That means other non-Muslim communities do not have the same political and cultural rights, and the Kurds in particular have been subject to waves of state violence and discrimination since the establishment of the Republic of Turkey in 1923.

Many people in Turkey are in agreement that Uyghurs share cultural and ethnic ties to their country's majority Muslim population, and anger about China's treatment of Uyghurs has sometimes gone hand in hand with the country's rising religious ethno-nationalism. Protests against the treatment of minorities in Xinjiang take place frequently in Istanbul near the Chinese consulate. As recently as March 2021, a large protest was held during a state visit by Chinese foreign minister Wang Yi.

As Turkey becomes increasingly estranged from the EU and the U.S., however, it is looking to strategically expand its economic ties with China and other non-Western countries. Despite political differences with Beijing, Erdoğan has been proactive in recent years in reaching out to President Xi to discuss economic cooperation, with the two meeting once or twice a year. Even though Turkey is a NATO member, Erdoğan has suggested that Turkey could join the Shanghai Cooperation

Organisation (SCO), a Beijing-headquartered regional security association made up of China, Russia, India, and several Central Asian nations that coordinate on counterterrorism and other security issues. Military analyst Daniel Darling hypothesized in a report that China sees the body primarily as a useful vehicle for promoting its New Silk Road investment projects in Eurasia, and in its current iteration the SCO is not a viable counterweight to NATO. Meanwhile, Turkey has been an active member of the Belt and Road Initiative since 2015.

In various European and North American media editorials on the decline of the West, analysts have often warned about creating a power vacuum to be filled by a cooperative cabal of authoritarian regimes. But in my interviews with Turkish experts, most thought Erdoğan's approach to China relations has been largely pragmatic and centred on what Turkey could gain economically. The two sides have historically never been close allies or trading partners, and the ideological underpinnings of the countries' ruling regimes are very different.

China's treatment of Muslims garners widespread anger and resentment in Turkey. What might happen if, as is more likely than forming a fearsome authoritarian cabal, the two regimes eventually clashed over their differences?

I MET MEMETELI TURKIYE, the manager of the Istanbul branch of the Uyghur Academy, at a tucked-away, plushly decorated Uyghur restaurant. Over plates of oily noodles with diced vegetables and lamb, and sweet tea in glass cups with golden handles, the soft-spoken but intensely focused man told me about how he had moved to Istanbul from Kashgar eighteen years earlier.

Turkiye didn't speak English well, but he had longed for an international education and to see the world and so chose Turkey. Once there, he quickly become fluent in Turkish, which is similar to his own Uyghur language. Memeteli didn't think the move would be permanent, however. Back then, while many Uyghurs felt uneasy living in Xinjiang, they were not yet fleeing for their lives.

The Uyghur Academy was founded in 2009 in Istanbul by nine Uyghur scholars who had settled in Turkey before the persecution of Uyghurs in Xinjiang had reached dire levels. Its international network now includes hundreds of researchers, writers, and specialists who collaborate with the goal of nurturing Uyghurs in higher education and preserving the Uyghur cultural identity.

The initial goal of the Uyghur Academy was to connect scholars and help students from Xinjiang pursue advanced degrees abroad. In the last several years, the academy, like other international Uyghur networks, has turned its attention to the growing human rights crisis in Xinjiang. It now conducts research and consults with world governments to try to raise awareness about what is happening in the camps.

While the academy does not explicitly endorse the goal of a separate East Turkestan state, some of its members are proponents of the independence movement, and an explanation of the history of East Turkestan is featured prominently on their website.

Turkiye was cautious to avoid telling me whether he advocated for East Turkestan, but he said it was important for journalists to understand why many Uyghur people identify more with the Turkic peoples around the world than they do with the modern Chinese state. After asking some questions about my project, he offered to connect me to survivors of recent persecution in Xinjiang who had made their way to Istanbul. When I offered to pay a researcher fee for his time, he staunchly refused and said it was his duty to help. "Everyone has a friend or family member who disappeared. It's inhumane. It's not right," he told me.

After dinner, Turkiye and two of his friends, including a linguistics professor who helped translate from Uyghur to Mandarin, took me on a tour of Zeytinburnu, a neighbourhood fifteen minutes from the city centre by train but affordable enough for a plethora of small Uyghur and other immigrant-run businesses to have sprung up there in recent years. In an alternate reality, one where migrants were coming for economic or personal reasons and not because of internment camps, tourist guidebooks might have called it "Little Xinjiang."

Children chased each other along the neighbourhood's dimly lit cobblestone streets or napped in strollers pushed by their mothers. Small bookshops sold Uyghur-language books, smiling halal butchers waited by their counters, and men played cards inside a sweets and nuts shop. In those simple bookshops, with their fluorescent lighting and utilitarian metal shelves, I detected an atmosphere of defiance and even muted joy. These displaced people were managing to preserve their traditions and cultural stories for future generations. Uyghur-language bookshops are heavily policed in China, so what Uyghur authors and publishers are doing in Turkey is out of the question back home.

We walked a while to take in the night life. The evening was neither warm nor cool, and people were socializing outdoors in the comfortable temperature. We must have looked like an odd group: a tall Chinese woman and several middle-aged Uyghur men, speaking in a mix of English, Uyghur, and Mandarin. I hid my camera under my scarf; my companions had warned me that local spies could report my presence to Chinese officials. Other foreign journalists had reported being followed in this neighbourhood.

Turkiye noticed a friend sitting at a low table in front of a café. He was Tibet Yücetürk, a textiles trader whose parents were among a small number of Uyghurs from Xinjiang who settled in Turkey decades ago. He was only five years old at the time, so Istanbul is all he has ever known. Pan-Turkic solidarity existed then as well, and his parents had quickly set up modestly successful textiles businesses that catered to a mixed working-class clientele in Zeytinburnu.

"When I was young, we were one of the only Uyghur families that locals knew here. They really welcomed us, but I think back then it was easy for them to accept us," Yücetürk said, sipping his tea. "But now, there are more and more Uyghurs coming. We care about them, but it is bittersweet, because they shouldn't need to come. They should be able to stay home instead of China trying to destroy their culture."

I asked if Yücetürk was worried that the Turks' welcome would wear thin. He said he hoped Muslims would never be turned away at the borders and forced back to China.

BEIJING'S PERSECUTION OF UYGHURS has lasted for enough years that some Uyghurs in Istanbul have long been able to "blend in" with locals. Their troubles in Xinjiang are a relatively faint memory, and they might not necessarily view themselves as political exiles. Even some more recent migrants from Xinjiang who had relatively privileged upbringings in China are able to assimilate quickly. At a gathering near Zeytinburnu on another day, I met a Uyghur woman in her mid-twenties who exuded warmth and kindness. She had fair skin, jet-black hair, and rounded features. In our conversation, she made more than one reference to her physical appearance, explaining that in China she'd struggled with guilt over being able to "pass" as Han Chinese and therefore escape daily discrimination there, and now, in Istanbul, where she's lived for five years, her fair complexion also conforms with beauty standards for Turkish women. She speaks Turkish fluently, and people usually assume she is a Turkish citizen of Central Asian descent. She didn't want me to use her name here, because she worried it would make matters worse for her family in Xinjiang.

She grew up in mainland China attending elite schools with Han students and could have earned a spot at one of the country's top universities, but at the urging of her parents she headed to Istanbul instead. They were happy she would be outside of China but in a place not too foreign or far away.

While she was working on her graduate degree, she learned through a friend that both of her parents had been taken to the camps. She couldn't determine if they had been detained out of suspicion over her whereabouts, as had happened to other Uyghurs in Xinjiang who had family members in foreign countries.

Chatting with her about life in Istanbul, I was struck by how calm she sounded. Recalling anecdotes from her childhood, she would laugh about little things, but I noticed flashes of anger, evident in the tightened grip on her cup or in her narrowed eyes. She was clearly trying hard not to let her emotions paralyze her. She told me that if her parents were able to get a message to her, they would likely tell her to complete her education.

"Uyghur parents are very serious about their kids' schooling," she said, as if we were comparing stories about our strict parents.

At one point, we sat side by side in a taxi, and I noticed that her phone had Chinese-language settings. She smiled apologetically and said people often asked her about that, but it was just what she was used to. Meanwhile, many of her fellow Uyghur exiles had forsaken all things Chinese and refused to speak Mandarin even if they were fluent in the language. "But I don't blame all Chinese people for what happened to my parents. Only the government," she said softly. "I miss my Chinese friends."

Despite the fact that she has a top degree and speaks several languages, and the ease with which she navigates Istanbul, her qualifications don't change her very precarious status. She only had a Chinese passport, and going to the Chinese consulate in Turkey wasn't an option when it expired. If she did, she feared, she'd be sent to the camps.

THE UYGHUR EXILE EXPERIENCE shows that the Chinese police state has gone global, skipping over geographical boundaries to haunt those on the run.

Ablet Jahanbag Yesi was the only member of his family to escape imprisonment. A slight man in his early fifties, Yesi was clearly nervous when I saw him, constantly clasping and unclasping his hands and looking askance at a group that had just entered and was seated at a table next to us. Still, he had decided that speaking to a journalist was one thing he could do to try to help his family, and he gave me permission to use his full name because he thought it made his story harder to ignore.

"Our troubles began with my younger brother's choice of school subjects," Yesi said. "He told us he wanted to learn Japanese and English, and we didn't know he was also taking a course on the Islam religion on the side."

After his nineteen-year-old brother was imprisoned somewhere in mainland China in 2012, Yesi stayed in Urumqi and tried to focus on growing his textiles businesses to support the rest of his large family, which included his parents, another brother, and sisters. Before long, he was the boss of eighty workers and had also opened a furniture shop in Hotan, in southwestern Xinjiang. Yesi enjoyed the setting of the ancient oasis town in the Taklamakan Desert. It felt like a reprieve from his community's non-stop anxiety.

But tensions continued to heighten, particularly in the regional capital of Urumqi. Heavily armed military police stood on every street corner of the city centre.

After engaging in a noisy argument with a neighbouring Han business owner who mocked him, Yesi began to feel like he too was being watched. His worries became justified during a business trip to Iran in late 2012, when Chinese police began calling him incessantly on his cellphone to ask when he was returning home. In the years that followed, he found it hard to sleep, fearing what had happened to his younger brother could happen to him. He kept his head down for the next several years.

Then came whispers of entire villages of people being taken away in the middle of the night. With the encouragement of friends living in Turkey, Yesi decided to apply online for an e-visa to Turkey, intending to overstay and never return to China. He was surprised when he got it. He arrived in Istanbul on May 1, 2015, with just a small suitcase so as not to attract suspicion.

He had barely settled in Istanbul when friends called to warn him not to come back for his family. "They said police were looking for me and searched my house. They turned everything over," Yesi told me.

Then phone calls started coming to his new Istanbul cell-phone number. Police told him they had found a CD about Turkish costumes and culture in his house. Yesi tried to explain that it was only for research for his textiles business, but they wouldn't believe him.

"I don't know how they got the number. They kept calling and calling, menacing me.... They'd threaten my family. They said, 'You have a mother and father and a brother and sisters here. Do you not care about what happens to them?'"

He tried to call his parents but couldn't reach them. Their phone had been disconnected. He couldn't reach any of his siblings either.

When I asked if he reported the harassment to Istanbul police, Yesi just shook his head. The Turkish government had given him a residency permit but no passport and no work visa. For the last five years, he had been living off his savings and the kindness of friends in Turkey. "I'm in no position to ask for help. What could police here even do?"

Instead, Yesi read with growing horror all the media reports he could find about the camps in Xinjiang. He still spoke with his friends there from time to time, but he didn't want to contact them too often or ask too many questions.

Meanwhile, police officers from Urumqi kept calling. For almost two years, they contacted him at random intervals. It didn't matter whether he changed his number. He was certain they knew where he lived, though he didn't fear for himself anymore.

On August 26, 2018, friends who lived near his Xinjiang home confirmed what he had already known: all his family members had been taken to the camps. Yesi showed me photographs of his large family in happier times, his brothers looking tall and healthy and smiling widely.

"My friend said he heard that police coerced my mother to give a forced confession," Yesi told me. He didn't know any more details. I thought about the piece of paper police tried to bully Jalilova Gulkbahar into signing. I wondered what extra powers a signed confession would grant Xinjiang officials, who had already detained hundreds of thousands of people without trial.

Of course, the harassment of members of the broader Chinese diaspora isn't new. For Uyghurs in particular, since at least the 1990s, there has been documented spying, harassment, and even extrajudicial kidnappings. But advances in surveillance technology now allow authorities to keep much closer tabs on the tens of thousands of Uyghurs residing outside China.

It starts even before they leave the country. To obtain a passport, some Uyghurs in Xinjiang had to go through extensive screening not imposed on Han Chinese. According to Rajagopalan, this included recording a voice sample and allowing police to take a 360-degree portrait and an eyelash hair.

I spoke with more than half a dozen Uyghurs who had recently escaped to Istanbul, and their stories echoed one another's. After each of them fled, police promptly found their new phone numbers and ordered them to return home, first politely and then belligerently, issuing threats to their family members in Xinjiang if they refused. In one case, an officer even put a man's frightened elderly father on the phone.

In each case, despite their anguish, the exiles decided not to return to Xinjiang, knowing they might be sent to a camp.

They hoped they would be able to lobby for assistance for their families from outside of China.

Yesi told me he had no plans for his future; he saw no choice but to live in limbo in Istanbul. He wanted me to help him get a message out: "Help save our children. Help them get a good education." He seemed to have lost hope that older Uyghur adults could regain normalcy in their lifetimes.

WHAT WILL BE THE fate of the tens of thousands of Uyghurs living in Turkey as the Erdoğan government continues to seek greater trade and economic relations with China?

Uyghur independence activists started immigrating to Turkey as early as the 1960s, building a community there in neighbourhoods like Zeytinburnu. They were followed start-ing in 2013 by a wave of migrants from Xinjiang who were fleeing the government's campaign against Uyghur "extrem-ists." Masses of Turkish people supported the newcomers with protests outside the Chinese consulate in Istanbul.

Many Turkish politicians are considerably more outspoken than Erdoğan on Xinjiang abuses. In April 2021, the Ankara city government raised eyebrows around the world when it responded to a vague threat from the Chinese embassy in Ankara by ordering a sudden public waterworks excavation in front of the embassy, which shut off its water supply.

Before the incident, China's embassy had lashed out against Ankara mayor Mansur Yavas, as well as an opposition party leader, in Twitter posts responding to the pair's criticisms of repression in Xinjiang. One post said "the Chinese side reserves its right to a rightful response," which was widely interpreted as a threat by outraged Turkish citizens. Ibrahim Haskoloğlu, a journalist for Turkish broadcaster Uluslararası Haberler, confirmed in an interview with Ankara city officials that government workers temporarily cut the embassy's water supply as a "message for China."

But recent examples in other parts of Europe and Asia, such as Greece, show that investment from China may increase the likelihood of political cooperation.

In Istanbul, I visited the Turkey China Culture Center, one of the few private institutions providing Chinese-language courses in the country. The president of the organization, Mustafa Karslı, told me Turkey's growing interest in China has been a boon for his business. "In the last two years, the government has required translators and people with knowledge of Chinese language and culture to help them in diplomacy, such as conferences on the Belt and Road," he said.

Some government officials had voluntarily signed up for regular Mandarin tutoring. "Five years ago, we employed seven teachers, and now we have twenty," Karslı said proudly.

In her address at the Turkey-China Business Forum in September 2019, trade minister Ruhsar Pekcan announced that China had become Turkey's biggest trading partner after Germany and Russia, with trade volume between the two reaching US$23.6 billion, up from $1.1 billion in 2001.

It's true that economic ties between Turkey and China have increased significantly in recent decades, but the flow of trade is very imbalanced. Out of the nearly $24 billion quoted by the minister, China imported only $2.9 billion in goods from Turkey. Local politicians had come to openly complain about the trade deficit.

Naturally, the New Silk Road project was seen by Turkey's leaders as a promising opportunity to strike a more balanced relationship with China at a time when the country was keen to diversify away from its traditional top investors, Germany and Russia. Ankara is trying to make the most of working with everyone regardless of ideology, showing no clear allegiances.

"Turkey actually has a much richer history of working with Korea than with China," Professor Altay Atlı, of Boğaziçi University, told me. "The Chinese are still very much newcomers so far. I see what the government is doing as trying to diversify and do business with different partners so that, you know, if something goes wrong with one of them, the whole ship doesn't go down."

As an example, he pointed to Ankara's eclectic sources of funding for its newest nuclear energy power plants. "One of them is being constructed by a company from Oregon, another by a Russian company, a third by a Japanese company, a fourth by a French company, and a fifth by a Chinese company," Atlı said. "Economically, it makes perfect sense to work more with China, but politically it's more complicated."

While Erdoğan backs the Belt and Road project, he is at the same time positioning Turkey as a champion for Muslim ascendancy in the world in order to appeal to his base of nationalist supporters.

The issue threatens to drive a wedge between Ankara and Beijing, Atlı told me. "It's basically the only point of tension. If not for Uyghurs, Turkey would have no problem with China at all."

Erdoğan has to tread carefully. Turkish officials welcome Uyghurs who show up at the nation's borders, but the government also has to honour its counterterrorism agreement with Beijing and investigate exiled Uyghurs accused by China of being terrorists, even though no accusations have been proven so far.

The acceptance of some Uyghurs into the country on residency permits is precarious and doesn't seem like a long-term immigration path for many. Most Uyghurs who have arrived in Turkey since 2014 have struggled to get residency permits, let alone passports that would allow them to travel internationally.

Other experts I spoke with agreed that the Turkish government's public emphasis on Uyghurs' ethnic ties to Turkey means the regime wouldn't allow something like a mass deportation of Uyghur exiles back to China. Since 2019, the Chinese government has been claiming it has shut down many of the "vocational training" camps and that residents have "graduated" to work placements around the country. But activists and experts warn that such placements likely involve forced labour or abusive conditions, and Beijing has refused to allow international investigators to assess the situation independently. Yet there are few countries in the Muslim world as influential as Turkey in terms of military strength and economic influence, and this country is only occasionally publicly raising human rights concerns with China. This doesn't bode well for Uyghurs counting on ethno-religious solidarity to secure their families' safety in Xinjiang.

On a July 2019 visit to Beijing, Erdoğan bluntly asked China to increase trade volume and reduce the trade deficit. He also poured extravagant praise on the Belt and Road project. Xi's vision, Erdoğan enthused, had "emerged as the greatest development project of the twenty-first century."

Erdoğan emphasized that Turkey lies at the geographical heart of the so-called Middle Corridor envisioned in New Silk Road plans. Those plans called for the building and upgrading of railways and logistics hubs to link Turkey to Georgia and

Azerbaijan, crossing the Caspian Sea and eventually reaching China through Turkmenistan and Kazakhstan.

"Among our goals is to double our bilateral trade volume with China to $50 billion and, subsequently, $100 billion on a more balanced and sustainable footing to serve the interests of both sides," he said. "I call on the Chinese business community to invest in Turkey—the crossroads of Asia and Europe, and the heart of the [Belt and Road]."

The question of whether Turkey will protect Uyghurs or stand with Beijing out of economic interests came to a head in December 2020, when Beijing ratified an extradition treaty with Turkey that was initially signed in 2017 between the two countries. Human rights groups urged the Turkish government to reject the treaty, warning that Uyghurs who had fled persecution in Xinjiang and settled in Turkey would be obvious first targets of Beijing's extradition requests.

While Chinese state media has refuted those claims, saying the treaty would be used for counterterrorism purposes, experts have pointed to a disturbing clause in the treaty that allows for broad interpretations of "terrorism." The text says, "It shall not matter whether the laws of both parties place the offence within the same category or describe the offence by the same terminology."

In spring 2021, Istanbul had yet to announce whether it would ratify the treaty. Uyghurs in Turkey remain in limbo.

8.

RUSSIA

Friend or Foe?

Vladimir Putin and Xi Jinping marched side by side down the steps of the Great Hall of the People to review the Chinese military guard assembled in Beijing's Tiananmen Square. In matching black suits and maroon ties, they made a perfect pair, though Xi's stroll was relaxed, while Putin kept his arms and back rigid.

A long red carpet was arranged in a large rectangle, and around the perimeter, rows of troops gripped their rifles and saluted as the leaders passed them by. I was crushed among a group of rather tall and wide-shouldered Russian reporters on one corner of the red carpet, as the military band blared grandiosely right next to us.

This display of compatibility, on June 8, 2018, wasn't typical for state visits to China and seemed to signal the two countries were entering a new phase of partnership.

The pomp didn't stop there. Chinese foreign ministry staff corralled the journalists and instructed us to pack up our equipment to relocate to the next event.

Inside the Great Hall, on a specially erected stage before an audience of dignitaries from Russia and China, Xi hefted a gaudy gold-plated chain and gingerly placed it around Putin's neck. The president fingered one of the oversized medallions in the chain and peered up at Xi with an intense gaze. I couldn't decide whether Putin's expression had an air of defiance.

Xi then announced, "This medal of friendship represents the Chinese people's lofty respect for President Putin and symbolizes the profound friendship between China and Russia."

China's "highest honour," bestowed for the very first time, recognized foreigners who had made "outstanding contributions" to the country's modernization and helped maintain world peace, Xi added. The award came in response to a similar gesture a year earlier, when Putin presented Xi with Russia's prestigious Order of St. Andrew.

In almost thirty meetings between the two by 2018, they had emphasized their friendship. They had given each other pride of place as guests of honour, exchanged birthday gifts, and even guzzled vodka and shared sandwiches "like university students," according to a Putin interview. Xi has called Putin his "best friend."

As a reporter for a European news agency, I witnessed several of these meetings up close. The two leaders did seem to share a genuine affection; even when the cameras weren't flashing, they almost always walked or sat shoulder to shoulder, slightly removed from other state leaders.

Ties between the two nations couldn't be better, the leaders say. In Beijing, Putin noted that bilateral trade between Russia and China had hit US$87 billion the year before and risen by 31 percent in the first quarter of 2018. China has been Russia's largest trading partner since 2010, and Russia is currently the largest crude oil and gas supplier to China.

"If we are able to keep up this rate of growth, we may be able set a record at the level we discussed achieving over the period of several years: $100 billion," Putin said. This goal was indeed achieved by the end of 2018, and in 2019 bilateral trade hit nearly US$110 billion.

Deteriorating relations with Washington have only drawn Russia and China closer. At the time of the 2018 medal ceremony, a trade war was looming between Beijing and the U.S., while the U.S. had imposed sanctions against Russia over Moscow's annexation of Crimea and support of Syrian leader Bashar al-Assad. With little goodwill to lose in the relationship, Russia continues to be brashly anti-American. And Beijing has moved closer to Moscow's position in recent years. The two leaders position themselves on the same side in economic disputes, agreeing that America has selfish motivations for criticizing China's trade practices and for expressing distrust of the New Silk Road strategy.

"We both believe that the current trade protectionism has increased, and there are many uncertainties in the recovery of the world economy. Economic globalization and regional economic integration are the trend of the times," Xi said at the June gathering.

To this day, Putin and Xi probably have more in common with one another than either has with any other world leader. They have both secured mandates to rule virtually for life: in March 2018, China's parliament lifted presidential term limits, paving the way for Xi to become the most powerful and longest-serving CCP leader since Mao; and in July 2020, after an overwhelming vote of confidence from the Russian electorate, Putin won the right to remain president until 2036, when he will be eighty-three years old. (However, it should be noted that Russian election results and democratic processes tend to come under serious dispute, not unlike the "voting" in Chinese parliament.)

Both are preoccupied with controlling information flows at home. Both have preached non-interference while running elaborate disinformation and political influence campaigns in other countries. And both are ready and willing to butt heads with America.

In late 2018, the two countries showed off their military prowess. Thousands of China's troops joined in Russia's biggest war games exercise in almost forty years, taking part in massive drills at a Siberian firing range.

Politicians like former U.S. secretary of state Mike Pompeo have definitely taken notice, warning of an authoritarian cabal led by Russia, China, and Iran that would threaten freedoms around the world.

But while there's not much to dispel international observers' assumption that the leaders of China and Russia are indeed "best friends," the future of their relationship is still uncertain. Putin's optimistic comments on trade growth haven't reflected the unequal nature of the flow of goods. Russia's economic reliance on China has increased year by year to 15 percent of total trade, while Russian goods make up only around 1 percent of China's world trade.

In Russia, there is growing concern that Moscow is no longer the "big brother" of the scrappy Chinese Communist Party of old. Someday, China could even encroach on Russia's traditional sphere of influence in Central Asia. A May 2020 analysis from the U.S.-based Kennan Institute found that while Russia's security sector presence has not diminished, China has dramatically increased its arms sales and joint military exercises in Central Asia. Chinese border forces have been operating inside Tajikistan to help monitor terrorist activity in recent years, since Beijing is concerned over possible terrorism spill-over to Xinjiang, when previously only Russia had a foreign military presence there.

Whether the relationship between the two countries leads to deepening cooperation or, conversely, conflict could mean a world of difference in global power dynamics.

AS NEIGHBOURS WITH THE WORLD'S sixth-longest international border, Russia and China share a long and bloody history of territorial disputes. But this dynamic suddenly changed when Communist revolutionary leader Vladimir Lenin seized power and ended centuries of monarchical rule in Russia.

The 1917 Bolshevik Revolution coincided with the early stirrings of Communist organizing in China, including the founding of the Chinese Communist Party in 1921. Many young Chinese intellectuals, including those who later rose to senior CCP leadership positions, spent formative years in Moscow as visiting students, writers, journalists, and scholars. It was fashionable for members of the new Chinese intelligentsia to learn the Russian language.

Qu Qiubai was one of them, and his writings provide a detailed record of how his time in Moscow helped shape his revolutionary ideas. Born to a once-powerful family whose patriarch succumbed to opium addiction, Qu had attended seminars on Marxism alongside a young Mao Zedong in Beijing while studying at the newly established Russian Language Institute. In 1921, he set off to Moscow as a correspondent for the Chinese newspaper *Morning News*.

There, he met Leo Tolstoy's granddaughter, watched Lenin deliver a speech, and absorbed Russian art and culture like a sponge. Living in a city that to him exemplified the virtues of the blurring of East and West, he wrote, "I am no longer solely a product of Chinese culture." In his memoir, Qu marvelled at the transformation of the "Red City," with its smoke stacks, industrialization, and casting away of old traditions. He thought China was on a similar path of grappling with the task of abandoning outdated beliefs and forging a new society.

Qu's story reflects the inspirational influence of the Russian Revolution on early Chinese Communist Party visionaries. Later, the Soviets would provide military aid and financial support as well.

After two years in Moscow, Qu accepted an invitation from CCP leader Chen Duxiu to return home and serve the Chinese revolutionary cause. He oversaw propaganda efforts before rising to the level of acting chairman of the Chinese Communist Party Politburo as the CCP gained enough power to challenge the ruling Nationalist party.

With Soviet support, the Communists won the Chinese Civil War and established the People's Republic of China in 1949. Chairman Mao Zedong wrote to Joseph Stalin throughout the war with desperate appeals. "We acutely need and hope that you will help us with 30–50 transport aircraft to ship food, clothing, key personnel and some of the troops," he begged in one letter before a planned invasion of Xinjiang. Stalin agreed, and the invasion was successful. When the Red Army needed aviation fuel and ten thousand tons of grain, the Soviets came through again.

On February 14, 1950, the People's Republic of China and the Soviet Union signed the Sino-Soviet Treaty of Friendship,

Alliance, and Mutual Assistance. The treaty included very concrete provisions that left little to interpretation. One section stipulated that in the event that one party was attacked by Japan or a Japanese ally, the other "shall immediately render military and other assistance by all means at its disposal."

Nevertheless, after Stalin's death in 1953, both sides soon began to quarrel. Stalin's successor, Nikita Khrushchev, softened the Soviet Union's combative stance toward the West and introduced liberal political and economic reforms. In 1956, Khrushchev denounced Stalin and Stalinism in a speech, "On the Cult of Personality and Its Consequences," which infuriated the hardline Mao. Beijing formally denounced the Soviets as "revisionist traitors," and the alliance between the two countries effectively dissolved.

For years after the Sino-Soviet split, the two sides jostled for influence over the Eastern bloc of fledgling Communist countries. Tensions ratcheted up until a brief seven-month border conflict between the two countries erupted in 1969 near Manchuria and ended in a stalemate.

Despite the conflict, both countries continued to observe the stipulations of the Sino-Soviet Treaty of Friendship, Alliance, and Mutual Assistance. China waited until the military alliance officially expired in 1979 before invading Vietnam, a Soviet ally, in the Third Indochina War.

It was not until July 16, 2001, one decade after the collapse of the USSR, that a new partnership was established. Putin, who had just come to power, and his Chinese counterpart, Jiang Zemin, signed the twenty-year binding Sino-Russian Treaty of Good-Neighbourliness and Friendly Cooperation. In contrast to the first treaty, this one was more abstract, outlining in broad strokes the two sides' commitment to restore and develop peaceful relations, economic ties, and diplomatic and geopolitical cooperation.

While the "friendship" treaty didn't say much on paper, it paved the way for dramatic economic and socio-political change. Government campaigns promoting exchanges between the countries had a significant impact on the movement of international students, businesses, and tourists. The introduction of visa-free entry for Chinese tour groups in 2015 sparked an explosion in the number of Chinese vacationers travelling to Russia, surpassing two million in 2018.

The two countries' international interests increasingly run parallel, as both have articulated their opposition to American hegemony. As Putin depicted it in an article for *Russia Today*, "The Chinese voice in the world is indeed growing ever more confident, and we welcome that, because Beijing shares our vision of the emerging equitable world order." Meanwhile, neither side has disabused international speculation about their two countries re-entering a formal alliance.

The situation is similar to Saddam Hussein refusing to deny that Iraq had weapons of mass destruction, Elizabeth Wishnick told me. "It probably follows a similar logic, because both countries want to be seen as more powerful," she speculated.

Wishnick, a Sino-Russian relations expert at Montclair State University in New Jersey, says that the two countries now enjoy a more stable and effective partnership than they did in the twentieth century. While Russia relies on China to buy its oil and gas resources, China benefits from Russia's military power.

"There is more equality between the countries, and a different international context. In those days [the mid-twentieth century], the Soviet Union was the older brother in the relationship, and now a lot of people call Russia the junior partner in the relationship, but I don't know if that is true," Wishnick says. The status quo is beneficial for both parties, she argues, and it's unlikely either side sees the need for a formal alliance.

"There's a lot of concern in Russia about its global position, but when you look at Russia's military forces, it's still ahead of China in many respects. I think they have different strengths, and that's the mantra both countries repeat: they have a complementary, win-win partnership."

To some critics, the prospect of the two authoritarian powers entering a military alliance spells trouble for liberal democracies. But even if the two never forged a formal alliance, they could still work together in ways that could cause major headaches for the United States, say Andrea Kendall-Taylor and David Shullman, senior academics at the Center for a New American Security. The Washington, DC, think tank receives millions in funding from the U.S. government and defence contractors.

"Imagine, for example, that Russia and China coordinate the timing of hostile actions on their peripheries. If China made aggressive moves in support of its sovereignty claim in the South China Sea at the same time that Russia made further incursions into Ukraine, U.S. forces would struggle to respond effectively to either gambit," Kendall-Taylor and Shullman wrote in a 2019 *Foreign Affairs* essay.

However, Australian foreign policy expert Bobo Lo characterizes the ties between an increasingly assertive China and disruptive Russia as an "axis of convenience," where the relationship is in fact marred by a lack of mutual understanding and lack of trust.

"Despite vociferous claims to the contrary, Beijing and Moscow are not engaged in a multi-dimensional plot to undermine the global order," Lo asserted in a 2020 Lowy Institute article that skewered fear-mongering rhetoric from Western policymakers.

It is a major topic of debate: if China clearly rises above Russia to become a dominant world power, experts are divided in their opinion on how Moscow would react, and how long their cheery union could last.

TO UNDERSTAND THE RELATIONSHIP between the two countries, there is only so much to glean from bombastic ceremonial displays and leaders' pronouncements.

Thanks to sophisticated propaganda and censorship regimes, it's difficult to gauge from a distance how ordinary people in Russia and China feel, but the COVID-19 pandemic put a sudden stop to my plans to visit Russia.

I was lucky to find Natalia Afanasyeva instead. The Moscow-based journalist has many years of experience working for Russian news outlets, including federal news agency RIA Novosti, as well as for a Swedish daily newspaper. We agreed to conduct video interviews independently and share transcripts with each other to compare notes, while Natalia would do in-person reporting outdoors whenever possible to reduce the risk of coronavirus transmission.

In the end, it was probably for the best. People were more open with Natalia than they might have been with me, someone who might appear more Chinese than Canadian to them. Another Russian journalist, who preferred not to be named in this book, provided translations of the reporting from Russian to English.

We wondered to what extent the anti-Asian racism and xenophobia that spiked around the world in 2020 with the spread of COVID-19 was present in Russia too. Officially, Moscow and Beijing were presenting a united front against international backlash over China's handling of the pandemic. In one of several phone calls on the coronavirus outbreak, Xi told Putin, "Politicizing and labelling the pandemic will not benefit international cooperation, and China and Russia should cooperate closely and safeguard global health care security together." Putin responded by agreeing that any attempt to discredit China and spread rumours about the virus's origins was unacceptable.

Meanwhile, both countries engaged in social media disinformation campaigns to deflect blame away from Beijing and toward Washington, according to research from the Oxford Internet Institute, a U.K.-based academic organization. China and Russia circulated conspiracy theories that the virus was either invented by the Americans or brought to China by the U.S. military. Even in the midst of a worldwide health crisis, global competition was at play, with China's propaganda departments working in overdrive to alter narratives about the outbreak's origins, while Russia was echoing China's propaganda to some extent and striving to boost its own reputation by being the first nation with a viable vaccine.

But what was the mood like on the ground in Russia? Did ordinary Russians agree with the rosy messages of friendship from both countries?

We also wanted to know if diverging public opinions could affect the two states' lofty goals. By March 2021, coronavirus cases totalled over four million in Russia, with more than two hundred thousand deaths, making it the third worst-hit country in the world for COVID-19 fatalities. Meanwhile, life in most Chinese cities had been relatively normal for months, and there were fewer than five thousand recorded coronavirus-related fatalities. Unsurprisingly, Chinese nationals in Russia flocked home.

In a Pew Research Center poll of thirty-four countries conducted from May 13 to October 2, 2019, China's most positive ratings came from Russian citizens. Drawing from a mostly urban survey sample, 71 percent said they held a favourable view of China, and only 18 percent held an unfavourable view. (There hasn't been similar polling of Chinese attitudes toward Russia.) But differences between high-level state relations and ground-level exchanges are probably not reflected well in general opinion polls.

During the early months of the pandemic, Beijing's embassy complained about Moscow's "discriminatory" monitoring of Chinese nationals living in Russia. And an IPSOS poll in February 2020 found that over a third of Russians would avoid contact with people of Chinese origin or appearance, and similar numbers said they would avoid purchasing Chinese products. The concern over Chinese products was noteworthy when the issue was COVID-19 and health safety.

In early January 2020, Natalia boarded a train to St. Petersburg, Russia's historic port city on the Baltic Sea, a place normally used to seeing many foreign visitors. She promised to be my eyes and ears, sending me photos and videos so I could get a sense of what the trip and the people were like.

In one of her first impromptu interviews, a controversial topic emerged concerning Chinese newcomers to Russia that is not discussed in either country's propaganda materials.

Apraksin Yard is a historic thirty-five-acre market occupying a city block in the centre of St. Petersburg. Every day, vendors set up in the former warehouse buildings, arranging their wares on tables and shelves. Colourful oversized umbrellas act as additional makeshift scaffolding and as shields from the sun, rain, or snow. But the morning Natalia visited, many of the rows of shops and open-air stalls were boarded up, with none of the usual Chinese shopkeepers and tourists. At the start of the pandemic, when tourism dried up, Chinese entrepreneurs had closed up shop to return to China.

In the near-empty streets, Natalia ducked into a café and struck up a conversation with Igor, a businessman in his early fifties, who took a keen interest in her reporting.

"I used to go to a canteen deep inside Apraksin Yard, since they serve real Chinese food there," said Igor, who was dressed in simple but elegant clothes. He explained that he spent a lot of time doing business in China as a trader in the 1990s, but while he clearly has fondness for Chinese food and culture, he's been unimpressed by the way some Chinese-owned companies operate in Russia. He thinks this reflects deep-seated corruption in the Russian business environment more than it does the character of the Chinese people, however. According to numerous local newspaper reports, Russian firms cooperate with Chinese businesses to register their companies in Russian citizens' names in order to get favourable tax rates. "Almost all of the businesses here in St. Petersburg that cater to Chinese tourists or Chinese citizens who work here are illegal. All the money goes back to China," Igor stated confidently.

"Even here, in the centre of St. Petersburg, they were still working for their country; they transferred everything through their own payment systems. The Chinese canteen was here for many years, but no one spoke Russian and they weren't planning on learning it."

Igor was referring to WeChat Pay and Alipay, the two most popular electronic payment systems from Chinese companies.

Transactions made through these apps can take place anywhere in the world as long as the buyer and seller both have a mainland Chinese bank account. So far, no government has robust enough measures to monitor and tax transactions through the apps. President Trump signed an order banning U.S. transactions on eight Chinese apps, including Alipay and WeChat Pay, but it was not yet in force by the time he left office.

On the windows of some shuttered shops, Natalia spotted stickers advertising tax-free goods and stating that mobile app payment methods were accepted. But even with all of these sales going untaxed in the so-called shadow, or grey, economy, the sheer number of Chinese tourists visiting Russia has pumped millions into the country's economy. Before the pandemic hit, Russia was one of the top three destinations for Chinese travellers, due in large part to the weak ruble, which allowed visitors to afford lavish accommodations and shopping sprees.

Russia's federal tourism agency estimated that more than two million Chinese tourists visited Russia in 2019, compared with around 160,000 a decade ago. Also in 2019, the Russian Central Bank said for the first time that Chinese citizens spent the most of all foreign visitors to Russia, an amount topping US$1 billion.

But Russian tourism industry leaders estimate that the US$264 million that Chinese tourists officially spent in the first three months of 2019 alone in fact accounted for no more than 40 percent of the real sum they spent in Russia, and locals were rankled about the proportion that went to Chinese-operated businesses that didn't pay foreign taxes. In some prime tourist areas, wholly Russian-owned businesses struggled to compete, Alexander Fedin, general director of the Kalina Travel agency, told *Kommersant*, a Russian business newspaper.

"There are exceptions, of course," Igor said. He told Natalia about his Chinese friend, a "very refined man," who spoke some Russian and registered his retail store legally in order to avoid trouble from the authorities. He wanted to settle in Russia long term, and his shop sold high-quality Chinese tea and ointments. However, once the pandemic hit, he couldn't pay rent each month. "He went bankrupt immediately, closed the store, and left," Igor said.

Within days of the pandemic's outbreak in Wuhan, the number of Chinese tourists in Russia had dropped to virtually zero. One year later, Natalia couldn't find a single Chinese entrepreneur anywhere in St. Petersburg to interview, since most had returned to China. Even in Chinese restaurants, there were only Russian servers and clientele. I tried calling Chinese-owned businesses I found listed on embassy websites and other platforms and didn't have much luck either.

It's impossible to predict how many Chinese business owners and tourists will return once the pandemic is over, but the swift exit of Chinese shopkeepers during the pandemic shows that concerns over their ability to overtake local competitors have been exaggerated, argues Ivan Vvedensky. He has worked in government as the former deputy director of the Department of Tourism's international bureau, as well as assistant to the head of the Federal Agency for Tourism. As a representative of Moscow, he travelled numerous times to China in the early 2000s, a time when cooperation frameworks for tourism, infrastructure, and trade between the two countries were being hammered out.

Vvedensky, who is now an independent investment consultant, has become familiar with the long-running debates in Russia over closer ties with China. "There are supporters of globalization, and there are nationalists," he told Natalia. "It's clear that [foreign competition] is a big challenge for the local community, and not everyone among the local population will be able to compete with the newcomers.... The scale of business that newspapers write about—all these little shops, et cetera—of course worries local Russian competitors, but on the scale of major state policy, they're worth nothing much."

Instead, Vvedensky said, international observers would be better served to look for signs of success in so-called trophy properties such as luxury hotels and businesses in Russia operated by large Chinese firms. He pointed to the sprawling Park Huaming business centre in Moscow, a project by a consortium of large Chinese companies and Shanghai banks. It had been "painstakingly under construction" for more than ten years. "And you know why?" Vvedensky said. "Because they don't have this depth of knowledge and understanding of how to work in Russia. They have constant scandals with contractors, with legal documents. And that's despite the fact that Huaming is a very big company."

Vvedensky's comments matched interviews I had done with other experts, who referred to lengthy and repeated delays in major Chinese-Russian joint infrastructure projects, such as the Moscow-Kazan high-speed railway.

If both countries were serious about substantially scaling up business exchanges, there would be a lot more support for companies and cutting of red tape, Vvedensky said.

FOR CONTEXT ON THE TENSIONS Natalia encountered in her reporting, I reached out to Maria Repnikova, an American citizen who grew up in Latvia and speaks fluent Russian. She is a scholar of China's political communication at Georgia State

University in Atlanta, and has done extensive field research in Moscow, Beijing, and the border areas of the Russian Far East and northeast China.

Repnikova has found that private media outlets in Russia tend to strike a critical tone toward China. Journalists in Russia are freer to express contrary opinions, whereas in China even nominally independent media outlets are under greater pressure to toe the government line. Which means that "in people-to-people relations, there is definitely more suspicion on Russia's side when it comes to Chinese economic migrants and China in general," Repnikova told me.

She initially assumed that the large number of critical reports and editorials about Chinese migrants in Russian media were exaggerated, but when she visited Russian markets for research in 2019, "there was a lot of talk about Chinese traders and buyers, and a lot of disregard and suspicion," she said. "The stereotypes are very strong.... The negativity some Russians harbour towards the Chinese is to do with the sense that there isn't an equal economic relationship between the two countries."

In 2017, China overtook Germany as Russia's top foreign investor, pumping an estimated US$35 billion into the Russian economy in 2018. The funding goes primarily into resource extraction activities, however, and much of the oil and gas produced is sold to China at relatively low cost. The Chinese government has been working to reduce consumption of coal—a major source of pollution in its megacities—in line with a state target to reach peak carbon emissions by 2030. While China's demand for oil from Russia and Central Asia will likely decrease over time, if the government remains serious about its commitment to mitigating climate change, China's demand for natural gas will likely grow in coming decades, as it is a relatively ecologically friendly fossil fuel.

Given that Russia is a Eurasian nation and in need of better infrastructure, it would seem like a natural candidate for the New Silk Road project. But foreign investors in general—including Chinese investors—seem reluctant to pour money into Russia-based projects.

A 2020 report for the Center for Strategic and International Studies from American analyst Jonathan E. Hillman looked at reasons why. "The issue is not simply risk aversion among Chinese investors, who have been willing to wade into some of the world's most challenging business environments," Hillman writes. "Russia is riskier than developed economies but holds less promise than many developing economies due in part to its declining population."

Nevertheless, in government forums, Chinese and Russian officials continue to emphasize that the two countries are very close, and only getting closer. They give copious examples of high-level exchanges such as diplomatic missions, and don't tend to talk about the more complex ground-level exchanges. "Equality and friendship" is the official message.

In Repnikova's earlier fieldwork in border areas such as Heilongjiang province in China, she met Chinese migrants who had trouble obtaining visas in time to get to work projects on farms and construction sites in Russia. "Racism or ethnic discrimination might play a certain role, but the inefficiencies are tied to corruption," she says.

In such situations, unsavoury similarities between the two countries were coming to the fore. Government and commercial corruption is rampant in China, and Xi has presided over a much-publicized anti-graft campaign since coming to power in 2012.

Frustration over bureaucratic obstacles to doing business is a major source of dissatisfaction among Chinese entrepreneurs and foreign companies in China. And tax evasion? That is a way of life in China too. In Beijing, real estate agents would instruct their expatriate clients on ways to obtain fake receipts to make their rent payments appear larger and therefore not subject to income tax.

All of this shows that international fears of the overwhelming power of two authoritarian countries banding together may indeed be exaggerated; on the ground level, exchanges don't seem as smooth as either country would like. And since both Putin and Xi draw their power in part from promises of economic growth and strengthened international standing, widespread disillusionment could weaken their legitimacy.

Even though Putin has been an early supporter of the Belt and Road Initiative, little Chinese funding to improve trade infrastructure is heading Russia's way. The idea that China's New Silk Road strategy deliberately "bypasses Russia" only adds to local critics' list of grievances, says Maria Repnikova.

Rather, Beijing is investing heavily in Central Asia's trade infrastructure along a proposed economic belt spanning the Pacific Ocean to the Baltic, with land and sea route projects in Turkmenistan, Kazakhstan, Uzbekistan, and Kyrgyzstan. These Central Asian countries happen to be firmly in Russia's sphere of influence, and so far the Russian government hasn't publicly opposed China's economic investments in the region. But if China were to deploy more military or security forces to Central Asia to protect its investments there, it could spark conflict with Russia, multiple experts told me.

Russia wants to maintain its dominant position as the security partner of choice for Central Asian countries, Elizabeth Wishnick says. "The implicit message from both countries is that China can play a complementary role to Russia in Central Asia by providing more economic support, but if China puts more [military] boots on the ground there, this would change the dynamics," she told me.

PERHAPS NOWHERE ELSE in Russia is China's presence more fraught than at Lake Baikal in Siberia.

Situated north of the Mongolian border and west of northeastern China, the massive lake, encircled by hiking paths and small villages, is the world's deepest. It is also the world's largest single source of fresh water. Yet in the winter, the entire surface freezes over to such a thickness that it can support most vehicles.

Although temperatures drop far below freezing in the winter, the Baikal climate tends to be dry and often more comfortable than Moscow's. The surreal deep-blue expanse draws over a million visitors each "ice season," from January to April, with mainland Chinese typically making up about two-thirds of foreign tourists: the destination, a three-hour flight from Beijing, became popular in China a decade ago, after the love song "Baikal Lake," by the Chinese singer Li Jian, became a huge hit.

Chinese entrepreneurs have opened hotels and restaurants in the area with romantic names like Baikal Dream, and honeymooners like how the lush pine forests and mountainous landscape enhance the beauty of the lake (and perhaps of their partners too).

Lovestruck couples likely give little thought to the tense history of the area, though Chinese tourism websites advertise that Lake Baikal was once a part of China. In 1858 and 1860, with the signing of two treaties, the Russian empire strong-armed China's Qing dynasty to cede more than a million square kilometres of its vast northeast territory, which today makes up the southern portion of the Russian Far East, including resource-rich Siberia.

Skirmishes broke out between the two nations a century later, in the 1960s, stopping short of all-out war, and tensions simmered until the 1990s. In 1994, officials signed the Sino-Russian Border Management System agreement to facilitate border trade, and Russia agreed to transfer far-eastern islands back to China as a gesture of reconciliation.

But many residents of Russia's Siberia remained uneasy. They were well aware how densely populated the Chinese side of the border was compared to their own sparse numbers and underdeveloped economy. In recent years, when Chinese state-backed firms signed multi-billion-dollar investment deals to expand tourism infrastructure in the region, and as Chinese-owned hotels proliferated, Siberian locals saw it as a coordinated land grab.

As she'd experienced in St. Petersburg, Natalia Afanasyeva couldn't find Chinese tourists or many businesspeople to interview in Baikal during the pandemic, but she saw evidence of the scale of the Chinese commercial presence in the area.

In Irkutsk, one of the largest cities in Siberia, on the banks of a river that flows into Baikal, Natalia chatted with a local woman who told her that signs in Chinese used to be every-where in the city centre—oversized billboards that dominated the streets, casting shadows onto the sidewalks. Many have since been removed, after the Chinese shops selling souvenirs, virtually exclusively to Chinese tourists, were forced to shut down. Local shopkeepers who sold jewellery at exorbitant prices were just managing to get by on the business they received from Russian tourists, but they sorely missed the deep-pocketed Chinese tourists.

The North Sea Hotel, which is Chinese-owned and operated, now functions as a quarantine facility for workers from other parts of Russia who come to Irkutsk for jobs in oil, gas, and gold mining. Contracts struck with Russian resource companies to provide workers with quarantine housing are profitable for such hotels, and local travel industry workers griped to Natalia that some lucrative contracts have gone to the Chinese.

In a nearby ramshackle indoor market known as "Shanghai City," most of the sellers actually hail from Central Asia or the Caucasus region. Natalia did meet four Chinese shopkeepers, a married couple and two younger women. They were talking animatedly to each other in Mandarin while tending to simple stalls selling warm hats, scarves, socks, gloves, and bags, but they also spoke proficient Russian.

When Natalia approached, they greeted her with friendly smiles but clammed up when she explained she was a journalist and started asking questions. "We are permanent residents here," the man told her, looking visibly nervous.

In response to local backlash, Irkutsk authorities have recently been enforcing a law that has long been on the books allowing only people with Irkutsk residence permits to sell goods.

"We've been living here for ten years and everything is fine," the man said, before saying they had to leave, and then turning away without another word. Moments later, a guard showed up to tell Natalia to stop taking pictures.

The sellers were clearly nervous, but Natalia told me it's not unusual for people in Russia to distrust strangers. In fact, the halt in Chinese tourism during the pandemic and the restriction of commercial activity to local residents seem to have calmed any pre-existing China-related tensions in Irkutsk. The city also benefits from a diversified economy, since it's a base for resource extraction companies.

But an hour's taxi ride away, in the small tourist resort town of Listvyanka, on the southern shore of Baikal, anger over the Chinese "occupation" is alive and well. Local newspapers have run numerous headlines about a Chinese "conquest" there and even compared the influx of investment and tourists to past Mongolian invasions.

In May 2019, the *New York Times* reported that a Russian motel owner took his chainsaw to the construction site of a Chinese-owned hotel that threatened to obstruct his views of the lake. He was lionized in the local community for standing up against the "invaders." "If we let them, the Chinese will take over," the man told the *Times*.

In Listvyanka, Natalia interviewed a prominent figure in the fight against "Chinese expansion" into the region. Sonya Buntovskaya has been active in protesting Chinese investment in general, including the building of hotels as well as a Baikal water bottling project owned by a Chinese company. A few years ago, she gathered hundreds of local residents to write to the regional prosecutor's office to complain about illegal sales of land to Chinese citizens for the building of hotels, and they were able to shut down some hotel projects.

With her husband, Yevgeny Kravkl, she founded a traditional musical theatre in Listvyanka some thirty years ago. Additionally, Buntovskaya offers tours of the Baikal area to tourists—but only to Russians, and she tells them the lake is Russia's "holy place."

When Natalia asked Buntovskaya why she is so opposed to a Chinese presence of any sort, she said, "The Chinese are children of the yellow dragon, and we are very different, we are children of a different god.... That's why we can never be friends. Because they want our territory. They are a very cunning nation. And they don't just want our land, they are actively trying to make it theirs."

She made several statements that I couldn't find any evidence for: "As far as I know, their government gives them money to do this to help them. For example, if a Chinese citizen buys a plot of land, the Chinese government subsidizes some 70 percent of the cost. I don't remember how much exactly. If a Chinese man marries a Russian woman, China gives him sixty thousand dollars!"

She was especially critical of marriages between Russians and Chinese citizens, claiming that the unions were a manoeuvre by the Chinese to set down roots on Russian soil and pillage natural resources. "These Chinese procure Russian wives, and when a Russian woman bears children, the Chinese blood is stronger, so they are in fact little Chinese children. Their country's population is ten times larger than our country's, and they have polluted all their rivers and soil, so that's why they are very interested in our territory. Our water.... What's good about this? Nothing."

Such sentiments, though extreme, seem to resonate with a significant number of people. When a petition on Change.org to stop the construction of the AquaSib water bottling plant in the dusty town of Kultuk, on the shore of Lake Baikal, surpassed a million signatures, Russian prime minister Dmitry Medvedev intervened, in March 2019, to order an inspection. AquaSib is a Russian enterprise owned by a Chinese company based in Heilongjiang province.

The petition emphasized that the water bottling plant was owned by a Chinese firm and its product was for the Chinese market. "On the shore of our Lake Baikal...they are going to build a Chinese plant for bottling drinking water. The plant's products will be supplied to China," it said.

Within days of the prime minister's intervention, a regional court ordered AquaSib to halt construction on the plant after inspectors found signs of an oil spill and industrial waste. Two years later, in 2021, Natalia found the area fenced off and deserted, with no sign the project would resume anytime soon.

While similar-sized water bottling plants have operated in the area, these did not attract scrutiny, likely because they were not foreign-owned. The incident shows that overwhelming public backlash can sway government decisions on China-linked investments in Russia, says Ilya Oleynikov, a senior lecturer in political sciences at the Irkutsk State University, who followed the situation closely. "Negative public opinion among locals just snowballed," Oleynikov told me. "It reached a point where famous Russian celebrities like fashion designer Sergey Zverev got involved by going out into the Red Square in Moscow with a banner saying 'Protect Baikal!'"

But even to environmentalists the issue seemed overly politicized and connected to broader anxieties about China's rising influence.

Maxim Tokarev, director of the Centre for Development of Ecological and Social Projects, an NGO operating in the Baikal area, says ecologists generally agree that the outrage over AquaSib glossed over a lot of the context. "Before this well-known story with the plant in Kultuk, there were already eight water bottling plants in the area. Russian ones, and some had some foreign investors," Tokarev told Natalia in a cautious manner, as if wary about offending activists but feeling the need to state some facts.

According to Tokarev, the Chinese plant was in an ideal location to efficiently pump water, and its level of potential environmental impact was comparable to other plants already in operation or further along in construction. "Water bottling is actually one of the cleanest productions," Tokarev said. "Some activists just went there, photographed the pipes lying on the ice, and started posting on social media that... this plant will pump all the water away and Baikal will be left empty." He added that he'd recently received a message from an activist spreading a conspiracy theory that the Chinese were building a tunnel directly from Lake Baikal to China.

Shaking his head, Tokarev said the hotel-building boom catering to the influx of Chinese tourists should have been a bigger cause of public concern, since it involved clear-cutting of the area's pristine forests. He said the Chinese weren't to blame, though; the Russian officials who let it happen were ultimately responsible.

WITH ALL THESE TENSIONS bubbling at the surface of Russian society, it's unlikely that either Moscow or Beijing is prepared to address the issues with any transparency. Doing so would undermine the countries' global message of being strong partners with perfectly complementary interests.

At a point when Washington is actively gathering allies to counter Chinese and Russian influence, Moscow and Beijing are expected to continue to present a coordinated front even if there isn't a strong sense of amity between its two peoples. In a way, overblown international speculation about a formal China-Russia alliance only pushes the two countries closer together when, in the absence of external pressures, their ties would probably experience more ups and downs.

After all, the chumminess between Putin and Xi can only go so far.

9.

THE UNITED STATES

"Virus" of Disinformation

"Have you seen this?"

In mid-2019, a friend, an American correspondent for a Hong Kong newspaper, sent me a link to a website for the film *Claws of the Red Dragon*, which was executive-produced by Steve Bannon, President Donald Trump's former chief strategist.

I laughed. The presence of "dragon" in any title about China tends to signal that it will be Orientalist and absurd. But to my horror, when I looked at the website, I saw that the film's main character, Jane Li, was "based on the Chinese Canadian journalist Joanna Chiu."

The website described my interview in January 2019 with former Canadian ambassador to China John McCallum. In the interview, McCallum directly contradicted the Canadian government's official line that it had played no role in the arrest of Huawei executive CFO Meng Wanzhou and that her fate—whether she should be released or extradited to the

United States, as the Americans had requested—was a matter for Canada's courts to decide. Prime Minister Justin Trudeau demanded McCallum's resignation the very evening the interview appeared.

"From Canada's point of view, if [the U.S.] drops the extradition request, that would be great for Canada," McCallum had told me at a fundraising event. "We have to make sure that if the U.S. does such a deal, it also includes the release of our two people. And the U.S. is highly aware of that," he added.

Trudeau never explained why he fired the ambassador for his comments, but Roland Paris, a former senior adviser to Trudeau on global affairs, told my *Toronto Star* colleague Michael Mui that Canadians should not be used as "bargaining chips." A senior government source later told my colleagues that Trudeau had already warned McCallum after he "misspoke" earlier in the week and told Chinese-language reporters misleading information about the government's view of the Meng case. When McCallum contradicted his government again in his interview with me, that left Trudeau little choice. China analysts derided McCallum's comments for playing into Beijing's strategy of arresting Canadians Michael Kovrig and Michael Spavor as leverage to push for the release of Meng from Canadian custody (by then, she was already out on bail and living in one of her Vancouver mansions). They warned that a capitulation from Canada to Beijing's demands would mean that Chinese officials could use "hostage-taking diplomacy" on more foreigners in the future.

I had no inkling that my attempt to get interesting comments from McCallum would lead to this series of events; I was only doing my job, but perhaps because of my Chinese ethnicity, some observers portrayed it as if I were "exposing" McCallum as some kind of ally of Beijing. China's state-owned hawkish tabloid *Global Times* smeared me as a "meddling" journalist, and countless pro-Beijing internet trolls bombarded my email and social media feeds with abusive comments. But after a few days, the comments trickled away.

On the website, Bannon's movie synopsis continued: "She interviewed the then-Canadian Ambassador to China, John McCallum, at a luncheon held in a Chinese restaurant in Vancouver, and she then truthfully reported his inappropriate remarks, which eventually led to McCallum being dismissed by the Canadian Prime Minister. . . . Jane is a Chinese individual born in the free society of the West and a journalist, who upholds and believes in the values of freedom and democracy."

Besides the basic facts of my interview with the ambassador and its aftermath, much of the plot was completely fabricated. In the movie, Jane's boyfriend is a "Huaxing" executive who sets out to betray her. Ominous music often plays, and Chinese officials whisper about a secret plan for world domination called "Made in China 2025." In reality, Made in China 2025 is a widely publicized Beijing government industrial policy that, while championing an expansion of China's high-tech sectors that could challenge other countries' economies, is hardly a secret plot.

The movie also includes disturbing fictional scenes in which a dead cat (which looks an awful lot like my cat in real life) is left on the hood of Jane's car and her parents are threatened. It felt like a violation, to say the least.

In an interview with Bloomberg, Bannon said he intended to screen the film to Trump to push the president to be tougher on Beijing. To my relief, the movie didn't have widespread distribution: it aired in October 2019 on the One America

News Network, which is considerably more right-wing than Fox News.

But Bannon continued to promote the movie as if it contained credible information, which prompted me to reflect on the outsized role that blatant misinformation plays in American politics in general, and particularly when it comes to discussions about China's threat to Americans. In the U.S., popular discussions on China have become dominated by politicians and pundits who don't have credible expertise. One such figure is Newt Gingrich, whose book *Trump vs. China: Facing America's Greatest Threat* contains many inaccuracies and nonsensical translations of Chinese phrases. Peter Navarro, who served in the Trump administration as assistant to the president and director of trade and manufacturing policy, has routinely made unsubstantiated allegations against the Chinese government, including that it was intentionally profiteering from the coronavirus pandemic. Navarro's 2011 book *Death by China: Confronting the Dragon—A Global Call to Action*, which was adapted into a 2012 film, was influential in the early days of the Trump administration. A *New York Times* reviewer called the film "alarming and alarmist." The film "undercuts its argument with an abundance of inflammatory language and cheesy graphics," wrote the reviewer, and was "unabashedly one-sided."

This puts reputable China scholars and researchers in an environment where "fake news" and overly simplified sound bites are given credence. There is a lot to criticize about Beijing's actions, but outlandish commentary and misinformation stoke anger and confusion while discrediting those who issue legitimate, fact-based criticism.

As U.S.-China tensions spike, disinformation campaigns could push the two countries ever closer to outright conflict.

Unlike misinformation, which is simply erroneous, disinformation is the deliberate spread of inaccurate and often very biased information intended to mislead. On China's side, anti-American propaganda is routinely published in state-run or state-affiliated media outlets. In the U.S., sources and motivations of anti-China screeds are much more varied.

Meanwhile, the stakes couldn't be higher. As Harvard University political scientist Graham Allison put it in a 2015 *Atlantic* magazine story, China's rise affects everyone. Allison says that the question of whether a new world order will emerge or the status quo be preserved is less important than the question of whether the outcome will be determined peacefully or China and America are destined for war.

U.S.-GROWN CONSPIRACY THEORIES related to China have shown a capacity to spread beyond America's borders. I discovered this while investigating another anti-Beijing venture related to Steve Bannon.

In a suburban Metro Vancouver cul-de-sac in September 2020, protesters began taking shifts outside the home of independent journalist and YouTube personality Benson Gao Bingchen. Almost every day, for up to six hours at a time, they waved signs stating that COVID-19 was a "bioweapon" made by the Chinese Communist Party and chanted slogans accusing Benson Gao of being a Chinese spy. They wore masks, sunglasses, and matching blue T-shirts and caps featuring a logo of crisscrossing loops of small yellow stars.

I arrived on day forty of the demonstrations to see what was going on.

Outraged local residents told me their children were afraid

to go outside during the afternoon demonstrations. "They claim our neighbour is a CCP spy," said resident Bob Petersen. "They put leaflets in mailboxes. [Benson Gao's] daughter is obviously freaked out by this, as is the neighbourhood."

The protesters I spoke with—eight of them had taken the shift that day—said they didn't mean to hassle the neighbours. They said they were peaceful "citizens" of the New Federal State of China, which was co-founded by Bannon and Chinese billionaire in self-exile Guo Wengui, who is also known as Miles Kwok.

"We support them so much," one man said in Mandarin, referring to Bannon and Guo.

The goal of the New Federal State of China, declared in June 2020 by banners towed by planes over American cities, was to take down the CCP and create an alternative Chinese state.

The group promoted its messages through popular social media sites as well as an online ecosystem of proprietary websites and video streaming platforms like G News and GTV, both named after Guo.

So why was the Canadian chapter of this American group concentrating its efforts on a quiet neighbourhood in Surrey, British Columbia?

As a journalist and activist, Benson Gao had for over a decade advocated against Beijing's authoritarian rule. He was the co-founder of the sixty-member Vancouver Society of Freedom, Democracy & Human Rights in China (formerly called Alliance of the Guard of Canadian Values). The group lobbied the Canadian government to resist Beijing's attempts to influence Canadian institutions. Benson Gao's outspoken stance would seem to make him an unlikely target for Bannon and Guo's group.

When I asked protesters why they believed Benson Gao was

a spy, a man replied, "It's because his videos distort the truth." Another interjected that Gao "spread misinformation about the scientist!" He was referring to Gao's YouTube videos in which he stated that he didn't believe a Hong Kong scientist's theories that COVID-19 originated in a Chinese laboratory.

Another protester handed me a pamphlet that told the story of Yan Li-meng, a scientist from Hong Kong and self-proclaimed whistleblower on the origins of COVID-19, who had fled to the United States. Fox News had aired an interview with Yan in mid-September in which she claimed her research provided evidence that COVID-19 was made in a Chinese lab and intentionally released into the world. Other scientists widely rejected the claim as unfounded, but Yan doubled down, publishing a second report, on October 8, titled "SARS-CoV-2 Is an Unrestricted Bioweapon." Both reports listed non-profit groups founded by Bannon and Guo as funding sources.

None of the protesters provided me with their names, saying they feared Beijing would kidnap them.

Meanwhile, Gao sat inside his house, watching the scene from his home office through security camera feeds. He tried to keep his ten-year-old daughter inside and to console his wife and mother-in-law, who were "angry and disturbed" by the protesters.

"The protesters accuse me of being a CCP spy and say I've sent their photos to China and their family members are affected. I absolutely don't know them, and I don't have their photos," he told me.

"These [protests] have happened in some five or six countries around the world... but I'm the only one I know of in Canada who has been targeted," he said in rapid Mandarin, gesturing emphatically with his hands. He said at first he hadn't realized it was a coordinated effort and didn't know of similar demonstrations, but he later found out that protesters elsewhere had been wearing the same clothes and shouting the same slogans.

In an August 2020 news release, the New Federal State of China announced it had organized general public protests in Tokyo, Osaka, and Nagoya, in Japan; Taipei, in Taiwan; Munich, in Germany; New York, Los Angeles, San Francisco, and Tucson, in the U.S.; and Vancouver, in Canada. Protests in Ottawa and Toronto took place in September. I independently confirmed that these protests had occurred in at least the Canadian cities and Texas.

Before the protests started, Benson Gao had posted several YouTube videos criticizing the "nonsense spouted by Guo Wengui." In social media posts, he accused Guo of whipping up supporters as a way to target influential Chinese-language critics and commentators, which actually seemed to forward the Chinese government's agenda. Benson Gao thought the Federal State's goals were questionable, since they were seeking to silence people like him who for decades had spoken out against Beijing's authoritarian rule.

A series of videos appeared online in which a man listed people's names, including Benson Gao's, and told his supporters the people "all deserve to die." Wearing a hat with a "G" logo and sunglasses, the man in the video looked and sounded like Guo Wengui, multiple people named in the video told me. Most of those listed in the video as "traitors" appeared to be pro-democracy figures openly critical of Beijing. The videos were later deleted on Twitter but were viewable on YouTube accounts that were not clearly affiliated with the New Federal State of China. It remains a mystery why Guo is so antagonistic to Beijing's strongest critics, and activists speculated that

Guo was vying to regain the favour of Chinese officials who had control over his assets in mainland China. I couldn't verify any of these theories.

In another video shared from the GTV platform, which at the time of writing is still publicly available, Guo's face is clearly visible. "Let's eliminate traitors in the world. Let's finish with these traitors first," he says, but he does not list any names. Bannon doesn't appear in most GTV videos, and it's unclear what role he plays in the organization.

I made efforts to contact Guo and Bannon, sending multiple requests through New Federal State of China members. I eventually reached Bannon's public relations manager, but instead of helping to arrange an interview with Bannon, she sent me links to Bannon's statements in support of Trump's 2020 re-election bid.

In Midland, Texas, Christian pastor Bob Fu, who is a prominent advocate for Chinese dissidents through his NGO ChinaAid, told me that shortly after Guo's videos were posted online, dozens of protesters gathered outside his home. Days later, he received online death threats and commenters mentioned planting bombs. "Federal FBI and local law enforcement had to evacuate us from our home to an undisclosed safe location," Fu told me. But protesters continued to gather outside his residence each day, and Fu was finding himself monitoring the situation on social media, not knowing when his family would be able to return home. Meanwhile, Federal State of China social media accounts were also busily spreading posts about lurid "sex tapes" involving Democratic Party presidential candidate Joe Biden's son Hunter.

In Vancouver, the daily protests soon turned violent. Benson Gao's friend Louis Huang, also a human rights advocate, was

smoking a cigarette outside Gao's home when two protesters jumped on him, dragging him to the ground and kicking
him repeatedly in the head. The brutal attack was recorded on
surveillance video, and police arrested the two men.

Then, in New Jersey, New Federal State protesters showed
up at the home of one of the highest-profile Chinese scholars-
in-exile, Teng Biao. A former lawyer in China, Teng has taught
at Harvard Law School and Yale Law School, and has criticized
Trump's policies and debunked Guo Wengui's conspiracy theories in articles and social media posts.

After many years of experiencing violence and racism around
the world, particularly at times of geopolitical tension and amid
the chaos of the COVID-19 pandemic, members of the Chinese
diaspora were incited by the American disinformation machine
to attack their own.

SINCE THE FOUNDING of the United States of America, para-
noia and xenophobia against migrants of Chinese descent have
worked to conjure the threat of the "yellow peril." During the
nineteenth century, Chinese immigrants worked as labourers
in industries like mining and construction and on transconti-
nental railroads, playing a key role in the development of the
country while suffering racial discrimination at every level of
society. A raft of exclusionary legislation and "yellow peril"
rhetoric amounted to systemic exclusion.

The targeting of Chinese Americans didn't let up until China
became a key ally for the Americans in fighting the Japanese
during the Second World War, and Chinese Americans only
won the right to vote in the United States in 1943.

It wasn't long before the Cold War started, however, which

pitted the Soviet Union and America, along with their respective allies, against each other. The McCarthy era, from the late 1940s through the 1950s, with its witch hunt for Communists and Communist "sympathizers," was a particularly dark time for Chinese Americans. Some employers were no longer willing to have a Chinese person on staff, and government committees dragged ordinary people in for questioning about their alleged affiliations with the Chinese Communist Party. Vandals attacked Chinese-owned businesses, and economic sanctions prevented thousands from remitting money to loved ones back home. Gilbert Woo, a popular Chinese American columnist at the time, described the mental state of Chinese Americans then as "numbed with fear," grappling with the sense that "being Chinese is itself a crime."

At the midpoint of the Vietnam War in the 1960s, a Gallup survey showed that 70 percent of Americans considered China, not the USSR, the greatest threat to U.S. security. This was surprising given that China didn't play a significant role in Cold War conflicts. At the time, the country was weak both politically and economically. The Communist Party leadership was dealing with the ongoing chaos of the Cultural Revolution and had yet to launch the market reforms that would lead to an economic boom. But despite being in dire economic straits, China was supporting North Vietnam in its fight against the South Vietnamese and the U.S., providing weapons, financial aid, and troops to play background roles such as reconstruction of destroyed areas. China continued to provide support after the Communist forces seized control of South Vietnam in 1975, but in 1978 it reduced its financial aid.

Next to Russia, China was the world's biggest Communist state. While Russia was considered part of the European world, the participation, however limited, of the relatively newly established Communist Party of China in the Vietnam War probably stoked anxieties among Americans about the rise of Eastern powers to challenge the West.

But, of course, people of Chinese descent do not all share the same beliefs and loyalties. To this day, life gets uglier for Chinese nationals and Americans of Chinese descent whenever political tides turn against Beijing. Too many Americans are still unable to differentiate the Chinese people from the Chinese government.

TO NEUTRALIZE THE PERCEIVED THREATS posed by Beijing during the Cold War, American politicians developed a theory that Western powers had the moral obligation to patiently draw China away from the USSR's orbit and that this was probably inevitable as the right course of history.

Sociologist Richard Madsen described the development of this thinking in his 1995 book *China and the American Dream*: "The dominant American myth about China, born in the 1960s, foresaw Western ideals of economic, intellectual, and political freedom emerging triumphant throughout the world. Nixon's visit to China nurtured this idea, and by the 1980s it was helping to sustain America's hopefulness about its own democratic identity."

From the 1949 founding of the People's Republic of China until the 1970s, China had been closed off from the Western world. Like the Soviet Union's, Beijing's experience of the Cold War was characterized by closed borders, ideological warfare, and the threat of nuclear conflict.

Beijing could have spent more years estranged from Western

democracies, without bilateral relationships or a seat at international organizations, if not for Richard Nixon's famous 1967 essay "Asia After Viet Nam," in *Foreign Affairs* magazine. Starting with this manifesto, and in subsequent remarks after he became president, Richard Nixon was able to convince a skeptical American public that it was wise to build trust with, rather than antagonize, Beijing. Many other countries would follow the same path.

It was possible to draw China away from Moscow's orbit, Nixon argued in "Asia After Viet Nam": "We simply cannot afford to leave China forever outside the family of nations, there to nurture its fantasies, cherish its hates and threaten its neighbours. There is no place on this small planet for a billion of its potentially most able people to live in angry isolation."

He laid out his strategy, whereby in the short term the U.S. would exercise "firm restraint" and use "creative counterpressure" to persuade Beijing that its interests could only be served through "accepting the basic rules of international civility." The goal was to bring China into the fold of the international community as "a great and progressing nation," not as the "epicenter of world revolution."

Nixon went on to win the presidency and in early 1972 was vying for re-election and needed a foreign relations victory. Winston Lord, who later served as U.S. ambassador to China in the late 1980s, recalled, "At home, you had riots, assassinations and people being disillusioned with executive power.... He thought if he opened China, the huge country, the drama and the importance of dealing with the giant would put in perspective the rather messy exit from Vietnam."

A declassified transcript provides an intimate view of Nixon's landmark February 1972 trip to meet with Chairman Mao

Zedong at his private residence. It was the first visit by an American president since the establishment of the People's Republic in 1949. At the time, it was difficult for most foreigners to get a visa to visit China, and Beijing still had no diplomatic ties with any major Western country. The two leaders sat side by side in plush armchairs, with white porcelain teacups on small tables between them, in a room lined with bookcases. A photograph shows Mao reclining in his chair and looking much older, being in his late seventies and dealing with health problems, while Nixon leans toward the chairman attentively.

Henry Kissinger, who would later rise to U.S. secretary of state in Nixon's second term and play a significant role in cooling Cold War tensions, was in attendance as Nixon's national security affairs assistant.

Nixon, Kissinger, and Mao exchanged flattering reassurances. Nixon told Mao that the United States had "no territorial designs on China" and wanted to find "common ground...to build a world structure in which both can be safe to develop in our own way on our own roads."

In an acknowledgement of the anti-Communist sentiment in America, and perhaps in direct reference to Nixon's previously negative stance on Communism, Kissinger implied they were in the wrong. "We didn't understand the different nature of revolution in China," he said.

Mao even shared his opinion that the risk of either country committing acts of aggression toward the other was "relatively small." He praised Nixon for being right to initiate friendly ties between the countries. Then he excused himself, since he was feeling ill, and left it to Premier Zhou Enlai to discuss the next steps with the Americans.

Later, scholars would speculate on whether Nixon truly

thought the U.S. and democratic allies would be able to turn China into a liberal democracy. Many argued that his move to strike friendlier ties with Beijing was really a strategy to gain an advantage in the Cold War, to neutralize a potentially strong Soviet ally.

Whatever Nixon's motivations, to a large extent the gambit worked spectacularly well. The two sides formally established diplomatic relations in 1979, and since then subsequent administrations have followed the path of engagement.

By the 1990s, hundreds of American companies were operating in China. The country had become a factory for the world, after all, churning out everything from cars to electronics to the latest fashions at lightning speed. And as its middle class grew in prosperity, foreign multinationals were eager to gain a foothold within its rapidly growing consumer market.

BUT CHINA'S RISING AUTHORITARIANISM and its flouting of international rules under President Xi Jinping has clearly shown that the American myth about China was wrong. A country *could* grow rich without becoming more liberal.

This reality has led to the emergence of a different kind of American attitude about China, and under President Barack Obama there were signs that the U.S.-China relationship was souring.

Starting in 2012, Obama pitched his "Pivot to East Asia" regional strategy as a rebalancing effort to move America's foreign policy focus away from the Middle East and toward the growing economic powerhouses of Asia. "Asia and the Pacific are increasingly the world's political and economic center of gravity," a November 2015 White House statement read. "At the same time, the region presents clear challenges in the years ahead, including concerns related to nuclear proliferation; intensifying maritime disputes; backsliding in democratic governance and respect for human rights in some countries."

While on the 2016 campaign trail, often with two hands on a podium, presidential candidate Donald Trump would spit out the syllables of "China," hitting the word hard, then pausing for dramatic effect. He did it over and over, in speech after speech, making sure his supporters took a moment to dwell on the word and what it made them feel. For many, it was resentment.

To roaring cheers at a campaign stop in Pennsylvania, Trump called Hillary Clinton part of "a leadership class that worships globalism." If he were president, he said, he would rip up existing trade deals with China, label the country a currency manipulator, and slap tariffs on Chinese goods.

"We can't continue to allow China to rape our country, and that's what we're doing," Trump bellowed before an electrified audience at a rally in Indiana. "We're going to turn it around, and we have the cards, don't forget it," he said. He referred to America's $346 billion trade deficit with China at the time as "the greatest theft in the history of the world." Experts are divided as to whether a nation importing more than it exports is necessarily harmful to its economy, but to Trump the imbalance was clearly a disgrace and Beijing's market manipulation was to blame.

In his campaign manifesto, Trump pledged to strike a new deal with China to "help American businesses and workers compete" and put "an end to China's illegal export subsidies and lax labour and environmental standards," even though climate change was a "hoax" concocted by China too.

Despite his status as a billionaire, Trump tapped into frustration among white working-class voters who felt they had lost jobs to foreign competition in an unfairly globalized world. Entrenched anti-Communist sentiment and rampant xenophobia helped make his audience receptive.

IN EARLY 2019, I visited several cities in the United States to try to take the pulse of the country.

It was unseasonably warm in DC. From my friend's apartment in the laid-back Adams Morgan neighbourhood, I walked downhill to Dupont Circle, where many think tanks and political consultancies are based. A haze over the city trapped the heat, and people were hurrying to and fro with blazers draped over their forearms.

The trade war with China was dominating the news cycle.

At a health food and juice bar, I met Stephanie Segal, deputy director of the Simon Chair in Political Economy at the Center for Strategic and International Studies. Until 2017, she had acted as co-director of the East Asia Office at the U.S. Department of the Treasury.

Poised, articulate, and wearing a smart suit, Segal perfectly matched my image of a high-level Washington bureaucrat who had transitioned into a career in the public eye at the nation's top-rated think tank. She told me that the DC establishment was shocked by Trump's willingness to set agendas and change the course of diplomatic relationships through unscripted statements and his Twitter account.

A few weeks prior to our meeting, Trump had told Reuters that he would intervene in the Justice Department's case against Meng Wanzhou if it would help secure a trade deal with Beijing.

"If I think it's good for what will be certainly the largest trade deal ever made, which is a very important thing—what's good for national security—I would certainly intervene," he said.

In the past, there had been separate lanes within the U.S. government for different aspects of foreign policy, including economic ties, national security, and the enforcement of trade sanctions, Segal explained. That separation was by design, to avoid the appearance of influence from partisan politics. Those lines had vanished.

"That's the power of Trump's statements and his Twitter feed, where he's setting the official view on things that pertain to legal violations and deviating from a government system predicated on the rule of law," Segal said. "Once you start to say everything is subject to negotiation, you're undermining a fundamental pillar of our system, and [in the Meng extradition case] Canada's system too. That's very odd," she said.

Even before Trump took office, complaints were piling up about China's trading practices and an unfair market environment for foreign companies in China, where Beijing's generous financial backing of its own "national champions" and various restrictions on foreign companies made it very difficult for outsiders to compete. International firms also argued that this contradicted China's commitments to safeguarding a free-market environment for international businesses to compete there.

In the past, however, people in the business lobby had more varied opinions on whether it was better to address such concerns through quiet discussions with Chinese counterparts or to push U.S. authorities to take a more aggressive stance on their behalf. Segal thinks sentiment gradually turned more negative because the "low-hanging fruit of market access in China had already been harvested," and now there were thornier issues, such as Chinese law forcing foreign firms to share technology know-how in exchange for market access; industrial overcapacity; and previously mentioned state subsidies that privileged Chinese companies and made it difficult for international firms to compete.

"Now it'd be hard to find anybody [in the White House] who would say something positive about China. The mood is very pessimistic. There has never been such a unified voice in regards to China and the need to be tough to get China to the table to talk about the structural reforms that the U.S. has been urging for a while now," she told me.

And very quickly, this turned from a shift in China policy to a new way to address all nations. "There's a feeling that the U.S. is basically telling other countries, 'You're with China or you're with us, so you have to show which side you're on.'"

The Trump White House must have been aware that allies were growing wary and wouldn't follow the U.S. blindly in any direction, but in the context of certain treaties and intelligence-sharing alliances, some countries may not have had a choice, Segal said. Trump's secretary of state, Mike Pompeo, had said that the U.S. would think twice before sharing intelligence with countries that allowed Huawei to develop its 5G networks, and a freeze on information-sharing with the U.S. could pose major obstacles for security agencies in its ally countries.

Segal also points out that the renegotiated North American Free Trade Agreement (NAFTA) between the U.S., Canada, and Mexico contained language that would oblige signatories to notify each other if they entered into trade talks with a "non-market" economy, effectively giving the U.S. a veto over the other countries' deals. A non-market economy is one in which government intervention is important in allocating goods and resources and determining prices rather than having supply and demand determine the price of goods and services.

"So that's China," Segal told me. "And it forced Canada to choose: Do you want NAFTA, or do you want an agreement with China? You can't have both."

The new free trade agreement, known as the United States–Mexico–Canada Agreement, went into effect on July 1, 2020, with the same binding language intact.

In DC, I also met with a representative of the International Crisis Group, where Michael Kovrig was employed as a senior analyst on Northeast Asia. The representative explained that the NGO wanted to avoid making political statements on Meng's case and keep the focus on Kovrig's inhumane treatment. As I write this, Kovrig and Michael Spavor are well into their third year in Chinese custody.

Similarly, when I met with scholars in DC who signed an open letter with more than a hundred other academics and former diplomats to call for the release of Kovrig and Spavor, we talked about how, in general, pundits in the U.S. tended to take a forty-thousand-foot view of bilateral relations. It was a struggle to get people to care about American citizens detained in China, let alone Canadian citizens.

Most Americans had never heard of the plight of the "two Michaels," the signatories told me. The narrative of an intense high-stakes global competition where America could "lose" and China might "win" seemed much more galvanizing.

BEFORE DECEMBER 2019, when news of a mysterious SARS-like virus emerged, many Westerners had never heard of Wuhan, the sprawling capital of China's central Hubei province. But twenty-nine-year-old Rui Zhong was born there, in Zhongnan Hospital, near the lush banks of Shahu Lake. While the city is densely inhabited and often polluted, it abounds in lakes and public parks.

Zhong's parents, who were ambitious junior academics, moved to America to attend graduate school when their only child was six years old. The family stayed but would return to their hometown at least once every several years to visit grandparents, aunts, uncles, and cousins.

As the situation in Wuhan unfolded, Zhong anxiously followed the news from the U.S., worrying for her relatives. People were literally dropping dead on the street. Police patrolled neighbourhoods, and community officials guarded apartment complexes to make sure the residents were staying home except to go out once every three days to purchase groceries. Videos showed mobs chasing people without masks. Heartbreaking diaries from the city told of what it was like to lose one's entire family within days.

Zhong also had to provide analysis of the crisis to the public: she is a China policy analyst for the DC-based non-partisan Woodrow Wilson International Center for Scholars. Journalists and broadcast networks sought her out for her perspective as a China expert who happened to hail from the epicentre of the outbreak. It was stressful to maintain her professional composure while anxious about her family members, and soon she also found herself dealing with online abuse.

Strangers sent Zhong pictures of bat carcasses floating in soup, though scientists had established that COVID-19 did not arise from consumption of bats. The abuse was part of a tidal wave of harassment and hate crimes targeting people of Asian descent all around the world. Victims were blamed for the spread of the coronavirus and spat on, beaten, and verbally abused.

When scrolling through social media, Zhong was horrified to see surveillance video of a man sneaking up behind a woman in New York and pouring acid on her. The victim suffered second-degree burns all over her upper body, face, and hands.

"Often, when racists target people, they target immigrants who skew older and don't speak English as comfortably as 1.5- or second-generation Chinese Americans like me," Zhong told me.

Yet politicians and public figures insisted on using the terms "Wuhan Virus" or "China Virus," despite pleas from advocates that such rhetoric was endangering lives. Undeterred, Trump piled on the racism and joked that COVID-19 was the "kung flu" at a June 2020 rally in Tulsa, Oklahoma. The theory gained ground that the virus was a biological weapon manufactured in Chinese labs.

As hawks in both countries seemed to be gearing people up for war, people of Chinese or Asian descent in the U.S. felt increasingly uneasy. Zhong thought of her cousin, a Chinese national on a work visa in the U.S. While he was excited to live in the States, he wasn't a citizen and had much deeper ties to China. He was feeling increasingly unwelcome.

"I think that's something baked into American society, to want to know where people's loyalties lie. It has been a question Asian Americans, including Japanese Americans, have faced throughout conflicts in the twentieth century," Zhong said. "Whose side are you really on?"

As a Chinese immigrant, she felt she had to push for space to take part in policy discussions in DC, where experts on Asia tend to be white men. At the Wilson Center, she planned programs and conducted research on how nationalist interests could impact business, technology, and cultural policies related to China. She wondered whether the scarcity of policy analysts with lived experience in China made it easier for fellow analysts to speak about geopolitical competition in the abstract.

"People are obsessed with being tougher on China," Zhong told me. "I don't have a problem with that, but when they use information that's wrong and misleading, that's spreading disinformation, which has consequences for people who aren't state actors. This is when I try to speak up."

She pointed to the precarious visa situation for Chinese scholars in America. In September 2020, the U.S. revoked the visas of more than a thousand Chinese students and researchers who were deemed to be a security risk. Many observers publicly stated that they did not trust that the decision had been made with proper consideration.

The actions of American authorities were undermined by the way Trump repeatedly generalized about the population of Chinese nationals in the U.S. Earlier in 2020, he said many Chinese nationals had ties to their country's military and had stolen data and intellectual property. At a dinner with American CEOs at his private golf club in New Jersey, Trump also characterized Chinese students in the U.S. as spies, according to a report in *Politico*. "Almost every student that comes over to this country is a spy," the president allegedly said.

Casting all Chinese students and scientists under suspicion had no place in a democracy, Zhong thought. It risked shutting out the very people who could provide insights into how China worked.

"It's not some kind of board game or video game," she told me. "What's happening now has consequences for real people."

Meanwhile, with the World Health Organization and governments struggling to stanch the spread of COVID-19 conspiracy theories, including racist ones about "bat soup," the origins of the virus became a battleground for competing U.S.- and China-originated propaganda.

Vanessa Molter, a former Stanford University graduate researcher, analyzed a massive data set on competing narratives and conspiracy theories related to China and COVID-19 in different countries in the spring of 2020. In China, Molter found, most of the spin was, unsurprisingly, created by state-controlled media to downplay Chinese officials' initial mishandling of the pandemic and emphasize the government's efforts to control the virus. There were many stories and videos about how Wuhan construction workers built a new hospital in ten days, for example.

In the U.S. and other countries, Molter found that conspiracy theories from various non-governmental sources flourished in the early weeks and months of the pandemic. "At this time, trusted sources didn't have good information yet. They either couldn't or were hesitant to make authoritative statements and guidances without complete information, which undermined public trust and created an information vacuum," she told me.

The misinformation and conspiracy theories, such as the idea that the virus was created on purpose in Chinese laboratories, were widely shared and widely read across platforms. "If you had outrageous articles, you were going to get clicks," Molter said. "For some actors, the motivation may have just been financial."

In response, Chinese state media put forward their own conspiracy theories, including one alleging that the American military had intentionally brought the COVID-19 virus to

China. "Domestically in China, state propaganda seems to have had significant success in shaping narratives and generating suspicion towards the U.S. Internationally, I don't think they were even expecting to be successful but wanted to at least sow doubt and confusion," Molter said.

INSTEAD OF PUTTING old grievances on hold, the pandemic only accelerated the trade and technology proxy war between the world's two largest economies. The U.S.-China rivalry expanded to new arenas, with journalists, students, and scientists on both sides bearing consequences.

In March 2020, Beijing revoked the press credentials of major U.S. media outlets reporting from China, including the *New York Times*, *Wall Street Journal*, and *Washington Post*. While China had done this in the past, this time the foreign ministry stated the expulsions were a response to Washington's new restrictions on dozens of journalists working for Chinese state-run media in the U.S.

The State Department ordered China to shut down its Houston consulate. In swift retaliation, Beijing forced the closure of America's consulate in southwestern Chengdu. Later, the State Department introduced new limitations on Chinese researchers in the United States that would shorten student visas in high-tech fields and restrict Chinese scientists' work at U.S. institutions. The American CEO of the world's most valuable startup, TikTok, quit after Trump signed an executive order on August 5, 2020, banning the Chinese-owned app from operating in the country, along with an order to ban WeChat.

Meanwhile, as Washington bungled the coronavirus response and the number of Americans killed by the disease climbed above two hundred thousand, Trump was trailing far behind Joe Biden in the presidential election polls. The White House needed a distraction, and the administration dropped any semblance of subtlety in evoking Cold War rhetoric to depict China as an urgent and existential threat.

The secretary of state, Mike Pompeo, declared in a fiery speech on July 23 that the last fifty years of engagement with China had been a failure. Standing outside the Richard Nixon Presidential Library in California, Pompeo said that, going forward, the approach to "Communist China" would be one of "distrust and verify." "I grew up and served my time in the army during the Cold War. And if there is one thing I learned, Communists almost always lie," he said. "We, the freedom-loving nations of the world, must induce China to change."

He called the People's Liberation Army of China a force designed to expand a Chinese empire rather than protect the Chinese people. That was why, he said, the U.S. military had ramped up patrols of the East and South China Seas and the Taiwan Strait. And, he added, "We've created a Space Force to help deter China from aggression on that final frontier."

Pompeo's militaristic remarks seemed to tip U.S.-China tensions toward a point of no return. Washington suspected that an increasingly coercive China wanted to drive the U.S. out of the "Indo-Pacific," a term American officials were now using over the previously accepted "Asia-Pacific" since it emphasized India's place in the region. It was a subtle way to counter China's dominance in Asia, international law expert Preston Lim told me. Beijing, meanwhile, believed that the U.S., worried about its global primacy, had fully abandoned its supposed neutrality on the South China Sea.

Haunted by an economic recession and the pandemic, and desperate for re-election, President Trump made a confrontation with China his last-ditch strategy to beat Biden. The risk of a mistake was high. It was one thing for the two countries to point their fingers at each other; it would be quite another if naval vessels were to collide in the South China Sea and trigger a direct conflict. In 2019, the U.S. Navy had conducted a record number of freedom of navigation operations there. Mark Esper, Trump's secretary of defense from July 2019 to November 2020, vowed to keep up the pace.

The era of engagement was over.

"'NUANCE' HAS BECOME a bad word in DC," says Elsa B. Kania, an expert on Chinese military strategy and emerging technologies at the Center for a New American Security policy institute. "But nuance is out there, no matter whether we like it or not. It's easier to be polemical, and much harder to assess U.S.-China relations in a way that captures the complexity of it all."

While working for the think tank, Kania served as an informal adviser on foreign policy and national security to former presidential candidate Elizabeth Warren and also provided informal counsel to Joe Biden's presidential election campaign.

"There's so much noise and fury and no clear sense of what a path forward looks like. I'm worried about unintended consequences," she told me. She wished there were more colleagues with personal or family connections to China who could bring more diverse perspectives into the mainstream.

Kania has skin in the game too. As an intelligence officer in the U.S. Navy Reserve, she could be called for active duty if a war with China breaks out. But this is far from what she wants to happen. She hopes to play some role in preventing it.

The Chinese Communist Party is promoting its own model and framework of governance as it undermines democracy and human rights around the world, Kania argues, and it is important for other countries to push back.

Although she opposes military intervention, Kania agrees that the future of democracy and a rules-based world order is at stake. When I asked what outcome she would want to see if war became inevitable, she said the human toll would be "tragic" and she would ultimately want the U.S. and its democratic allies to prevail. "But the U.S. is also undermining human rights and democracy at home, and, through leading with a terrible example, damaging our own causes worldwide."

Despite her position within the U.S. military and political establishment, Kania is scorching in her criticism of those who act as if they desire war. "I think there is this nostalgia for the Cold War, where competing with a strong peer is something Americans were born to do, and now we're pretending we're back in the time of Reagan and ready for this grand quest. The jingoism in both the U.S. and China is eerily similar," she told me. "It's a strange unreality, watching this all play out."

To Jerome A. Cohen, a widely respected scholar and one of the first American researchers to visit the PRC in the early 1970s, it seemed that history had come full circle: President Nixon used China policy to assure his re-election; President Trump was using China policy to try to assure *his* re-election.

People like Cohen, who had devoted their entire lives to building mutual understanding and respect for human rights in both countries, called for calm in 2020 as the superpowers seemed to be hurtling headlong toward conflict.

Cohen told me there was no doubt that the Trump administration's overreach in response to China's provocations "makes the CCP—and the Chinese nation subject to the Party's manipulation of the media—less likely to accept legitimate criticisms regarding the PRC's many violations of the rule of law at home and its international human rights obligations.

"This presents a dilemma for people like me and many other students of China who feel a duty to continue to voice our criticisms of PRC misconduct but who are uncomfortable about providing more ammunition for the Trump-Pompeo campaign. Of course, the PRC could relieve us of this dilemma by ending its violations!"

Many experts I spoke with didn't actually think a military confrontation would break out in the near future but agreed that a second Cold War mentality in both countries could bring unknown consequences. In China, where the media landscape is heavily controlled by the state, the narrative was consistently nationalistic, with news reports and editorials painting the U.S. government as dysfunctional, vengeful, and petty, and putting the blame on Washington for the conflict.

On May 24, 2020, during a video press conference, Chinese foreign minister Wang Yi accused American politicians of warmongering. "Some U.S. political forces are taking hostage of China-U.S. relations, attempting to push the ties to the brink of so-called 'new Cold War,'" Wang said. "This is dangerous and will endanger global peace." Meanwhile, Chinese state-owned and state-run media ran numerous English-language articles fanning the flames of U.S.-China tensions and posted them on Twitter and Facebook. The *Global Times* tabloid frequently publicized the commentary of Chinese experts like Renmin University of China professor Diao Daming, who said in November, "China needs to precisely retaliate against the Trump administration and make it feel the pain if the provocations harm Chinese core interests; on the other hand, if the provocations are just bluffing with no concrete damage, China can ignore them and focus on communicating with Biden's team to minimize the damages." Another expert said, "Being prepared for a long fight is always the wise choice for China."

The situation in the U.S., with its free press, is more complex, since even within government, opinions on China vary widely. The general trend into 2021, however, was that portraying oneself as a China hawk seemed to be immensely politically popular. A competition continues to play out among American politicians and pundits to one-up each other; in a field where so many people profess to be tough on China, some resort to saying increasingly outrageous and exaggerated things to stand out.

The posturing has reached ridiculous levels, including in law enforcement. In a brief January 2021 press conference by the FBI in Boston to announce the arrest of an MIT professor for allegedly failing to disclose his work for the Chinese government, officials used the term "Chinese Communist Government" five times. This needless anti-Communist rhetoric only distracts from, and can even discredit, legitimate facts and findings about Beijing's foreign influence activities in America. As my friend Margaret Lewis, a U.S.-China relations expert put it to me, "It's better to use People's Republic of China, or CCP. But 'Chinese Communist Government' is not a defined term and it emphasizes a red scare."

. . .

IT IS EASY TO IDENTIFY the problems that inhibit level-headed discourse on U.S.-China relations, such as online and political environments in both countries that foster disinformation and fear, but it's harder to imagine better American policy approaches.

I reached out to Charles Edel, who at the time we spoke was a senior fellow at the United States Studies Centre at the University of Sydney. He was previously associate professor of strategy and policy at the U.S. Naval War College and served as staff adviser to former secretary of state John Kerry on political and security issues in the Asia-Pacific region. I met Edel when we were both speaking at a conference in Sydney, where I was struck by his ability to analyze problems of his own country as if he were both an insider and an outsider. He has since returned to Washington, DC, to research the United States' history of dealing with authoritarian regimes.

He is the co-author of the 2019 book *The Lessons of Tragedy: Statecraft and World Order*, a fascinating exploration of how Americans have "forgotten" that descent into violence and war has been all too common throughout human history. This "amnesia," Edel and historian Hal Brands argue, has become more pronounced as the modern global order, which America helped to shape, looks as if it may become undone.

When President Trump and other American figureheads fail to uphold supposedly foundational American ideals like rule of law and democracy, this naturally invites outside accusations of hypocrisy. China's philosophy about global order is also opposed to allowing values like human rights to dominate international governance systems. Together, these factors, American and Chinese, weaken rules-based global institutions like the United Nations.

Like the original Cold War, the current conflict between the U.S. and China appears to be in part a battle of clashing ideologies, with both sides defending an ideology they believe is under threat. China practises a "live and let live" model in others' domestic governance and foreign policy, which is not values-based, according to Edel. "Here, the proposition is clear, if implicit: American foreign policy, inextricably linked to its values, will always attempt to impose itself on others; China promises non-interference in the internal affairs of other nations, offering an alternative model of governance that privileges economic growth over political liberalization, and social stability over individual rights," he told me.

It's important, however, for American policymakers to take into account that they're not dealing with a monolithic entity in Beijing. As much as President Xi would like it to be the case, there isn't ideological unity within Chinese Communist Party members. There are voices in China that seem cognizant of the harm done to the country's international reputation by its combative "wolf warrior" diplomacy and its human rights violations at home, particularly in Xinjiang. The leaks of Xinjiang government documents to the *New York Times* detailing Muslim internment camp strategies, which could only have come to international media through government insiders, demonstrates that Xi has opponents, Edel said. "However, the reality of Xi Jinping's consolidation of power, purges of political opponents, and near-total control of the party's security organs suggest that it is unlikely that these voices will prevail," he added.

Edel's comment made me think of how some American institutions have welcomed persecuted scholars from China to the U.S. with guest researcher or full-time professor positions. One of these scholars is Chen Guangcheng, a blind self-taught

human rights lawyer in China who astonishingly scaled a wall
in 2012 to escape his house arrest and seek refuge in the U.S.
embassy in Beijing. New York University's law school provided
him with a scholarship and one-year fellowship, and Chen
now works as a senior fellow at the Witherspoon Institute in
Princeton, New Jersey.

There is little the rest of the world can do to change the
CCP's monopoly of power in China, but reformed asylum
and sponsored work visa programs can provide safety to more
people at risk of persecution in China. "While public pressure
on Beijing has at times proven ineffective, private pressure on
China's rulers also has its limitations," Edel told me. "A better
approach for those like the United States, Canada, and others
is to stick to their principles, seek to negotiate from a position
of strength, and consistently coordinate their actions in a meaningful way."

But instead of pursuing a cooperative approach to China-
related challenges with U.S. allies, many actions from Trump's
administration seemed to surprise and irritate those outside
the West Wing. While American politicians like Republican
senator Marco Rubio and Speaker of the House Nancy Pelosi
consistently spoke out about human rights abuses in China for
years, the president didn't seem to care.

In his book *The Room Where It Happened*, former national
security adviser John Bolton wrote that on two separate occa-
sions, Trump told Xi that he "should go ahead with building
the [concentration] camps in Xinjiang, which Trump thought
was exactly the right thing to do."

BACKED BY AN ENTIRE political party and much of the American electorate, Donald Trump has single-handedly given Beijing more material than it could possibly use for its propaganda against Western democracies. Chinese state media boasted of how officials deftly controlled the pandemic so that by the summer of 2020, life in China was back to normal. The message in the articles, which contrasted China's handling of the pandemic with the response by Western nations, is that a loss of civil liberties was a fine price to pay for safeguarding lives.

Already, major Western nations were facing a credibility issue with embarrassments like the U.K.'s disorderly handling of the Brexit vote. And after Trump had violated democratic norms throughout his presidency, it became more difficult still for the U.S. to stand as a bastion of democracy when, on January 6, 2021, millions of people around the world watched as rioters stormed the Capitol building because they couldn't accept the results of the presidential election. The deadly insurrection in Washington was spurred by a rally in which Trump falsely claimed he had won the presidential election "by a landslide" and told his supporters, "If you don't fight like hell, you're not going to have a country anymore."

When Americans cherish their political system enough to champion democracy around the world, what to make of a U.S. president facing impeachment for inciting violence because he refused to accept an election loss? It makes it easy for Beijing to promote a narrative that Americans are hypocritical and that U.S. criticisms of China's human rights record stem from fear of being unseated as the world's superpower.

In Bobo Lo's 2020 Lowy Institute essay "Global Order in the Shadow of the Coronavirus," the Australian political expert is unrelenting in his assessment of how Western democracies have failed: "The coronavirus pandemic has thrown a harsh spotlight on the state of global governance.... Western leaders blame today's global disorder on an increasingly assertive China and disruptive Russia. Yet the principal threat lies closer to home. Western governments have failed to live up to the values underpinning a liberal international order."

Lo argues that policymakers are in denial, believing that with some adjustments—like a change of U.S. president— normal functioning of institutions like the United Nations can continue. In fact, the idea of democratic nations automatically holding moral authority has long been in question, he writes. Western countries' bungled responses to the coronavirus reveals that, "more than ever, nations operate according to narrow self-interest, not international norms or shared values." This has led to a crisis of international leadership where the problem is a "collective failure that cuts across continents and systems of governance."

Lo cites the 2003 Iraq invasion, the endless war in Afghanistan, and the 2011 NATO intervention in Libya as earlier failures encouraging China, Russia, and other non-Western countries to feel justified in similarly flouting international laws and norms.

To move forward from this very low point, Lo says, policymakers must do more to bridge the gap between liberal principles and illiberal practices and take responsibility to end hypocritical state behaviours. Western democracies then have to show that liberal-values-based governance can indeed deliver greater public benefits than exist in authoritarian regimes.

I recommend a close read of Lo's entire essay, and for Americans to heed the observations of reputable political analysts based outside of the U.S. in general, since their position at a distance can provide helpful clarity.

Within Biden's first months in office, Washington has shown that it is far more willing to coordinate with allies than the previous administration was. In March 2021, the U.S., Canada, the U.K., and the EU took joint action to impose parallel sanctions on senior Chinese officials involved in the mass internment of Uyghurs in Xinjiang. Biden has also brought back together the informal alliance of the U.S., Japan, India, and Australia—called the Quad, or Quadrilateral Security Dialogue—which Beijing has lashed out against as emblematic of a "poisonous" Cold War mentality. But Quad members have so far emphasized cooperation on benign measures such as greater coordination on the coronavirus pandemic.

In addition to such measures, the U.S. must tackle internal crises and address its own belligerent international behaviour. Ultimately, America will be convincing as a global defender of democracy and human rights only if Washington practises what it preaches.

CONCLUSION

Ten years into his self-imposed exile, the political cartoonist who calls himself Badiucao was agonizing over a decision: Should he reveal his identity or stay hidden behind a mask? It was May 2019, and he was contemplating showing his face in an upcoming documentary.

Badiucao—the pen name is a nonsensical string of characters in Chinese—had been skewering the CCP ever since he quit law school in Shanghai to study art in Australia. His darkly humorous work, witty versions of red-and-black Communist propaganda posters, brings attention to Beijing's abuse of power.

One day, when Badiucao was struggling to decide what to do about the documentary, he looked up from his seat on a bus to see four men board together. Asian men, in a predominantly white Melbourne suburb, wearing suits and with matching Bluetooth headsets.

The men split up to take different seats around him, and Badiucao knew he needed to get off at the next stop. Two of them followed.

Alarmed, Badiucao quickly crossed to the other side of the

street and then glanced over his shoulder to see if the pair was still tailing him.

"They noticed me looking at them. Instead of coming towards me, they headed into a shopping mall," the artist recalled.

His family, artists and intellectuals themselves, had suffered immensely during the Cultural Revolution. Two of his grandparents died in prison. When Badiucao told his mother and father that he felt his calling was to become a political cartoonist, they told him that he must leave and never return to China again. It was their loving way of giving him their blessing.

After completing art school in Adelaide, Badiucao decided he didn't want his separation from his family to be for nothing. He moved to bustling Melbourne, rented a studio space, and set to work satirizing the China-related news of the day. He shared most of his art for free, utilizing his bilingual social media accounts to great effect, and accepted commissions and donations to make a modest living.

Badiucao's reputation grew. Soon he was travelling around the world to speak at events. Each time, remembering his parents' pleas to stay safe, he pulled a ski mask over his head before meeting with a reporter or stepping onstage. He hid his artistic pursuits even from the people closest to him.

Despite his caution, Chinese authorities somehow discovered the cartoonist's identity, and in late 2018 he was forced to cancel his debut solo exhibition in Hong Kong. It was going to be a big production, with the Russian protest band Pussy Riot and local democracy activist Joshua Wong scheduled as headliners for the opening ceremony.

Police had shown up on the doorstep of Badiucao's family's apartment in Shanghai and asked them to pass on a message to their son: cancel the art exhibition; otherwise, the police would not treat him or his family with courtesy. Badiucao felt he had no choice but to do as they said.

But at that moment on the sidewalk in Melbourne, seeing the two men in suits across the street, he came to a different decision. He followed the men into the shopping mall.

"I had to stand up and fight back," he said. "They stopped and looked at me. We stared in each other's eyes for a couple seconds, and then they walked into a grocery store."

The men grabbed random items off the shelves, then went to separate self-checkout machines. They struggled to use the computer systems, and cashiers had to go over to help them.

Badiucao knew that if he gave up hiding his identity, he might risk more strange encounters like this. But it was clear his secret was already out, and he hoped that if he cut all ties to his family, the authorities would choose to target him directly and leave them alone.

"If I had to choose between protecting my family or myself, I would protect my family," Badiucao told me when we met in mid-2019, days before the release of the documentary, *China's Artful Dissident*. The last scene showed Badiucao unmasked and staring into the camera with a sad yet defiant expression. Since then, he has become an even more prominent voice on Chinese political issues and has donated protest art to support democracy movements in Thailand and Myanmar.

While writing this book, I have thought often about Badiucao's peaceful confrontation with the men who followed him. If he hadn't stood up, hadn't looked them in the eye, he might still be living in fear of some amorphous threat. And while the whole encounter was unnerving, the comedic scene of those flustered men struggling at the self-checkout machines is a reminder that Beijing's influence is often less powerful than it seems.

After years of reporting on China from countries around the world, I have come to the conclusion that United Front activities have gone unchecked for as long as they have only because people in positions of power in the West are failing at their jobs.

When journalist Benson Gao was facing daily protests outside his Metro Vancouver home—culminating in the savage beating of a friend who was critical of Beijing—police told me the language barrier was one reason they didn't step in sooner. This isn't a valid excuse when half a million people of Chinese descent live in Metro Vancouver alone. Many in the West treat information in Chinese as if it were in secret code.

And instead of drawing on reliable primary evidence, too many officials promote hyperbole, disinformation or xenophobic rhetoric about China. This is unnecessary when the truth is compelling enough. Details about Beijing's aims and activities are widely available online.

BETHANY ALLEN-EBRAHIMIAN DIDN'T NEED to go undercover to identify multiple Chinese Communist Party branches at universities across America.

The idea for her 2018 *Foreign Policy* article came from a news item that visiting Chinese scholars at the University of California, Davis, had formed a small CCP branch at the school. The founding members realized they might have contravened U.S. federal law and willingly disbanded the group, but it wasn't immediately obvious whether this was a more widespread practice. "So I went on Google and searched in Chinese, 'CCP branches in American universities,'" Allen-Ebrahimian told me. That simple search came up with pages of information.

"Honestly, from the very beginning, I was shocked, once I started looking, that it was unbelievably easy to find things. All you have to do is be able to read Chinese and know what to look for," she said. She added that it's still unclear whether such groups are actually illegal, but she hopes her story sheds light on a method Beijing uses to maintain ties with overseas Chinese scholars.

Allen-Ebrahimian's practical approach to her work is an example of how China-related research shouldn't come from a place of aggressive posturing toward Beijing. Better policy rests on trying to understand issues deeply from all angles while considering the best ways to hold Beijing accountable for human rights abuses and maintaining as much nuance and context as possible.

In every country, there is an urgent need for better education on China's complex political realities, but instead of expanding China studies or Chinese-language courses, many universities are cutting such programs. As a result, Western governments lack a pool of China experts with Chinese-language skills—and governments cannot rely on media reports when the global journalism industry is struggling and most publishers cannot afford to support full-time staff overseas.

While many of these limitations come down to money, governments on all sides have also put up barriers to acquiring knowledge on China. For its part, Beijing regularly kicks out foreign journalists, researchers, and NGO workers. And in 2020, despite predictable outcry, Washington shut down Fulbright junior scholar exchange programs for Hong Kong and mainland China, an institution that had launched the careers of generations of China-focused academics and professionals in the United States.

Thankfully, eager people can find ways to gain expertise on China without having to move there, as I discovered from my travels in the last several years. The China story is global, and there are interesting people with valuable insights to share everywhere.

Engaging with China remains crucial, and not only because it's an economic powerhouse with one-fifth of the world's population. Despite the "wolf warrior" stance dominating China's foreign ministry of late, Beijing's leaders are still willing to meet with their Western counterparts.

Governments should make smart use of these opportunities before avenues of productive diplomacy close further. The CCP is not a monolith — moderate individuals remain within the Chinese leadership. Those voices seem to have mostly fallen silent in a very tense political atmosphere, but this isn't necessarily a permanent state of affairs. And when it comes to extremely serious issues such as Beijing's "hostage-taking" of Canadians, crackdowns in Hong Kong, and territorial claims in the South China Sea, there are no quick fixes.

In Canada and the U.S., optimistic policymakers champion a closer relationship with India, hoping to support its rise to a dominant role in Asia at China's expense. Carleton University international relations professor Stephanie Carvin says this glosses over the decline of rights and freedoms in India. "It's like, things aren't going well with this Asian superpower; let's go to the next Asian superpower! It's faulty analysis," she told me.

Democratic countries do not automatically share the same goals. The inept handling of the coronavirus pandemic in rich Western countries shows that democracies can be fragile and

that they still favour the most privileged. Laws protecting freedom of speech do not guarantee that everyone in a country will
feel safe to speak without intimidation from fellow citizens and
foreign agents.

Much can be done, domestically and internationally,
to protect critics of Beijing better. In the case of the large-
scale persecution of Uyghurs and other Muslim minorities in
Xinjiang, international bodies could push harder for investigations or even take matters into their own hands to punish
perpetrators. Preston Lim, who specializes in the study of legal
solutions to global human rights issues, told me that countries have domestic and international tools to charge Chinese
officials, find them guilty, and either enact sanctions or throw
offenders in jail if they set foot again on sovereign soil.

It would be a mistake to rally around the status quo on the
assumption that what is already in place is the best iteration of
the world order. We have an opportunity to set a higher standard for global governance and ethics centred on protecting
universal human rights.

The coronavirus pandemic has shown that borders are
extremely porous and often arbitrary, and in the same manner,
conditions that empower authoritarian governance to flourish in certain countries have human consequences around the
globe, as we've seen with the targeting of foreign citizens by
Chinese authorities. For decades, people of non-white descent
have been harassed or subject to this coercion from foreign
powers, and it shouldn't be more alarming if someone who is
white experiences the same, yet when this happens, Western
media reacts as if it were a much greater offence.

As I finish writing this book, a long overdue discussion
about anti-Asian hate is taking place. Beijing has for many

years taken advantage of Western discomfort with speaking about race to inject its own narrative, arguing that it is racist to criticize the CCP. But to accept this assertion, treating the Chinese people and the Chinese state as one and the same, means accepting that people of Chinese descent essentially belong to Beijing.

We must be diligent to distinguish the actions of the Chinese leadership from the will of its people and to eradicate any language that evokes the old "yellow peril." These mistakes only serve to alienate those who can contribute so much to solving a dysfunctional state of world affairs.

NOTES

INTRODUCTION

Canadian officials tricked my great-great-grandfather: "Canadian Pacific Railway," *The Canadian Encyclopedia*, https://www.thecanadianencyclopedia.ca/en/article/canadian-pacific-railway.

Beijing uses racism from the West: Yangyang Cheng, "'China-Watching' Is a Lucrative Business. But Whose Language Do the Experts Speak?" *The Guardian*, January 13, 2021, http://www.theguardian.com/commentisfree/2021/jan/13/understand-china-speak-chinese-english-language.

CHAPTER ONE

Thousands of international websites are now only accessible: For an engaging study of China's online censorship regime, see James Griffiths, *The Great Firewall of China: How to Build and Control an Alternative Version of the Internet* (London: Zed Books, 2019).

I was researching Christianity: This section draws from my reporting in Beijing for "Underground, Overground," *Economist*, April 9, 2016, https://www.economist.com/china/2016/04/09/underground-overground.

The government vets the appointment of all pastors: For a detailed study of the CCP's agenda to separate ties between Chinese and global Christian churches, see Joseph Tse-Hei Lee and Christie Chui-Shan Chow, "Methodological

Reflections on the Study of Chinese Christianities," in *World Christianity: Methodological Considerations*, edited by Martha Frederiks and Dorottya Nagy (Boston: Brill, 2020).

The Chinese Communist Party is above the law: For insights on domestic efforts to improve China's justice system from one of China's top lawyers, see He Weifang, *In the Name of Justice: Striving for the Rule of Law in China* (Washington, DC: Brookings Institution, 2017).

Historians say the Party's obsession with control: For an overview of Chinese history, there are many timelines available online, and a classic book on modern Chinese history is Jonathan Spence's *The Search for Modern China*, 3rd ed. (New York: W.W. Norton, 2013).

Xi Jinping has declared his admiration for the Chinese classics: For more on how Xi draws from ancient Chinese philosophy, see Chris Buckley, "Leader Taps into Chinese Classics in Seeking to Cement Power," *New York Times*, October 11, 2014, https://www.nytimes.com/2014/10/12/world/leader-taps-into-chinese-classics-in-seeking-to-cement-power.html.

Beijing's preoccupation with social order: Kerry Brown, "Why Is Beijing So Obsessed with Order? It Fears the Alternative," *South China Morning Post*, April 28, 2018, https://www.scmp.com/week-asia/opinion/article/2142926/why-beijing-so-obsessed-order-it-fears-alternative.

Waves of CCP attempts to "reform" and "re-educate" the masses: See Timothy Cheek, *Living with Reform: China since 1989* (London: Zed Books, 2006). On China's reform years through the perspectives of Chinese artists, see Madeleine O'Dea, *The Phoenix Years: Art, Resistance, and the Making of Modern China* (Old Saybrook, CT: Tantor Media, 2017).

The Pew Research Center found: "Chinese Views on the Economy and Domestic Challenges," Pew Research Center, October 5, 2016, https://www.pewresearch.org/global/2016/10/05/1-chinese-views-on-the-economy-and-domestic-challenges/.

Studies on the Chinese middle class: David S.G. Goodman, "Why China's Middle Class Supports the Communist Party," *Christian Science Monitor*, October 22, 2013, https://www.csmonitor.com/Commentary/

Global-Viewpoint/2013/1022/Why-China-s-middle-class-supports-the-Communist-Party.

For same-sex couples, unmarried couples, and single parents: This reporting draws on my research for "Single Parents: Pariahs," *Economist*, February 27, 2016, https://www.economist.com/china/2016/02/27/pariahs?zid=306&ah=1b164dbd43b0cb27ba0d4c3b12a5e227.

In the southern Chinese city of Kaiping: Joanna Chiu, "Historic Chinese Town Resists Eviction for Theme Park," Agence France-Presse, July 25, 2018, https://news.yahoo.com/historic-chinese-town-resists-eviction-theme-park-031220355.html.

Professor Chen Guiqiu and her two daughters: Joanna Chiu, "China Lawyer's Wife Seeks US Asylum after Brazen Escape," Agence France-Presse, May 10, 2017, https://news.yahoo.com/china-lawyers-wife-seeks-us-asylum-brazen-escape-064035115.html.

Such language is really a self-interested manifesto: For an analysis of Xi's vision for global governance, see Liza Tobin, "Xi's Vision for Transforming Global Governance: A Strategic Challenge for Washington and Its Allies," *Texas National Security Review*, November 12, 2018, https://tnsr.org/2018/11/xis-vision-for-transforming-global-governance-a-strategic-challenge-for-washington-and-its-allies/.

CHAPTER TWO

"The idea was to win trust": Peter Martin, *China's Civilian Army: The Making of Wolf Warrior Diplomacy* (London: Oxford University Press, 2021).

"Big country diplomacy": Ting Shi and David Tweed, "Xi Jinping Outlines 'Big Country Diplomacy' for China," *Sydney Morning Herald*, December 2, 2014, https://www.smh.com.au/world/xi-jinping-outlines-big-country-diplomacy-for-china-20141202-11yaj5.html.

"All the existing triad groups in Hong Kong are patriotic": "HK Triads Turned 'Patriotic' after 1997 Handover: Michael Chan," *EJ Insight*, December 10, 2014, https://www.ejinsight.com/eji/article/id/951640/20141210-HK-triads-turned-patriotic-after-1997-handover-says-Michael-Chan.

"Unity is iron, steel, and strength": "Xi Urges Unity in Rejuvenation," *China Daily*, October 1, 2019, https://www.chinadailyhk.com/articles/143/160/116/1569912563261.html.

"Magic Weapons": Anne Brady, "Magic Weapons: China's Political Influence Activities under Xi Jinping," Wilson Center, September 18, 2017, https://www.wilsoncenter.org/article/magic-weapons-chinas-political-influence-activities-under-xi-jinping.

The report called the United Front's overseas expansion: Alex Joske, "The Party Speaks for You," Australian Strategic Policy Institute, June 9, 2020, https://www.aspi.org.au/report/party-speaks-you.

Geoff Raby, former Australian ambassador: Geoff Raby, "Hong Kong's Relationship with Beijing Has Been Changed Forever," *Australian Financial Review*, June 23, 2019, https://www.afr.com/world/asia/hong-kong-s-relationship-with-beijing-has-been-changed-forever-20190623-p520fl.

The Hong Kong Journalists Association's yearly surveys: "Hong Kong Press Freedom Index," Hong Kong Journalists Association, https://www.hkja.org.hk/en/survey-report/hong-kong-press-freedom-index/.

The Party's "local-centred approach": Shui-Yin Sharon Yam and Jeffrey Wasserstrom, "Hong Kong Is a Local Tragedy, Not a Geopolitical Shuttlecock," *Foreign Policy*, August 18, 2020, https://foreignpolicy.com/2020/08/18/hong-kong-local-us-china-history/.

I arrived in Hong Kong: My reporting in this section draws from original research for "How Canadians Are Part of an Underground Network Helping Hong Kong Protesters in Their Struggle against Chinese Control," *Toronto Star*, July 14, 2019, https://www.thestar.com/news/canada/2019/07/14/how-canadians-are-part-of-an-underground-network-helping-hong-kong-protesters-in-their-struggle-against-chinese-control.html.

Cheung says the national security legislation: See Alvin Cheung's parliamentary testimony, "Committee Report No. 2 - CACN (43-2)," House of Commons of Canada, November 9, 2020, https://www.ourcommons.ca/DocumentViewer/en/43-2/CACN/report-2/page-45, and Alvin Cheung, "Road to Nowhere: Hong Kong's Democratization and China's Obligations under Public International Law," *Brooklyn Journal of International Law*, August 27, 2015, https://papers.ssrn.com/abstract=2428220.

In April 2021, the Hong Kong High Court: Helen Davidson, "Hong Kong: 47 Key Activists Charged with Subversion and Face Life if Convicted," *Guardian*, February 28, 2021, https://www.theguardian.com/world/2021/feb/28/hong-kong-47-democracy-activists-charged-with-subversion-under-security-law

In June 2021, the unabashedly pro-democracy Hong Kong newspaper: Candace Chau, "'We belong to Hong Kong': why the brash pro-democracy *Apple Daily* could not survive in a new political era," *Hong Kong Free Press*, June 25, 2021, https://hongkongfp.com/2021/06/25/we-belong-to-hong-kong-why-the-brash-pro-democracy-apple-daily-could-not-survive-in-a-new-political-era/.

"Hong Kong has fallen into this strange dynamic": Antony Dapiran, *City on Fire: The Fight for Hong Kong* (London: Scribe, 2020).

CHAPTER THREE

United Front's chairwoman, Sun Chunlan: Sara Custer, "United Front Bureau to Focus on Overseas Returnees," *The Pie News*, August 8, 2016, https://thepienews.com/news/china-united-front-bureau-to-focus-on-overseas-returnees/.

Report on the topic by the international NGO Human Rights Watch: Yaqiu Wang, "Why Some Chinese Immigrants Living in Canada Live in Silent Fear," Human Rights Watch, March 4, 2019, https://www.hrw.org/news/2019/03/04/why-some-chinese-immigrants-living-canada-live-silent-fear.

I spoke with Brad West: Joanna Chiu, "'They're That Fearful': Why This B.C. Mayor Is Talking about the Harassment of Chinese Canadians in Metro Vancouver," *Toronto Star*, November 15, 2019, https://www.thestar.com/vancouver/2019/11/15/theyre-that-fearful-why-this-bc-mayor-is-talking-about-the-harassment-of-chinese-canadians-in-metro-vancouver.html.

For democracies to function: Ronald J. Deibert, *Reset: Reclaiming the Internet for Civil Society* (Toronto: House of Anansi Press, 2020); see also Alexander Dukalskis, *Making the World Safe for Dictatorship* (Oxford: Oxford University Press, 2021).

Rukiye Turdush at McMaster University: Gerry Shih and Emily Rauhula, "Angry over Campus Speech by Uighur Activist, Chinese Students in Canada

Contact Their Consulate, Film Presentation," *Washington Post*, February 14, 2019, https://www.washingtonpost.com/world/angry-over-campus-speech-by-uighur-activist-students-in-canada-contact-chinese-consulate-film-presentation/2019/02/14/a442fbe4-306d-11e9-ac6c-14eea99d5e24_story.html.

In 2006, Kwan testified: "Mr. Cheuk Kwan (Chair, Toronto Association for Democracy in China) at the Subcommittee on International Human Rights," Open Parliament, November 21, 2006, https://openparliament.ca/committees/international-human-rights/39-1/5/cheuk-kwan-1/only/.

The director of the Canadian Security Intelligence Service had revealed: "Foreign Influence 'Ongoing Threat': CSIS," CBC News, January 7, 2011, https://www.cbc.ca/news/canada/foreign-influence-ongoing-threat-csis-1.1000606.

Guests at one dinner included a businessman who subsequently donated C$1 million: Robert Fife and Steven Chase, "Trudeau Attended Cash-for-Access Fundraiser with Chinese Billionaires," *Globe and Mail*, November 22, 2016, https://www.theglobeandmail.com/news/politics/trudeau-attended-cash-for-access-fundraiser-with-chinese-billionaires/article32971362/.

One such dinner: Jeremy Nuttall, "Secrecy Surrounds Watchdog's Review of Trudeau's Fundraisers," *Tyee*, February 13, 2017, https://thetyee.ca/News/2017/02/13/Trudeau-Fundraisers-Review/?PageSpeed=noscript.

China's share of Canada's trade: "State of Trade 2020," Global Affairs Canada, June 3, 2020, https://www.international.gc.ca/gac-amc/publications/economist-economiste/state-of-trade-commerce-international-2020.aspx?lang=eng.

Huawei has received as much as US$75 billion: Chuin-Wei Yap, "State Support Helped Fuel Huawei's Global Rise," *Wall Street Journal*, December 25, 2019, https://www.wsj.com/articles/state-support-helped-fuel-huaweis-global-rise-11577280736.

"Canada…long used to a unipolar world dominated by the United States": Wendy Dobson, *Living with China: A Middle Power Finds Its Way* (Toronto: University of Toronto Press, 2019).

Waiting for the first day of Meng's bail hearing: Michael Mui, Perrin Grauer, Joanna Chiu, and Jeremy Nuttall, "Bail Hearing for Huawei Exec Reveals Fraud Allegations at Heart of International Strife," *Toronto Star*, December 7, 2018, https://www.thestar.com/vancouver/2018/12/07/what-to-expect-at-wanzhou-mengs-bail-hearing.html.

Kovrig was one of the first people I met in Beijing: Joanna Chiu, "My Friend Michael Kovrig Was Arrested in China. Please, Pay Attention," *Toronto Star*, December 11, 2018, https://www.thestar.com/opinion/2018/12/11/my-friend-michael-kovrig-was-arrested-in-china-i-beg-you-to-pay-attention.html.

Huseyin Celil, a Uyghur Muslim: Chris MacLeod, "Huseyin Celil Is the Forgotten Canadian Detained in China," *Toronto Star*, March 15, 2021, https://www.thestar.com/opinion/contributors/2021/03/15/huseyin-celil-is-the-forgotten-canadian-detained-in-china.html.

Argued that Canada had been foolish: Charles Burton, "Is China a Friend to Canada or Not? — Lessons from Aristotle," Macdonald-Laurier Institute, April 17, 2019, https://www.macdonaldlaurier.ca/china-friend-canada-not-lessons-aristotle-charles-burton-inside-policy/.

China's ambassador to the Netherlands warned: "Chinese Ambassador Warns Dutch Government against Restricting ASML Supplies," Reuters, January 15, 2020, https://www.reuters.com/article/us-netherlands-asml-china-idUSKBN1ZE1Z8.

2020 report on coercive economic measures: Ashley Feng, Elizabeth Rosenberg, and Peter Harrell, "A New Arsenal for Competition," Center for a New American Security, April 24, 2020, https://www.cnas.org/publications/reports/a-new-arsenal-for-competition.

CHAPTER FOUR

Landbridge would take over Port Darwin: Angus Grigg, "How Landbridge's Purchase of the Darwin Port Killed Perceived Wisdom on China," *Australian Financial Review*, July 7, 2017, https://www.afr.com/world/asia/how-landbridges-purchase-of-the-darwin-port-killed-perceived-wisdom-on-china-20170706-gx66r8.

Acknowledged he shouldn't have made public statements in support of Beijing's positions: Quentin McDermott, "Sam Dastyari's South China Sea Stance Revealed in Secret Recording," ABC News, November 29, 2017, https://www.abc.net.au/news/2017-11-29/sam-dastyari-secret-south-china-sea-recordings/9198044.

Canberra's new foreign policies: For an assessment of Beijing's influence in Australia, see "Appendix 2: Chinese Influence in Selected Countries" in the report "China's Influence & American Interests: Promoting Constructive Vigilance," edited by Larry Diamond and Orville Schell, Hoover Institute, November 29, 2018, https://www.hoover.org/research/chinas-influence-american-interests-promoting-constructive-vigilance.

"I'm some nerd from a rural municipality": Alan Harris, "Running for Municipal Office, I Was Targeted by China," *Toronto Star*, August 24, 2020, https://www.thestar.com/opinion/contributors/2020/08/24/running-for-municipal-office-i-was-targeted-by-china.html.

"Municipal politicians are often the prime target": The Carvin and Prest interviews originally appeared in Joanna Chiu, "'Prime Targets': Are Canada's Local Politicians in the Sights of Beijing's Global PR Machine?" *Toronto Star*, August 8, 2020, https://www.thestar.com/news/canada/2020/08/08/are-canadas-local-politicians-a-target-for-beijings-global-pr-machine.html.

A follow-up volume on international trends: Clive Hamilton and Mareike Ohlberg, *Hidden Hand: Exposing How the Chinese Communist Party Is Reshaping the World* (London: Oneworld, 2020).

Hamilton posited in a 2018 lecture: Clive Hamilton, "Commentary: Learning from Australia about China's Influence Activities," November 2, 2018, https://macdonaldlaurier.ca/files/pdf/201801026_Commentary_Hamilton_FWeb.pdf.

H. quoted the Berlin-based author and former political prisoner Liao Yiwu: "'My Dream Is That China Splits Up into 10 or So Countries': Beijing a 'Threat to World' Says Dissident Writer Liao Yiwu," Agence France-Presse, April 6, 2019, https://hongkongfp.com/2019/04/06/dream-china-splits-10-countries-beijing-threat-world-says-dissident-writer-liao-yiwu/.

Vicky Xu: See profile of Xu by Jennifer Feller and Susan Chenery, "From 'Perfect Chinese Daughter' to Communist Party Critic, Why Vicky Xu Is Exposing China to Scrutiny," ABC News, March 8, 2020, https://www.abc.net.au/news/2020-03-09/vicky-xu-exposing-chinas-human-rights-abuses/11954794.

Australian journalists reported that less than a year earlier: See update on Yang's case by Ben Doherty, "Yang Hengjun: Australian Writer Held in China for Almost Two Years Officially Charged with Espionage," *Guardian*, October 10, 2020, http://www.theguardian.com/world/2020/oct/10/yang-hengjun-australian-writer-held-in-china-for-almost-two-years-reportedly-charged-with-espionage.

China's foreign ministry even faced widespread criticism: "Chinese Official Fuels Outrage with Doctored Image Depicting Australian Soldier Cutting Afghan Child's Throat," *Washington Post*, November 30, 2020, https://www.washingtonpost.com/world/asia_pacific/china-australia-tweet-afghanistan/2020/11/30/546a2512-32b8-11eb-9699-00d311f13d2d_story.html.

An analysis from Bloomberg News: "China's Fight with Australia Risks Backfiring as Biden Era Nears," Bloomberg News, November 30, 2020, https://www.bloomberg.com/news/articles/2020-11-30/china-s-clash-with-australia-risks-backfiring-among-u-s-allies.

Nearly one in five Chinese Australians: "Experiences of Discrimination," Lowy Institute, March 2, 2021, https://interactives.lowyinstitute.org/features/chinese-communities/topics/experiences-of-discrimination.

CHAPTER FIVE

Historians have since questioned: See Frances Wood, *Did Marco Polo Go to China?* (London: Vintage, 1997).

Intellectual property theft and forced technology transfers: For a collection of international scholars' work on these issues, see *China's Quest for Foreign Technology: Beyond Espionage*, edited by William C. Hannas and Didi Kirsten Tatlow (London: Routledge, 2020).

The European Commission in Brussels: "EU-China—A Strategic Outlook," European Commission and the High Representative of the Union for Foreign Affairs and Security Policy, March 12, 2019, https://ec.europa.eu/info/sites/info/files/communication-eu-china-a-strategic-outlook.pdf.

In 2017, the project even became enshrined: "'Belt and Road' Incorporated into CPC Constitution," Xinhua, October 24, 2017, http://www.xinhuanet.com/english/2017-10/24/c_136702025.htm.

Bruno Maçães wrote in his book: Bruno Maçães, *Belt and Road: A Chinese World Order* (London: Hurst, 2020).

In a 2019 interview, the Sri Lankan ambassador: Laura Zhou, "Sri Lanka rejects fears of China's 'debt-trap diplomacy' in belt and road projects," *South China Morning Post*, April 22, 2019. https://www.scmp.com/news/china/diplomacy/article/3007175/sri-lanka-rejects-fears-chinas-debt-trap-diplomacy-belt-and

Xi's numerous other speeches: "Pence, Xi Trade Barbs in Speeches at Pacific Summit," Associated Press, November 16, 2018, https://www.seattletimes.com/business/chinas-xi-world-faces-choice-of-confrontation-cooperation/.

The *Washington Post*'s Rome bureau chief wrote: Chico Harlan, "A Defiant Italy Becomes the First G-7 Country to Sign On to China's Belt and Road Initiative," *Washington Post*, March 22, 2019, https://www.washingtonpost.com/world/europe/defiant-italy-becomes-the-first-g7-country-to-sign-on-to-chinas-belt-and-road-initiative/2019/03/22/54a732d4-4bdf-11e9-8cfc-2c5d0999c21e_story.html.

Fanned the flames further by telling the *South China Morning Post*: Sarah Zheng and Liu Zhen, "Italy's Critics Are Jealous of Its China Deal, Says Rome's Lead Negotiator," *South China Morning Post*, March 27, 2019, https://www.scmp.com/news/china/diplomacy/article/3003406/more-european-countries-set-follow-italys-lead-down-chinas-new.

In a March 9, 2019, tweet: "NSC 45 Archived," Twitter, March 9, 2019, https://twitter.com/whnsc45/status/1104402719568203776.

Thinly sourced media stories suggesting the Port of Palermo: See, for example, "China Considers a New Silk Road Role for Italy's Palermo Port," *Ports Europe*,

March 14, 2019, https://www.portseurope.com/china-considers-a-new-silk-road-role-for-italys-palermo-port/.

The work of Lorenzo Mariani: Mariani's reports are online at Lorenzo Mariani, "Publications," Istituto Affari Internazionali, https://www.iai.it/en/persone/lorenzo-mariani.

Under the headline "Who Put China in Government": Giulia Pompili, "Chi Mise La Cina al Governo," *Il Foglio*, March 7, 2019, https://www.ilfoglio.it/esteri/2019/03/07/news/chi-mise-la-cina-al-governo-241742/. See also Giulia Pompili, "Huawei Tramples Its Employees' Freedom of Speech, a Confidential Document Reveals," *Il Foglio*, October 24, 2019, https://www.ilfoglio.it/esteri/2019/10/24/news/huawei-tramples-its-employees-freedom-of-speech-a-confidential-document-reveals-282639/.

The Diplomat magazine remarked: Jojje Olsson, "China Tries to Put Sweden on Ice," *Diplomat*, December 30, 2019, https://thediplomat.com/2019/12/china-tries-to-put-sweden-on-ice/.

Had to shut down its Confucius Institute: Stuart Lau, "Belgian University Closes Its Chinese State-Funded Confucius Institute after Spying Claims," *South China Morning Post*, December 11, 2019, https://www.scmp.com/news/china/diplomacy/article/3041617/belgian-university-closes-its-chinese-state-funded-confucius.

The Economist Intelligence Unit reported in 2019: "Democracy Index 2018: Me Too?" Economist Intelligence Unit, October 22, 2019, https://www.eiu.com/public/topical_report.aspx?campaignid=Democracy2018.

CHAPTER SIX

Greece does score sixth in the world: "Trade in Counterfeit and Pirated Goods," Organisation for Economic Cooperation and Development, April 18, 2016, https://www.oecd.org/corruption-integrity/explore/topics/illicit-trade.html.

Not only did Xi immediately agree to help: Jessie Yeung, "Xi Jinping Offers to Help Greece Retrieve Contested Parthenon Marbles," CNN, November 13, 2019, https://www.cnn.com/style/article/xi-jinping-greece-marbles-intl-hnk-scli/index.html.

As the *New York Times* reported: Jason Horowitz and Liz Alderman, "Chastised by E.U., a Resentful Greece Embraces China's Cash and Interests," *New York Times*, August 26, 2017, https://www.nytimes.com/2017/08/26/world/europe/greece-china-piraeus-alexis-tsipras.html.

"We have the power": Vivienne Walt, "Boxed in at the Docks: How a Lifeline from China Changed Greece," *Fortune*, July 22, 2019, https://fortune.com/longform/cosco-piraeus-port-athens/.

Greek research agency Dianeosis asked Greeks: "What Greeks Believe in 2017," Dianeosis, April 28, 2017, https://www.dianeosis.org/en/2017/04/greeks-believe-in-2017/.

According to financial advisory firm Deloitte: "If You Want to Prosper, Consider Building Roads: China's Role in African Infrastructure and Development Projects," Deloitte, March 22, 2019, https://www2.deloitte.com/us/en/insights/industry/public-sector/china-investment-africa-infrastructure-development.html.

Howard W. French detailed in a story in *The Atlantic*: Howard W. French, "The Conflict in China's African Investment," *Atlantic*, April 13, 2010, https://www.theatlantic.com/magazine/archive/2010/05/the-next-empire/308018/. See also Howard W. French, *China's Second Continent* (New York: Knopf, 2014).

Global Risk Insights: Hadeeka Taj, "China's New Silk Road or Debt-Trap Diplomacy?" Global Risk Insights, May 5, 2019, https://globalriskinsights.com/2019/05/china-debt-diplomacy/.

An editorial by Seymur Mammadov: Seymur Mammadov, "Why Should Europe Be Friends with China?" CGTN, November 14, 2019, https://news.cgtn.com/news/2019-11-14/Why-should-Europe-be-friends-with-China--LCsiOcrx1m/index.html.

The Montenegro government had earlier failed: Valerie Hopkins, "Montenegro Fears China-Backed Highway Will Put It on Road to Ruin," *Financial Times*, April 10, 2019, https://www.ft.com/content/d3d56d20-5a8d-11e9-9dde-7aedca0a081a.

CHAPTER SEVEN

By 2018, the United Nations: "UN Says It Has Credible Reports That China Holds Million Uighurs in Secret Camps," Reuters, August 10, 2018, https://www.reuters.com/article/us-china-rights-un-idUSKBN1KV1SU.

Uyghurs are a mostly Muslim group: Books and podcasts on the history of Xinjiang and its peoples include: James Millward, *Eurasian Crossroads: A History of Xinjiang* (New York: Columbia University Press, 2017); Justin Jon Rudelson, *Oasis Identities: Uyghur Nationalism along China's Silk Road* (New York: Columbia University Press, 1997); Gardner Bovingdon, *The Uyghurs: Strangers in Their Own Land* (New York: Columbia University Press, 2020); Laszlo Montgomery, "The History of Xinjiang Part One," *The China History Podcast*, March 23, 2020, https://chinahistorypodcast.libsyn.com/chp-244-the-history-of-xinjiang-part-1.

David Tobin, a research fellow: David Tobin, *Securing China's Northwest Frontier: Identity and Insecurity in Xinjiang* (Cambridge: Cambridge University Press, 2020).

Beijing has repeated the policies of the last Imperial Chinese dynasty: For sources on Chinese state promotional campaigns for Han Chinese migration to Xinjiang, and demographic data, see Amy H. Liu and Kevin Peters, "The Hanification of Xinjiang, China: The Economic Effects of the Great Leap West," *Studies in Ethnicity and Nationalism* 17, no. 2 (2017), https://onlinelibrary.wiley.com/doi/pdf/10.1111/sena.12233.

President Xi instructed senior officials to "show absolutely no mercy": Austin Ramzy and Chris Buckley, "'Absolutely No Mercy': Leaked Files Expose How China Organized Mass Detentions of Muslims," *New York Times*, November 16, 2019, https://www.nytimes.com/interactive/2019/11/16/world/asia/china-xinjiang-documents.html.

The approach has been to pre-empt criminal activity: See Sheena Chestnut Greitens, Myunghee Lee, and Emir Yazici, "Counterterrorism and Preventive Repression: China's Changing Strategy in Xinjiang," *International Security* 44, no. 3 (Winter 2019/20), doi.org/10.1162/ISEC_a_00368.

Benjamin Dooley: Dooley's reporting in Xinjiang, with photos by Johannes Eisele and Greg Baker, includes "Inside China's Internment Camps: Tear Gas,

Tasers and Textbooks," Agence France-Presse, January 30, 2019, https://www.afp.com/en/inside-chinas-internment-camps-tear-gas-tasers-and-textbooks.

According to a report from Megha Rajagopalan for Buzzfeed News: Rajagopalan's investigative reporting on Xinjiang with Alison Killing includes "Inside a Xinjiang Detention Camp," Buzzfeed News, December 3, 2020, https://www.buzzfeednews.com/article/meghara/inside-xinjiang-detention-camp.

Uyghurs who had recently fled from China: For more on the Uyghur community in Turkey, see Simina Mistreanu, "The Capital of Xinjiang is Now in Turkey," *Foreign Policy*, September 30, 2019, https://foreignpolicy.com/2019/09/30/the-capital-of-xinjiang-is-now-in-turkey/.

Military analyst Daniel Darling hypothesized: Daniel Darling, "Is the SCO Emerging as Eastern Counterweight to NATO?" *Real Clear Defense*, August 30, 2019, https://www.realcleardefense.com/articles/2015/08/31/is_the_sco_emerging_as_eastern_counterweight_to_nato_108426.html.

Professor Altay Atlı, of Boğaziçi University: See Atlı's analysis of Turkey and China's relationship, "Making Sense of Turkey's Rapprochement with China," German Marshall Fund, November 26, 2018, https://www.gmfus.org/publications/making-sense-turkeys-rapprochement-china.

CHAPTER EIGHT

"This medal of friendship": Reporting originally appeared in Joanna Chiu and Laurent Thomet, "Xi Touts Putin Ties as US Tensions Bring Them Closer," Agence France-Presse, June 8, 2018, https://sg.news.yahoo.com/xi-touts-putin-ties-us-tensions-brings-them-095441727.html.

In almost thirty meetings between the two: For an analysis of Putin and Xi's relationship, see Elizabeth Wishnick, "Putin and Xi: Ice Cream Buddies and Tandem Strongmen," PONARS Eurasia Policy Memo, October 25, 2019, https://www.ponarseurasia.org/putin-and-xi-ice-cream-buddies-and-tandem-strongmen/.

Politicians like former U.S. secretary of state Mike Pompeo: Matthew Lee, "In Europe, Pompeo Warns of China, Russia Authoritarianism," Associated Press, August 11, 2020, https://apnews.com/article/beijing-belarus-iran-world-war-ii-technology-9554c4757183431d6228f6de10db5c4c.

A May 2020 analysis from the U.S.-based Kennan Institute: "In Russia's Shadow: China's Rising Security Presence in Central Asia," Kennan Institute, May 2020, https://www.wilsoncenter.org/publication/kennan-cable-no-52-russias-shadow-chinas-rising-security-presence-central-asia.

Qu Qiubai was one of them: For more on Qu's time in Moscow and an account of interactions between Chinese and Russians throughout the last century, see Ed Pulford, *Mirrorlands: Russia, China, and Journeys in Between* (London: Hurst, 2019).

To some critics, the prospect of the two authoritarian powers: Andrea Kendall-Taylor and David Shullman, "A Russian-Chinese Partnership Is a Threat to U.S. Interests," *Foreign Affairs*, May 14, 2019, https://www.foreignaffairs.com/articles/china/2019-05-14/russian-chinese-partnership-threat-us-interests.

"Despite vociferous claims to the contrary": See Bobo Lo, *Axis of Convenience: Moscow, Beijing and the New Geopolitics* (Washington, DC: Brookings Institution Press, 2008).

In a Pew Research Center poll: "How People Around the World View China," Pew Research Center, December 5, 2019, https://www.pewresearch.org/global/2019/12/05/attitudes-toward-china-2019/.

Told *Kommersant*, a Russian business newspaper: "How Chinese Tourists Are Received in China and Why They Have Become a Problem," *Kommersant*, 2019, https://www.kommersant.ru/projects/chinatourism.

Repnikova has found that private media outlets: Maria Repnikova, "Contesting the State under Authoritarianism: Critical Journalists in China and Russia," *Comparative Politics*, October 1, 2018, https://static1.squarespace.com/static/57d4491d15d5db80cad99cb7/t/5c1294c1cd83665d18f6ca0b/1544721602010/Contesting_the_State_under_Authoritarian+%281%29.pdf.

Given that Russia is a Eurasian nation: Jonathan E. Hillman, "China and Russia: Economic Unequals," Center for Strategic and International Studies, July 15, 2020, https://www.csis.org/analysis/china-and-russia-economic-unequals.

In May 2019, the *New York Times* reported: Neil MacFarquhar, "As Chinese Flock to Siberia's Lake Baikal, Local Russians Growl," *New York Times*, May 2, 2019, https://www.nytimes.com/2019/05/02/world/europe/chinese-lake-baikal-tourism-russia.html.

Stop the construction of the AquaSib: "Russian Prosecutors Seek to Stop Chinese Bottling Factory at Lake Baikal, *Moscow Times*, March 11, 2019, https://www.themoscowtimes.com/2019/03/11/russian-prosecutors-seek-to-stop-chinese-bottling-factory-at-lake-baikal-a64771.

CHAPTER NINE

My interview in January 2019 with former Canadian ambassador to China John McCallum: Joanna Chiu, Wanyee Li, and Michael Mui, "Ambassador John McCallum Says It Would Be 'Great for Canada' if U.S. Drops Extradition Request for Huawei's Meng Wanzhou," *Toronto Star*, January 25, 2019, https://www.thestar.com/vancouver/2019/01/25/it-would-be-great-for-canada-if-us-drops-extradition-request-for-huaweis-meng-wanzhou-ambassador-says.html.

Made in China 2025: See Lance Noble, "China Manufacturing 2025 Report," European Union Chamber of Commerce in China, March 7, 2017, http://www.europeanchamber.com.cn/en/china-manufacturing-2025.

Graham Allison put it in a 2015 *Atlantic* magazine story: Graham Allison, "The Thucydides Trap: Are the U.S. and China Headed for War?" *Atlantic*, September 24, 2015, https://www.theatlantic.com/international/archive/2015/09/united-states-china-war-thucydides-trap/406756/.

In a suburban Metro Vancouver cul-de-sac: Some reporting in this section originally appeared in Joanna Chiu, "These 'Citizens' from Steve Bannon and a Chinese Billionaire's 'Federal State' Have Been Protesting in a Metro Vancouver Cul-de-Sac for Nearly 50 Days. What Do They Want?" *Toronto Star*, October 31, 2020, https://www.thestar.com/news/canada/2020/10/31/these-citizens-from-stephen-bannon-and-a-chinese-billionaires-federal-state-have-been-protesting-in-a-metro-vancouver-cul-de-sac-for-nearly-50-days-what-do-they-want.html.

The McCarthy era: "Numbed with Fear: Chinese Americans and McCarthyism," PBS, December 20, 2019, https://www.pbs.org/wgbh/americanexperience/features/mccarthy-numbed-with-fear-chinese-americans/.

"The dominant American myth about China": Richard Madsen, *China and the American Dream: A Moral Inquiry* (Berkeley: University of California Press, 1995).

Nixon argued in "Asia After Viet Nam": Richard Nixon, "Asia After Viet Nam," *Foreign Affairs*, October 1, 1967, https://www.foreignaffairs.com/articles/united-states/1967-10-01/asia-after-viet-nam.

A declassified transcript: "Mao Zedong Meets Richard Nixon," University of Southern California, February 21, 1972, https://china.usc.edu/mao-zedong-meets-richard-nixon-february-21-1972.

"Now it'd be hard to find anybody": A portion of Stephanie Segal's interview originally appeared in Perrin Grauer and Joanna Chiu, "'You're with China or You're with Us': Global Relations Hinge on Outcome of Trade Talks, U.S. Analysts Say," *Toronto Star*, March 11, 2019, https://www.thestar.com/news/canada/2019/03/11/youre-with-china-or-youre-with-us-global-relations-hinge-on-outcome-of-trade-talks-us-analysts-say.html.

As the situation in Wuhan unfolded: See Rui Zhong's interview "A Wealth of Anger and a Wealth of Time—Wuhan and the Coronavirus," *Nü Voices* podcast #25, February 23, 2020, https://nuvoices.com/2020/02/23/nuvoices-podcast-a-wealth-of-anger-and-a-wealth-of-time-wuhan-and-the-coronavirus/.

Analyzed a massive data set; Vanessa Molter and Alicia Chen, "Mask Diplomacy: Chinese Narratives in the COVID Era," Stanford Internet Observatory Virality Project, https://fsi.stanford.edu/news/covid-mask-diplomacy.

Chinese foreign minister Wang Yi accused: "China Warns U.S. Politicians Pushing Nations into 'New Cold War,'" Bloomberg News, May 24, 2020, https://www.bloomberg.com/news/articles/2020-05-24/beijing-urges-u-s-to-drop-wishful-thinking-of-changing-china.

The *Global Times* tabloid frequently publicized: "Beijing Prepared for Trump's Final Madness, Hysteria on China Policy," *Global Times*, November 16, 2020, https://www.globaltimes.cn/page/202011/1206986.shtml.

The Lessons of Tragedy: Hal Brands and Charles Edel, *The Lessons of Tragedy: Statecraft and World Order* (New Haven: Yale University Press, 2020).

The Room Where It Happened: John Bolton, *The Room Where It Happened: A White House Memoir* (New York: Simon & Schuster, 2020).

"Global Order in the Shadow of the Coronavirus": Bobo Lo, "Global Order in the Shadow of the Coronavirus: China, Russia and the West," Lowy Institute, July 29, 2020, https://www.lowyinstitute.org/publications/global-order-shadow-coronavirus-china-russia-and-west.

CONCLUSION

Days before the release of the documentary: Director Danny Ben-Moshe, *China's Artful Dissident*, Identity Films, 2019, http://www.identity-films.com/films/chinas-artful-dissident.

Bethany Allen-Ebrahimian didn't need to go undercover: Bethany Allen-Ebrahimian, "The Chinese Communist Party Is Setting Up Cells at Universities across America," *Foreign Policy*, April 18, 2018, https://foreignpolicy.com/2018/04/18/the-chinese-communist-party-is-setting-up-cells-at-universities-across-america-china-students-beijing-surveillance/.

Visiting Chinese scholars at the University of California, Davis: Nectar Gan and Zhuang Pinghui, "Why a Chinese Communist Party Branch at the University of California, Davis, Was Disbanded," *South China Morning Post*, November 20, 2017, https://www.scmp.com/news/china/policies-politics/article/2120707/why-chinese-communist-party-branch-university.

Governments should make smart use of these opportunities: For further reading on scenarios of China's rise, including potential actions taken by other nations and their implications, see David Shambaugh, *China's Future* (Cambridge: Polity Press, 2016).

Study of legal solutions to global human rights issues: Preston Jordan Lim, "Applying International Law Solutions to the Xinjiang Crisis," *Asian-Pacific Law and Policy Journal* 22, no. 1 (January 4, 2021), http://blog.hawaii.edu/aplpj/files/2021/01/APLPJ_22.1_Preston-Lim-1.pdf.

ACKNOWLEDGEMENTS

I would like to first thank Janie Yoon for approaching me with an idea for a more ambitious book than I imagined I could tackle. You believed in me from the start and your faith in this project and masterly initial edits carried it through to the end.

I adored working with brilliant editors Alex Schultz, Michelle MacAleese, Maria Golikova, Peter Norman, and Sue Sumeraj as well as with the rest of Team Anansi including Bruce Walsh, Alysia Shewchuk, Karen Brochu, Laura Chapnick, Zoe Kelsey, Siusan Moffat, and Peter Jacobsen. You became my trusted colleagues — providing support, keen insights and moments of fun while we were all working from home.

I'm very fortunate to have an incredible literary agent, Carly Watters, and publicist, Debby de Groot, who must be the two best in their fields in Canada. I learned so much from the both of you.

I would also like to take the opportunity to thank the wonderful teams at Hurst Publishers and Lemniscaat, who prepared the U.K. and Dutch editions of *China Unbound*, respectively.

My friend Kevin Hamilton was my "secret weapon" during the writing process. Thank you for reviewing the rough drafts that I was too embarrassed to show other editors. You seemed to understand the main points I wanted to make before I did, and you helped bring the book to life.

I owe an enormous debt of gratitude to the journalists and researchers I worked with on the road: in the United States, Colleen O'Connor; in Australia, Alex Joske; in Italy, Catarina Martins; in Greece, Alexandros Kottis; in Turkey, Memeteli Turkiye. Your invaluable contributions helped me avoid some pitfalls of "parachute" journalism, and any mistakes that remain are solely my own.

I couldn't report in Russia as planned because of COVID-19 and was anxious about what to do, until I had the good fortune of finding journalist Natalia Afanasyeva, who traveled across the country during the frigid winter on my behalf. Another immensely talented journalist, who prefers to not be named in the book, provided coordination and translation. Thanks to Bernhard Mohr for the introductions.

I am immensely grateful to those who generously provided detailed and constructive feedback on one or more chapters. A huge thank you to Jeffrey Wasserstrom, Terry Glavin, Megha Rajagopalan, Giulia Pompili, Raquel Baldwinson, Alvin Cheung, Kevin Carrico, Didem Tali, and Steve Dunthorne.

Additionally, I would like to thank my current and former colleagues in Hong Kong, Beijing and at the *Toronto Star*. The book is partly a summation of what I witnessed in the last decade, and those years of reporting wouldn't have been possible without the work of fellow reporters, including Chinese journalists (the unsung heroes of foreign correspondence), and guidance from my editors.

Thank you to my sources, who generously shared their expertise or courageously shared their personal stories with me.

Support from a wider network of friends and media industry colleagues was critical while reporting in a difficult environment like China. My thanks also go to the teachers and professors who prepared me to meet the challenges.

I'm glad to be part of the wonderful NüVoices community of China specialists. Anne Henochowicz helped identify an epigraph for this book, and Ming Di and Neil Aitken kindly granted permission to reproduce part of their translation of the poem by Zang Di.

To my family around the world, thank you for all your support, taking my calls to answer questions about Chinese vocabulary, and for all the advice and nourishing home-cooked meals.

To my parents, who shaped their lives around giving me opportunities to pursue my dreams, and my brother, who is always there for me with his special brand of wisdom: I love you and words can't express how much I appreciate you.

Lastly, to Joel, my best friend and favourite adventure partner, thank you for being my most astute reader, my travel coordinator, my live-in historian, and my debate opponent, and for generally keeping me healthy and happy. You make every day brighter. I'm so excited to continue living this life with you.

INDEX

JOANNA CHIU is an internationally recognized authority on China whose work has appeared in the *Guardian*, *Foreign Policy*, BBC World, *The Atlantic*, *Newsweek*, Quartz, Al Jazeera, GlobalPost, CBC, and NPR. For seven years she was based in China as a foreign correspondent, reporting for top news agencies such as Agence France Presse and Deutsche Presse-Agentur, and in Hong Kong she reported for the *South China Morning Post*, the *Economist*, and Associated Press. In 2012 her story on refugees in Hong Kong won a Human Rights Press Award, and in 2018 her report on #MeToo cases in Asia was named one of the best *Foreign Policy* long-form stories. She is the founder and chair of the NüVoices editorial collective, which celebrates the creative and academic work of women working on the subject of China. She is currently a senior journalist covering China-related topics for the *Toronto Star*, Canada's largest newspaper, and has previously served as bureau chief of the *Star Vancouver*. She speaks frequently at major events and conferences.